PRAISE FOR
RECLAIMING THE SACRED SOURCE

"Lynn Creighton's *Reclaiming the Sacred Source: The Ancient Power and Wisdom of Women's Sexuality,* invites readers to join her for a sociohistorical exploration of sexuality. Her sculptures have celebrated women reclaiming all that is joyful and powerful in their sexual identities and experiences, and her book deepens readers' understanding of the ways in which sex/gender hierarchies of power and privilege have shaped sex and sexuality throughout the millennia. Creighton's words and art inspire readers to discover and recover the sacred in women's sexual experiences and identities."

— Adina Nack, Ph.D., Chair and Professor, Department of Sociology; Administrative Fellow, Public Health; California Lutheran University; Senior Scholar, Council on Contemporary Families

"Lynn is a mother, grandmother and great-grandmother, college professor, and ceremonial leader who has supported literally thousands of women in the path of healing their sexual traumas. Her book is much needed in our world that is out of balance with Nature. Her treatise is about sex as a sacred act and female orgasm as a direct connection with the source of creation. It is a subject that is controversial and uncomfortable for many in our society, and is much needed for us to understand so we may heal our world and stop destroying it. Lynn's understanding comes from the integration of her life's experiences, her scholarship, her Red Road spirituality and her art. This book comes from deep within her being and is her gift to us and those to come."

—River Sauvageau, Spiritual Leader in Ojai, California, *designs to fit your life, studiosauvageau.com*

"As one who has participated in numerous purification lodges, a vision quest and other ceremonies with Lynn Creighton, I am so grateful she put her experience and insights into the written word so that many more women (and men) can benefit from her wisdom. *Reclaiming the Sacred Source* is a valuable story, both of one woman and of all women, and their journey of losing connection with the power of their sacred sexuality and a path forward to regaining it."

— Dahra Perkins, MD

"'I am arguing for sex as a sacrament.' Lynn Creighton has fully taken the shamanic journey. Many quests for vision in the indigenous spiritual tradition. Many years of leading purification lodge for women traumatized by sexual abuse. Profound delving into the mythos of the primal goddess cultures—and her own art as a sculptor celebrating feminine orgasmic energy. This book is a Healing Work on a grand scale."

— Brock Travis, Spiritual Counselor

"Lynn Creighton has devoted her life-long work to creating art forms to express the joyful celebration of the sensual female body. Using her life experience, coupled with her exceptional talents as sculptor and as an author, she is now showing her synthesis of this work. Ms. Creighton gives us her views of how acceptance of our bodies and our sensuous drives can free us from past trauma and cultural misconceptions. This liberation can then lead to freedom in, perhaps, exceptional areas of creative expression and more joy in living today."

— Daniel A. Droke, MFT, MBA. Retired Psychotherapist. Berkeley, CA

RECLAIMING THE SACRED SOURCE

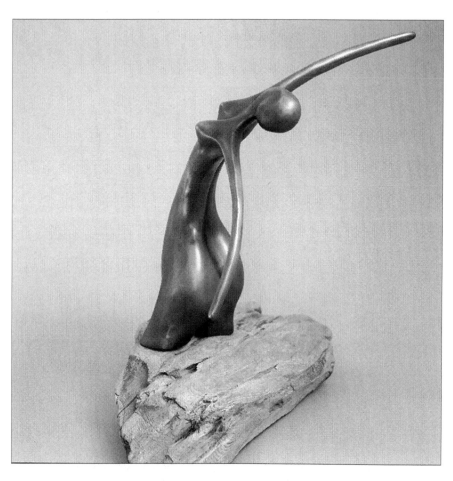

MORNING GLORY SAYS:

We express the highest level of our being through our sexual nature.

RECLAIMING THE SACRED SOURCE

The Ancient Power and Wisdom
of Women's Sexuality

Lynn Creighton

Reclaiming The Sacred Source:
The Ancient Power and Wisdom of Women's Sexuality

Cover: **DANDELION SAYS:** *What do women want? Freedom to be who they are.*

ISBN 978-1-7371423-1-7 Paperback Black and White Edition
ISBN 978-1-7371423-2-4 Hardcover Black and White Edition
ISBN 978-1-7371423-4-8 Paperback Color Edition
ISBN 978-1-7371423-5-5 Hardcover Color Edition
ISBN 978-1-7371423-0-0 Digital Edition
ISBN 978-1-7371423-3-1 Audiobook Edition

Library of Congress Control Number: 2021908728

Printed in the United States of America

X01-v23

TABLE OF CONTENTS

INTRODUCTION:
THE AWAKENED WOMAN

Most of us in the developed world think of ourselves as living in modern society with its many scientific and technological advantages, and increasingly rational and liberal understanding of what it means to be civilized.

However, when one begins to scratch at the surface of this facile view by asking some basic questions about the role of women, gender equality, and sexual mores, we're confronted with a stubborn history of irrational discrimination that belies our assumptions. For decades, I have worked with women in Native American purification ceremonies. Again and again I heard their tragic stories of rape, incest, and abuse. I witnessed the soul-crushing effects of the largely unconscious and hostile repression they suffered, the way it robbed them of joy and self-esteem. I began to see these patterns just beneath the surface in women all around me, only slightly disguised by their seemingly "normal" lives, prompting a flood of questions:

- Why have women so often throughout history been branded as the source of sin, uncleanliness, witchcraft and worse?
- Why has sexuality—women's in particular—been such a taboo subject in most of our world, while remaining a source of pain and trauma?

- Why are assertion of power and sexual violence so closely intertwined?
- Why is open and frank discussion about sexuality, especially between parents and children, so often met either with hostility or embarrassed avoidance?
- Why, despite centuries of attempts to contain and control sexuality, do we find such proliferation of pornography and deviant behavior today?
- How did even the slightest display of a woman's body in places like Catholic churches and fundamentalist Muslim cultures become profane, or even punishable?
- How did we come to think of the body (especially women's bodies) as corrupt and corrupting, and think of rationality and the mind as transcendent of our bodies and of nature?
- Why is sexuality never depicted in centuries of religious art, and virginal purity depicted as sacred while the very act that miraculously brings us into being is considered perverse?
- Why do so many women report that they do not experience orgasms?

Increasingly appalled by having no answer to these questions, I set off on a journey to discover the roots of the problem. Initially it was a personal journey, questioning my own assumptions about sexuality, marriage and the role of women in society. I came of age and married during the fifties and sixties when women were starting to challenge cultural expectations that they should stay at home, raise children, and serve their husbands. I became increasingly frustrated that equal rights and equal pay for women constantly were met with such resistance.

As my questioning gained power in my consciousness, I sought answers in my studio and found satisfaction for many years in the sculptural forms that appeared in my clay. Expressing the idea of "Reclaiming the Sacred Source," I was excited by the ecstatic female figures empowered by their reawakened sexuality that began to emerge from the clay. I felt I was finding in my artwork images that would inform, hoping to establish a path to healing sexual ignorance and imbalance, and open the space for women to be all that they are meant to be.

Eventually, as I pursued a deeper understanding, I discovered the historical revelations of various pioneering archeologists and anthropologists such as Marija Gimbutas and artist and activist, Merlin Stone. These brilliant women painstakingly unraveled the prevailing views of their male counterparts, shedding light on the extraordinarily long history of peaceful, harmonious, and abundant Goddess-worshiping, matriarchal cultures that predated male-dominated cultures, which traditionally have been thought of as the founders of "history."

This led me to investigating the historical records found in textbooks and dominant religious texts such as the Bible and the Koran, searching for clues as to how these "prehistoric" cultures had existed for tens of thousands of years, and yet had been so thoroughly expunged from our awareness. I traveled to sacred and historic places around the world, searching for and finding visual remnants of these ancient Goddess worshipers, despite centuries of attempts to banish them from our collective memory.

I discovered the writings of early feminists, such as Simone de Beauvoir, and psychoanalysis pioneers, Sigmund Freud and Wilhelm Reich, who through the power of their intellect and willingness to challenge the assumptions of their times, began to shine a light on the truth about how repression of women and sexuality lay at the root of neurosis and war.

I had become an archeologist to my own soul, excavating

beneath the layers of the cultural trance to which we all are subject, finding the teachers and practices that awakened in me knowledge of the sacredness of my body, the historical barriers to my power, and the healing power of sexuality. As an artist, I was manifesting in my sculptures of clay ancient forms celebrating the divine feminine and sacred sexuality.

Ultimately, I came to realize that my journey was not only a personal one, but one that we all must embark upon if we are to bring ourselves back into balance with nature, with one another, and save ourselves and our planet. To that end, I have written this book, and hope that by sharing my discoveries others will awaken from the violent and self-destructive trance that robs us of so much of the joy and creativity available to us.

ꣷꣷꣷ

**Our sexual potential provides the built in means to
celebrate ourselves and life itself.**

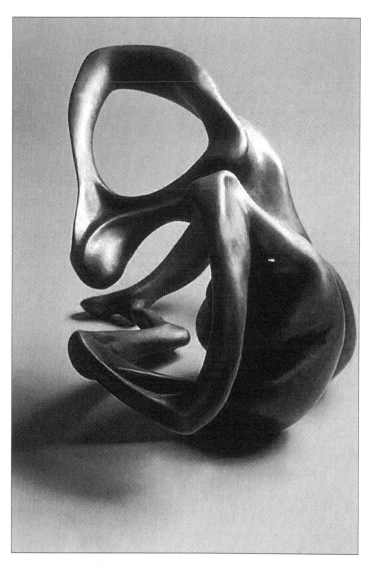

BRIDGET SAYS:

Sexuality is one of the most powerful aspects of our being to be celebrated and developed along with our minds, bodies, emotions, and spirits.

CHAPTER I

A JOURNEY OUT OF DARKNESS

I grew up in a time when the Women's Movement was getting underway in the 1960s. Despite the continued resistance to women seeking equal pay and equal rights with men, the general feeling in the culture was that women were making progress in this quest. After all, way back in 1920 women had triumphed after a nearly 100-year-long struggle to gain the right to vote. World War II had brought many women into the workforce to take the place of their male counterparts who went off to fight, demonstrating that women can be just as capable as men. Many of the previous barriers to equality, such as the right to own property and pursue a career, had been swept away.

But by the 1950s, American culture had reverted to the idea that women's place was in the home as nurturers, doing housework and raising children. Then in 1963, Betty Friedan published her bestselling book, *The Feminine Mystique*, which illuminated the myths women had been telling themselves that allowed them to remain behind the doors of their homes long after the deepening sense of dissatisfaction and hopelessness had driven them to drug use, affairs with their neighbors, and the need for help from psychologists. The backlash was strong. Critics, including many women, accused Freidan of plotting to destroy families. Nonetheless, another wave of American feminism was begun.

Gloria Steinem appeared on the scene in 1971, founding Ms.

Magazine, writing and lecturing on feminist issues, questioning the idea that male hegemony was a God-given right. Numerous other women came forward to fight this good fight.

Many people felt that that the movement had created significant change, and that there was nothing to worry about in regard to woman's place in the culture. However, I was seeing something quite different. I had begun leading Native American-based purification lodges, something I have now done for nearly 30 years. What I experienced in these deeply personal and cathartic rituals was soul wrenching: persistent and profound evidence that, despite fits of progress, we remain under the unconscious and sociological influence of masculine-dominant thinking. The women revealed all kinds of abuse, and many women continually wept and prayed for healing, particularly from sexual abuse.

These experiences forced me to look at the issue of women in relation to their sexuality, and the imbalance of power between women and men that leads to abuse. I began asking forbidden questions: Why have women so often throughout history been branded as the source of sin, uncleanliness, witchcraft and worse? Why has sexuality—women's in particular—been such a taboo subject in most of our world, while remaining a source of pain and trauma? Why could so many women in the purification lodge reveal what they had experienced, but had to hide it elsewhere? As an artist, I wondered why virginal purity was depicted as sacred while the very act that miraculously brings us into being is considered perverse. Why for so many centuries have women been second-class citizens (or not citizens at all), and been subjected to so many heinous acts of torture and subjugation? So many questions.

Eventually, I discovered authors and researchers such as Merlin Stone, Riane Eisler, Naomi Wolf, Marija Gimbutas, and others who revealed the largely forgotten (and even denied) history of women on Earth. Dominant religious texts such as the Bible and the Koran offer clues. I learned that "prehistoric" Goddess-worshipping, matriarchal-based and largely peaceful civilizations had existed and prospered for 20,000 to 30,000 years before being conquered by the male-dominant, warlike, Indo-European tribes, who rewrote "history," as if it began only 5,000 years ago.

My eyes were opened. The more I learned, the more I realized how the deep, unconscious trance in which we have been living for 50 centuries has poisoned our souls, been the source of our ignorance, our self-destructiveness and violence, and how critical it is today for us to awaken to our true nature and understand that sexuality is a sacred, healing force needed to restore balance in the human race, and return us to living in celebration of life.

In the next chapters, I will share with you how working with clay as a sculptor has helped me awaken, and then some of the historical revelations the researchers I mentioned have brought forth that will help women understand what has been lost for thousands of years, and what we must restore if we're to save the planet and ourselves.

ॐॐॐ

Women praying in the purification lodge for healing from abuse led me to look at the issue of women in relation to their sexuality, and the imbalance of power between women and men that leads to abuse.

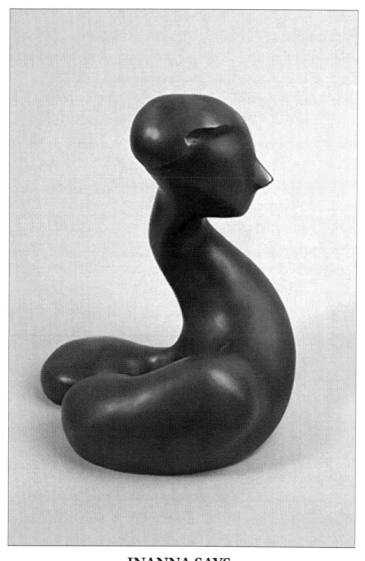

INANNA SAYS:

*It is my right to feel the pleasure of desire and to find
my way to fulfill my desires.*

CHAPTER II

FINDING MY WAY WITH CLAY

Regaining the truth of my being has been a long journey. Had I received all that I needed from my family, there likely would have been no need to undertake that journey. I would not have searched for the wisdom of Native Americans or the reality of the Goddess. I would not have sought divine love.

Along the way, I have realized the gifts inherent in a difficult childhood and had the opportunity to see the distortions I had constructed, to gradually burnish them away, discover the more authentic person within, and transmit these ideas to you.

Much of the childhood pain that twisted my original growth resulted from the lack of honoring of the feminine. My father was not God, though I certainly thought he was, and at times he may have thought so, too.

Five Daughters a Son Does Not Make

We were five daughters, all disappointments to my father and mother. He wanted sons, and she felt, even with her Phi Beta Kappa and Master of English Literature, that it was her duty to fulfill his wish. After three pregnancies, nervous breakdowns took Mother away from us, including the newborn, for long periods. Aunt Fanny came and made order out of the chaos of our household, but she could not erase the disappointment or the knowledge that we were all girls. We competed jealously to garner the bits of available love and attention, failing to see the love and warmth we could have given each other. There was hate, envy, and little comradeship or support among us. Even as an adult, I still yearned for what our family falsely said it had: caring.

Shot out of the reality of basic unfulfilled wants and needs, in my freshman year at UCLA I hungrily attached myself to the first sexual encounter that came along. In those days, we would not allow ourselves to go "all the way," but orgasms were possible and a huge comfort of pleasure. Struggles with my oldest sister continued into college, and in the aftermath of the skirmishes between us, I would rendezvous with my boyfriend. The constant need for comfort (which began with hugging and kissing and became orgasmic) eventually led to marriage. It took me only a few months after we exchanged rings to realize I had little in common with my husband beyond the comforting form of sexuality that had brought us together.

I had followed the man who gave me relief from family trauma into marriage, sure that our love would last forever. It took more than twenty years to gain the courage to acknowledge that the myth of "forever" did not apply to my marriage, and that it was suffocating me. I was unaware that sexuality could be more than a mechanical release that allowed me to transcend human difficulty. Not until my middle years did I open to a way into my own being through high-level orgasms. With these, and my growing love of clay stimulated by a fourth-grade memory of a caring art teacher and a perfect yellow bowl I made then, I became transformed.

Clay's plasticity, its formlessness that will become any form, and the mystery of what it might become in response to my energy, made it the perfect partner in my search for the feminine aware of its true self: me. It is how I found my way to the message of my sculpture and, eventually, this book.

The Purification Lodge as a Womb of Discovery

I had finished graduate school when I first went into a purification lodge with Wallace Black Elk at the Ojai Foundation. I was seeking spiritual guidance, believing that beyond the realm of coffeemakers, classes, and economics lay an understanding of my life's purpose—my own and all of life.

My first sweat lodge, a Native American purification ritual, was like spending time inside magic. In the low-willow structure, the glistening naked forms gathered around the pit filled with glowing red rocks, onto which Wallace Black Elk poured water. I felt at home there, and in my belief that a depth of understanding was necessary if I were to become the artist I wanted to be—one who addressed the mysteries of life, revealed them through her work, and awakened others to a deeper understanding of their own lives and life all around them. I saw a way forward for myself.

Although he had never met any of the women there, Black Elk knew the women's concerns, and was helpful in his interpretation of their prayers and the Great Spirit's response offered in the lodge. In the steam-filled, womb-like structure, healing was taking place. I became conscious of hints of truth I had never known. I committed myself to exploring Native American transformational ceremonies. It was the beginning of my long awakening process.

Soon after that first lodge, I was introduced to another local medicine man, Harley Swiftdeer, who taught the ancient wisdom of his ancestors, and led transformational ceremonies for the awakening of people who had never been aware of spirit in their lives. I apprenticed to him for ten years. Among the many changes he brought about in my thinking and way of living was the idea that fully developed sexuality was a necessary ingredient in a fully actualized life. My French lover and I practiced the prescribed techniques, and my own access to inner wisdom was opened. We even made cassette tapes of the flow of information that occurred during and after our trysts.

Following my teacher's instruction, my own extraordinary orgasmic experiences sensitized me to the stories of women in the sweat lodges who wept as they told of the abuses that mired them in pain, shame, and guilt about their sexuality. I learned that, for many women, the beauty had vanished from this most wonderful and sacred event. Measured against their distress, my own growing sense of delight and power forced me to look at the destructive issues of abuse.

One of the techniques found in Native American spiritual practices is the vision quest—time spent alone in nature, often while fasting, performing certain rituals and praying for guidance, a new vision for one's life.

While on one such vision quest in the desert of Joshua Tree, California, I received an important gift. I had chosen the spot in the daylight and returned at sundown after the leader's pipe ceremony that began the "night on the mountain of fear" for 16 initiates. I built the prescribed medicine wheel of eight rocks, one for each cardinal and non-cardinal direction. Sprinkling tobacco around the circle made it sacred; sprinkling cornmeal was a gift to the ancestors; sprinkling cayenne and garlic powder protected the circle for the coming night. Only with a special tapping could I leave the circle. A lit candle on the altar in the center of the circle was my children's fire (the original essence of who I am).

Throughout the night, I shook my rattle in each direction again and again, starting in the south and moving clockwise from point to point, asking the ancestors from each direction to be present and tell me what I needed to know. I wrote down each message.

At one point, this memory fragment came forth:

Whenever I'm thinking that a man should treat me in a certain way, I am thinking my father should pick me up. He is closing the door instead of coming in to pick me up and comfort me. I am furious, but impotent to make things any different in my pre-verbal state of development. Because as an adult I am wanting and waiting for my father to pick me up, I am not present for what is here now in the moment I am in. I entered this recognition in my journal.

I saw clearly my father's profile, illuminated by the crack of light from the hallway as he closed the door and left me to my suffering. This vision released me to experience each new interaction on its own terms. During another transformational ceremony, a prayer-dance, I experienced being dropped by my mother. I do not know whether this was a metaphorical drop indicating her inability to know the me that I am, or an actual drop which might have occurred when she had had too much wine.

I continued this kind of discovery process for ten years, working with the medicine-man teacher, doing many vision quests, and one- and three-day prayer dances, including three days and nights in a cave, and six days and nights on the mountain. These were extreme situations that cleansed me to the marrow of my being and gave me a new starting place from which a truer me could emerge. Vision questing has since become a way of life.

Another of the healing practices is Sundance, which has provided much of what I have discovered over thirty-five years since I first began working with my medicine-man teacher. At these rituals, there were mostly meti (white) people dancing. The form did not include the piercing of pectoral muscles and hanging from leather thong used in South Dakota by the Lakota tribes enacting their ancient ceremonies. Swiftdeer designed our sundances for mostly non-native people who wished to benefit from constant prayer in distressed, therefore, altered states of consciousness. As many as 100 dancers danced for three days and nights with no food and very little water. The idea was to become a new self, the one who could witness the unknown invisible world. Each step toward the sacred tree in the center of the circle of dancers was a prayer. Backing away from the tree toward my space in the dance arbor, I was given more information with each step. The world made known to me had no malls, automobiles, or war machines. The Great Spirit became real for me. Life began to glow with the magic of undreamed of possibilities. The worry I carried of who I was and what I was supposed to do evaporated. My steps lightened; the crease between my eyes was erased, and my smile appeared, and I laughed. This writing is a result of the life-journey undertaken after seven Sun Dances in which I learned to dance for myself, calling in the powers of the four directions, the as-above and the so-below, to witness and guide me.

Purification Lodges Provide a Safe Environment for Speaking the Truth

From the prayers of women sitting naked in the dark and steamy heat of the purification lodges, I learned of their struggles. The women had no idea who they were or how to navigate toward the truth. I became more and more aware of the terrible imbalance women experienced around their sexuality, and I saw the many ways the feminine was dishonored. These women's natural growth had been snagged by the sexual improprieties of the men in their lives. As my own experience was leading me out of my own quagmire, I could empathize with theirs.

Praying is an act of admission that there is a guiding principle to life. We are not dumped here by accident with no real reason for being. Native Americans believe that the consciousness of the Great Spirit wants to see itself and be celebrated in our actions. Praying in the lodge, praying as drumming, praying as dance, exposes the sacredness of being to the light of life.

I prayed to understand the disturbance in their lives, and the assumption of the secondary position they held. I heard about their monumental struggles to disengage from the barnacles hindering their growth and emergence into their authentic selves. Though their pursuit had been sidetracked, they knew this authenticity existed—their own true natures, their own voices, and the engagement in life that would excite and satisfy their souls. Women capable of only meager contributions because of meager belief systems stymie us all, draining possibilities from a society that is barely working.

I was deeply affected by their prayers and what these women said about the level of contribution they make to themselves and their culture, and their shouts of liberation as they emerged from the steamy hot womb of the lodge and jumped into the pool. As they swam in the reviving amniotic fluid, they were jubilant. It revealed something to me about healing. These were exuberant women reveling in their inner capacity to celebrate life, and in this I found inspiration for my sculptures.

From the Awakening in the Lodge to Realization in Clay

From such Native American transformational ceremonies, I carried into my studio my concern for the abuse women revealed in the purification lodge. There I began to form in clay representations of the inner nature of women, forms impregnated with cause, forms that would not clutter the world with more stuff, as I saw the works of so many artists do. I began to see my role as an artist was to call attention to the sacredness of life as was intended when life was created.

I found more and more pleasure in the malleable nature of clay, how with a little pressure here and there, it responds and takes an unexpected shape. I witnessed the clay reveal the mystery of what life is or can be; what we want to know but do not allow ourselves to know; the mystery that part of us does know, but has forgotten how to access.

The clay in my hands responded just like the fantastic possibility dividing genes unlock as they follow the impulse of their being. As the clay artist, I initiated this creative impulse just as the impregnated ovum is stimulated by the sperm to begin its journey into becoming. Once begun, the process proceeds until it is complete.

For me, the artist's job is to get out of the way. Creation is the invisible making itself visible, and I experience a deep thrill knowing that something of lasting beauty and importance will occur if I can keep myself—my brain that wants to name everything, my imperfect understanding, and my effort to direct—out of the way. The result is beyond what I could conceptualize or do, even if I wanted to.

Instead, my mantra became, "Life is a mystery unfolding as we allow recognition of the Great Spirit's presence and involvement in everything in and all around us." We do not know what will become any more than we know the vibrancy of the appearance of any single blossom or child forming in the womb. And so, I sing my spirit song each time I begin a new task in my studio, approaching the wet clay with anticipation of what will be revealed in my hands. I nourish the creative impulse by providing an environment in which my work flourishes, in which the excitement of discovery is an ongoing reality, revealing what must be said through my sculpture. If I remember that my gift has a sacred intention, I think that I may keep everyone attuned to the sacredness of life. An event evolves that requires me as the vehicle to be attentive and allowing, but not controlling.

Now, my attention is drawn into what is happening in my hands. Is there anything there of interest? Has anything revealed itself? Who is this child emerging from the womb, this form emerging in my hand? The mother witnesses her child and celebrates the increments of growth that reveal who she/he is becoming. The artist engages in the delight of what is becoming known as the clay takes shape.

I ask the clay to reveal to me what celebration looks like, what the woman free in her own mind, body, and spirit to be will be. An immense de-masking is required. I am asking for the mystery of possibility to present itself in the clay, trying to say, "Let yourself have your own exuberance. It is possible. In that exuberance, the truth of your own being is revealed and offered to your life and all of life."

This leads to forms that reveal, first to me and then to the viewer, the vibratory energy of the feminine in full awareness of itself, in celebration of life each figure encouraging—no, demanding—that all women awaken to the full possibility of who they are and what they can and must do. My artwork reveals life as a mystery: that I am the material of my own possibility. In response to my energy, the embryos of the final forms that emerge in my sculptures are forms of women reaching for their own truths, dancing into their own aliveness, erupting into joy.

Given such a sacred mission, how can it be that women are demeaned, that they demean themselves and do not celebrate this miracle that performs itself in their bodies? All of this comes into my awareness as I search for form in clay.

As I am working, I remain awake, aware, and alert until ... there it is! Something has begun to happen, a hint! I keep going, usually with a wooden paddle to extend my effort beyond my hand, farther from any consciousness that might interfere with the movement that stretches the clay into its potential, into the mystery of what it contains in its infinite capacity to reveal form, into what cannot be seen or known but may be discovered. I follow the impulse, the gesture, discovering possibility in the emerging form. The clay leads the way and the form gradually reveals itself.

There is no hurry. I have complete confidence in the outcome of the process. From not knowing what will occur I gradually become aware of what is occurring. Eventually, my inner critic begins to make judgments about what does and does not work, what needs to be edited, where clay must be taken away or added.

Finally, the figure in front of me—first in clay then in bronze—tells me what being alive in the ecstasy of life looks like...and I celebrate. My own joy increases; my own sense of purpose and wholeness grows; I gradually release the impediments to my own growth and recognition of myself. The purpose of my work as an artist has been given to me.

Importantly, my work is stimulated by the realization of the greatest pleasure and joy available in the sexuality my teacher showed me how to awaken in myself, in the sexuality marred for the abused women in the purification lodges. It is the subject of the workshops I offer across the country to awaken and celebrate feminine energy and the four-day ceremonies for men and women in open spaces near Los Angeles. We bring our concerns to the lodge for purification. Sitting in a tight circle around the hot stones, we pray for understanding, for recognition of our birth from the consciousness of the Great Spirit, for understanding that we are perfect, and that it is possible to remember our perfection, and we pray to live our perfection. We have returned to this symbolic womb to experience the ORIGINAL perfection of our being.

The Spark of Inspiration is Equal to the Spark of Orgasm

I am a clay artist because clay responds immediately to my impulse, and the resulting form makes me happy. The possibilities for form are as infinite as the possibilities for the creative impulse of the Great Spirit. This is why I love clay, love its response to my touch, its capacity to become exhilarated forms and shapes that I have neither predicted nor tried to make. My attention follows what the inert clay magically reveals as I manipulate it, a process of discovery. As I interact with it, stretching it to its maximum capacity to hold form, the energy of the feminine fully awake to itself reveals itself. There is no model attempting to hold a pose she cannot attain, does not know exists, and never has experienced.

The clay shows the way past the limits of possibility into the potential of form made possible by taking off the shackles placed on us by laws of our forefathers, by fear, and by ignorance of the blessings of the Creators' gifts. Far from my controlling brain, my tool, a paddle, allows me to create beyond what I know, to encourage stretching beyond limitation, and experience the full extent of celebration for life given by life itself.

Like these sculptures, orgasm shows women the way. It is the catalyst by which women stretch into unimaginable potential, into celebration of their own energy and of life. How is it, then, that we lost our ability to live so exuberantly, to experience the transcendent power inherent in our full-blown sexuality and orgasm, to fully participate in our world as co-creators?

We must understand how we got to this place if we are to find our way back. This book is an exploration of what has happened in history to rob us of our potential to discover the truth of our own being in its interaction with life.

DESDEMONA SAYS:

Orgasm is a re-enactment of the creation of all things—the creative bang.

CHAPTER III

LOST HISTORY: SEXUALITY AS CELEBRATION OF THE DIVINE

One thing I have discovered is the enormous part ancient history plays in present-day society and the ways in which we think of ourselves. One of the great tragedies of human history occurred when we lost the connection between our sexuality and the divine, our bodies and the sacred source of all life and energy.

For so many years I questioned what is stopping so many women from owning themselves and celebrating their lives. The standard answer is that the masculine principle intimidates and dominates. But, why is that? Why have women allowed men to reign over their lives? Why do they await the awakening of men when so many men are seeking to own and curtail women's energy? What is missing in women's lives? How do we get it back?

Who are we intrinsically, and what do we have to offer besides more of the same power-hungry greed that our brothers have learned and are teaching us? How would our offerings be unique? How would these be helpful in viewing our difficulties differently and bringing about changes, not only in a different way, but with different goals in mind? What constitutes the feminine? The changes must be about more than jobs and pay. Gender equity requires re-evaluation of the roles of both sexes.

How will we bring delight into life that holds us in the joy of being while preserving the resources that provide for continued life? How do we rise above the trivial to what is important in life? Why don't we acknowledge that war destroys life and truth connects spirit with substance? How do we convince ourselves that success is life fully expressed for both men and women? What does it take to be healthy, happy, harmonious, humorous, hopeful, respectful, responsive, compassionate, intimate, and loving? What is it our culture is aiming for? What do we want? Why are we alive? What is life for?

It seems perfectly obvious to many that success is not about getting to the moon; doing so has not made us happier, more peaceful, or more fulfilled. It is not about a few people getting very rich and many still aspiring to achieve more riches. It is not about acquiring a giant house in the suburbs or private schools for the children, or about the freedom to buy and access hallucinogenic and other drug-induced moments of rapture or having the right to an abortion. It is more than desegregating the schools or affirmative action. Bringing peace to our souls requires a new frame of reference, with goals adjusted to the reality of what life is meant to be as the gift of creation. How do we clear away the visions that have given us the illusion of well-being as we traipse toward our demise?

The sadness and confusion I found in the sweat lodge, awakened by sexual abuse, was not only the pain of the attacks, but also the recognition of the dichotomy between how these women were experiencing their lives and what they sensed was possible.

I began to see indications all around me of the dominant and controlling role many men still take for themselves, and the subservience of many women. Riane Eisler heard the slogan regarding the Viet Nam war: "Make love not war," and she recognized that much of the relationship between men and women is making war, and the fighting words are "bitch, bastard, motherfucker, fucker." "Cunt" is hurled at women to express hatred or contempt. Men take territory in war, men take women in sex. A man who makes many female "conquests" is a "lady killer." A man's sexual organ is his "gun." Nuclear weapons give more "bang for the buck," as in 'banging' women."[1] In all this I could hear the lack of respect. Our heroes are often killers. Movies, television, video games, and songs attract attention with violence, and women are often depicted as objects. "Pornography ... institutionalizes male supremacy the way segregation institutionalizes white supremacy." It cannot be ignored. We are in a "cultural trance... [in which] abuse is buried in the consciousness."[2] It erupts as sexual abuse at home, as violence in our neighborhoods and towns, and as war with countries of the world. The beautiful and powerful sexuality of our ancestors that was connected to the sacred became sexuality as power over women. Men are as much trapped in this awful script of scornful interaction as women.

The resistance in my own family to the concept of this book brings the message very close, and I pressed on to unravel the mystery of women's second place status.

I realized continuing imbalance hiding in the sexual cultural-revolution. "It is easy under the guise of sexual freedom...for those who hold power to effectively dominate those who have been socially disempowered. Just as 'free enterprise' can be a smoke screen for domination and exploitation of economically disempowered people, 'sexual freedom' has often led to even more exploitive sexual predation, as women are pressured to be sexually available to men simply because they have been taken out."[3] We call this "date rape," a clear expression of domination. Recent revelations leading to the #MeToo movement make it clear how prevalent the problem is.

Often when sex becomes the topic of conversation, it is cast in a negative light. Rock and Roll and Rap music often degrade women and "extoll the most brutal sex as good manly fun."[4] In some parts of the planet, male rule has intensified. It's hard to imagine how the situation could worsen for women in parts of the Middle East today.

My questions seemed endless, and the answers elusive. Then, little by little, awareness of ancient history began to provide some: I discovered that *women have not always taken second chair to men.* They have not always done what men expected, but they found the part they were meant to play, and played it!

The Goddess is Revealed by Archeology

Modern archeological discoveries have revealed that in ancient cultures, the Goddess was understood as the Great Creatrix. As such, She prevailed over all aspects of creation. She was the force behind the creation of new seeds (multiplied by cultivation), and She was called upon at every planting and harvest for Her blessing. The Goddess was in charge of sexuality. She was understood to be the sacred force behind sexuality—human sexuality for women and for men was known as a basic drive reflecting the divine will and allowing celebration at the maximum vibration of the life-force energy. My purpose here is to show the way to retrieving the gift of sexuality.

Such understanding prevailed for 20,000-30,000 years in the fertile crescent of the Mediterranean, and the practice of sacred sexuality endured in the valleys of the Tigress and the Euphrates and in Old Europe along the Danube until about 5,000 years ago when Indo-Europeans invaded the centers of these cultures from the north and east. I will cover this takeover in greater detail in a later chapter.

According to the late Marija Gimbutas, UCLA archeologist and author of many groundbreaking books on ancient peoples,

Goddess worship grew out of the attitude that *the creation of new life by the feminine was sacred and prevailed with the discovery that a plant seed produced multiple new life sources, and cultivation eliminated the continual need for gathering food, a necessity since the beginning of human life on the planet.* Human enactment of our own creative process in sacred sexual practices was thought to give human influence over the outcome of planting and harvesting. The welfare and riches of the communities were measured in the number of full grain jars. Thus, sacred sexual practices were central to the ongoing, balanced, bountiful life, and the continuation of the species.

Think about this understanding, and how radically different our attitude toward sexuality is today. The prolific author and cultural historian, Riane Eisler, describes this ancient forgotten history in her book, *Sacred Pleasure: Sex, Myth, and the Politics of the Body.* "Institutionalized distortion of human sexuality —particularly severe and cruel control over female sexuality—has been the primary mechanism for maintenance of dominator ... societies."[5] Eisler mentions Austrian psychoanalyst and author, Wilhelm Reich, who talks about the psychological effects of the trauma of sexual abuse: "Psychological armory (deadening of positive emotions and eventually even the addiction to pain) is the consequence of severe traumas."[6] I will discuss Reich's findings later in this book.

In addition, if we look toward art, she notes, "Our sacred images focus on death, punishment, and pain, not sex, birth, and pleasure... [it is] shocking how few of our religious images express love as intimate relations. We have no sacred images of sexual love or sexual pleasure since...only sex for procreation was condoned by the Church...even the Madonna and Jesus lack tenderness. ...What we call sacred imagery came out of a time that was far more male dominated and authoritarian, a time when violence was sanctioned as divinely ordained."[7] By comparison, archeologic evidence of the ancient Goddess worshippers offers abundant evidence in their art that sexuality was celebrated as a gift of living.

The Pleasure of Sexuality and Birth Were Once Magical Mysteries

The disclaiming of women's sexuality has been so complete that it is hard to imagine a time and place when breasts, vulvas, and pregnant bellies were commonly celebrated, and caves represented the inner mystery of the vagina itself. Eisler says, "In traditions that go back to the dawn of civilization, the female vulva was revered as the magic portal of life, possessing the powers of both physical regeneration and spiritual illumination and transformation... the cave was a symbol of the Great Mother's womb—opening as a sacred portal—the vaginal opening."[8] British archaeologist and writer, Jacquetta Hawkes, wrote about the sacredness of sexuality in her book, *Dawn of the Gods:* "...fertility and abundance were the purpose and the desire, sex was the instrument and the reason its symbols were everywhere."[9]

Eisler reports that "Our Paleolithic and Neolithic ancestors imaged woman's body as a magical vessel...it says in *The Malleus Maleficarum* [one of the most famous medieval treatises on witches], 'it is precisely woman's sexual power that was in the older religion venerated and sanctified.'"[10] In the earlier religion sexuality was sacred, a spiritual act, a religious sacrament celebrated by women and men.

Looking around them, our ancestors were attempting to grasp what life was all about and find ways to live in comfort and harmony. They recognized that nature operated in repetitive cycles. "In the cosmic cycle, sex...symboliz[ed] the divine energy that makes the world go around: the erotic power of the Goddess."[11] Our ancestors celebrated the cycles of the sun and moon, of seasons and weather, and of woman's menstruation. "Menstrual blood was a divine gift,"[12] not the awful curse our young women today are forced to face each month. We must awaken our awareness to right this wrong, and restore our attitude toward blood and sexuality as an honoring of the sacred capacity to celebrate and to create new life.

Spring was a time in the cycle of seasons to celebrate all new life, an erotic rite as a "ritual of alignment with life-giving female and male powers of the cosmos...partaking in the pleasure of sex would not have been sinful but...a way of coming closer to their Goddess."[13] Much attention was given to the union of the Goddess with her consort. Sex and spirituality were blended in the performance of *hieros gamos* (recorded in a sculpture found at Catal Huyuk in Anatolia from 9,000 years ago.) "The sacred union between women and men [was] part of a larger cosmic cycle to which erotic pleasure [was] integrated—a cycle that begins with sex and birth and ends with death and regeneration." And further: "The sexual union between female and male principles was a form of sacrament. Celebration of pleasure was primary... socially sanctioned for public good for [an] important religious purpose: alignment of higher consciousness through sense of oneness with the divine."[14] As we will see later, it was exactly that importance that made sexuality the primary target of those who wished to take control of the cultures captured through invasion. Knowing that there was an arbitrary curtailment of the sexual sacrament can provide the place of focus to reclaim sexual celebration as a spiritual possibility and right today as we seek gender balance and full and truthful contributions of the feminine. My purpose is to establish a pathway toward healing the wounds inflicted by the wrenching reversal of very ancient sexual practices.

There has been a lack of recognition of the role of the Goddess in human history. Archeological findings of prehistoric images of pregnant women, breasts, and vulvas routinely were ignored for many years, or called insignificant by men so configured by their male-oriented cultures that they could not recognize what they were uncovering. Eisler notes that "Anything pertaining to women... [was] unworthy of extensive or serious study...When images of female genitalia were even recognized as such, they were dismissed as mere pornography, expressions of what one writer quaintly called 'expressions of male imagination'... not considered of great cultural significance ...Against enormous resistance these biases are beginning to change."[15] Eisler says despite the fact that "...there are those who still cling to the male-domination views of prehistory, a growing number of archeologists, linguists, geographers, evolutionary scholars, sociologists, systems scientists, historians of art, religion, and myth... today try to reconstruct a very different picture of Western cultural evolution,"[16] one which includes the Goddess as she was worshipped for more than 20,000 years. This book is meant to expand this crack in resistance.

Gimbutas is recognized for deciphering mass quantities of archeological findings, and determining the vast area and enormous time in which the Goddess tradition existed, indicating that "in Western culture, religious art focusing on sexual imagery goes back more than twenty thousand years to the Paleolithic or Old Stone Age showing sacredness of woman's body—more precisely the sacredness of woman's vagina, breasts, and womb."[17] The male-dominated field of archeology gave these periods of the Paleolithic and the Neolithic the pejorative title, "pre-history," in an effort to dismiss the goddess worshippers as insignificant.

To the contrary, for our ancient ancestors, sexuality was an obvious natural function of life, and was celebrated. Eisler notes, "As these people observed, sex is necessary for life to go on. So, it is not irrational of our prehistoric ancestors to view sex and birth as sacred manifestations of the mysterious life- and pleasure-giving powers of the cosmos, not fear of divine punishment for our sins…it is rather a wholly different way of looking at both sexuality and spirituality: one that does not negate the spiritual dimension of pleasure—particularly of ecstatic pleasure—as an experience of wholeness with ourselves, one another, and the universe."[18]

Perhaps even more significant to the effort to understand and fully participate in life and the unseen aspects of the world around them, our ancestors recognized "sexual orgasm as an altered state of consciousness,"[19] an attitude far different from what we mostly imagine today when couples often simply "hook-up" for immediate gratification using the techniques they learn from pornographic enactments. My aim is to bring the reader to the realization of what has been lost and the personal value of reclaiming the sense of sacred in sexuality and its power to reveal inner dimensions of pleasure and purpose.

For thirty-thousand years prior to occupation by god-fearing peoples, sexuality was a sacrament—the way the people gave thanks and celebrated the fact of life. "The emphasis in prehistoric [times was] not on women as merely baby containers. Rather it [was] on woman's sexual power that to our prehistoric ancestors was natural and sacred."[20] Not engaged with waging war and acquiring wealth, the people had time and attention to view "the human body as sacred and woman's sexuality—her vulva, her pregnancy, her birth-giving— as associated with a deity rather than something shameful, unfit for polite discussion, much less religious art."[21] The Goddess was sacred, and she "sacralized love, life, and pleasure…flowing from the 'sweetness of her loins.'"[22]

Seen in this light, the vanished celebration of sacred sexuality seems a terrible loss. So, what happened to so radically change our view of sexuality and women's bodies? Why do we no longer understand sexuality as a portal to the sacred?

What Happened to the Goddess and the Concept of Sexuality as Sacred?

The way of life of our ancestors, who apparently lived in peace with no fortifications or weapons, was savagely interrupted when the Indo-Europeans arrived from the north. Over time celebration and pleasure were forced out of the sexual experience. The Goddess was subdued along with the sacred sexuality with which she was celebrated. Fifteen-hundred years after the Indo-Europeans originally invaded, they morphed into the Hebrews, during which time written evidence documents the suppression of women through the complete disruption of the practice of celebrating the Divine Creatrix: sacred sexuality. "It required an almost total reversal and vilification of precisely what was once revered: nature, sex, pleasure, and above all, the life creating, the life sustaining, sexual power of women."[23]

Eventually the Church turned the screw even tighter: "The Church did not condemn the association of sex with violence and domination or with the sadomasochistic inflicting of pain...it condemned sexual pleasure."[24] Power and control were the influencing goals. "If the Church was to consolidate power and establish itself as the one and only faith, the persistence of myth and ritual from an earlier well-entrenched religious system in which the Goddess and her divine son or consort were worshipped, women were priestesses, and sexual union between men and women had a strong spiritual dimension, could not be condoned. These remnants had to be eradicated at all costs either through co-option or suppression. So the Church took the position that sexuality was tainted with sin unless used by a man solely for the obviously necessary act of procreation...."

Witch hunts were a condemnation of sex and a violent persecution of women in an attempt to terrorize women."[25] Thus the Church provided a means to maintain control of women's lives. "From acts associated with the sacred, with religious rites, with the Goddess herself, sex became associated with power over women."[26] Since the new rules governing the lives of women took root, cruel and severe power over women's sexuality has been the mechanism of control. With women's sexuality demonized, men's sexuality sought new ways of accommodating itself with often violent overpowering of women.

This is our situation today, while the more peaceful, harmonious way has faded from reality and memory.

Simone de Beauvoir, the famous 20th century feminist and social theorist, believed that position of women as the Second Sex had been a required step in the evolution of "mankind." Eisler stated the dominator philosophy a little differently: "The configuration of male dominancy, warfare, and strong-man rule (in both the family and the state) is somehow of a higher order, indeed, the 'mark of civilization.'"[27] Recognizing that the invaders had imposed a completely different way of relating having nothing to do with pleasure and celebration helps us understand de Beauvoir's confusion, and opens a direction toward gender balance as sexuality is again viewed as sacred and an enactment of consenting lovemaking.

We must now know how the aspects of pleasure and celebration that were central to the Goddess worshippers were harshly suppressed. "Men...[beginning about 5000 years ago] radically altered the course of Western civilization...for them, violent domination, be it man over women, man over man, tribe over tribe, or nation over nation, was not a regrettable human failing but a highly institutionalized, glorified, and even deified way for men to live and die."[28]

A Long History of Abuse

A huge proportion of women have suffered in the way the abused women had who first brought me to this study. Through the centuries, abuse has been sanctioned as a means of maintaining control of the female population, especially required in the time of transition during the initial thousands of years after the invasions in which women and men refused to give up the way of life they had always known. In the case of incest, "incest works to maintain male control over women...a violation of bodies and trust by men who are supposed to care for and protect."[29] Whenever a breach was observed of women lapsing into their old ways or in any way expressing independence, self-confidence, or self-awareness "... societies oriented to the dominator model built in devices that distort[ed] and repress[ed] sexuality, vilifying sex and women."[30] Western religions teach that sex is dirty and evil, and woman is sinful, "a carnal creature suitable only for propagation—or providing men with sons. Therefore, women along with human sexuality must be rigidly controlled."[31]

These forefathers engaged in consolidating their own power and access to riches continuously sought and enforced methods of control. "What better way of unconsciously programming women to accept subservience and domination than through the eroticization of female submission."[32] Additionally, even though women had held the highest positions in the religion and the government of the Goddess worshippers, they were too inferior to be priests in the male-oriented religions of their conquerors.

For modern women, pornographic visualizations of the acts of sex mark a very low level of what is possible. "Rather than being associated with a female deity, pornographic sex is often linked to male coercion, violence, and female submission and degradation—not erotic—not associated with love or caring—often contempt of women is shown and sometimes hatred—more like making war than making love."[33] The beauty and pleasure that our ancestors had known in the peaceful cultures of the Goddess worshippers is gone. "The requirements for maintaining dominator way of life and maintaining life itself were in opposition."[34] This stance is as confusing and confounding for men of the culture as it is for women who all wonder who we actually are to each other. At the same time, in many places on the planet, the wonderful jewels of nature have also gone.

The Path to Healing

To heal ourselves and our world, we must become open to the discussion of our ideas about sexuality and how they affect the contours of our reality. There is profound reluctance to explore the topic. It is forbidden by our relatives, our religions, and/or our institutions of education. We are expected to know and ashamed to admit that we do not. The fact that we do not talk about sexuality (except in mostly negative or profane terms) and the reasons we do not are the same: sexuality as a function of Goddess-worshipping cultures was declared immoral and evil by invaders who overthrew those cultures some 5,000 years ago. We have been taught not to accept sexuality as a gift.

Desire as a gift is minimized and ignored. We have forgotten the role of desire as a motivator, to direct our attention, showing us where the action of life must go. There is no connection to the idea that the object of desire is the vehicle of the gift of desire, that desire makes no demands, that desire radiates with joy from the one who possess it. Desire as a positive motivator for sexual engagement must be affirmed as one of the gifts of the Creator who gave sexuality as a form for celebrating life. When acknowledged in this way, desire need not be manufactured: it has been given!

When we were children sexuality was hidden from us or sharply dismissed as not our business and/or beyond our grasp. Thus, sexuality stays in the shadows—perverse—because the major religions continue to declare women inferior and unclean, and sexuality an evil necessary to perpetuate the races. These are the ideas our families expose us to. We don't know the history of the Goddess-worshipping cultures, their worship of their Goddess through sacred sexuality, and their destruction. I am writing to right this wrong.

Healing requires that we wash away concepts implanted by the major religions that tarnish the truth of who the Goddess had been before the God arrived. We must return to an understanding of the sacredness of sexuality and its function in maintaining a connection to the sacred energy that has created all things.

We must blast through inhibitions, distortions, and brutality, and rise above technique to reclaim the sacredness of sexuality. We must reclaim the place where full and open contact is possible with deep and truthful intimacy that calls forth the gifts available to be given and total openness to receive. We can and must realign ourselves with the sacredness of our orgasm to bring ourselves back to the sense that all of life and living is a blessing.

The medicine man who was my teacher in the '80s told me a Native American genesis story reflecting how the orgasm is the reenactment of creation itself. In this story, the Sacred Creator of all life implanted in human life the capacity to recreate the moment of the beginning of all things in order that each human might recreate him/herself again and again: the climax of orgasm. The Goddess worshippers held this aspect of sexuality as sacred as well. They understood that the sacred was witnessed inside and all around by the worshippers who celebrated their sexuality in the temples of the Goddess.

A basic ingredient of the belief structure of Goddess worshippers was that orgasm is the catalyzing moment in which the sacred is experienced. Orgasm, given by the Creator, is a special gift of pleasure containing the ignition of the life-force and the recognition of life as sacred. Orgasm reveals our divine nature. The energy of our orgasm at a high vibration offers the means to move out of denial, forgetfulness, and repression.

I easily grasped this understanding because it was already familiar to me through my study of Native American philosophies. I recognized that this gift has been sullied, misused, and not acknowledged as sacred any more than life itself is seen as a blessing or the gift of consciousness.

Lots of healing is needed. Women are still afraid of being truly open because of what will be taken from them—so much has been taken for so many thousands of years. Women may initiate their own healing by learning their own sexual natures. By exploring her own sexuality as a way of extending into knowledge of herself, she gains energy and freedom to experience new possibilities in life. She does not need a partner—intimacy with self can satisfy much of the need for intimacy. Self-pleasuring is one of the many gifts of life. The more she knows about her own pleasure, the more she can share with whoever her partner is, and the more satisfaction she will receive when intimacy with another is possible. Like the iris that opens to fifteen versions of its own beauty, she learns to visit herself with unfettered, unselfconscious, totally confident, open sense of her own perfection. To be open to it she must trust that pleasure allows opening to knowledge (and she must remember herself as a source of knowledge).

I believe that a world in which women are full participants with shared responsibility for fulfillment of the highest-level vibration will be a world in which the men no longer seek abhorrent sexual engagements. Rape, incest, molestation, harassment, and abuse will recede as punishment to women who have not known the power of their own sexuality, and the reward of higher vibration won by meeting men's sexual drive with their own. Abuses will no longer testify to testosterone overpowering estrogen.

This is the true meaning of yin/yang: giving and receiving with the giver able to receive and the receiver able to give, a form of intimacy also symbolized by the sign for infinity. In the Native American tradition, the infinity sign is the sign for the life-force energy. An infinite exchange of giving and receiving is a celebration of the divine in life. In a world free of sexual abuse in which women are free to experience the highest vibration of their own orgasms, women will make full contributions of their creative energy to restore balance and harmony to our planet. My devotion for more than 40 years to the subject of sexuality as a blessing demonstrates my belief that there is a sexual problem and that healing is possible.

As we courageously re-examine orgasm, pulling the subject out of the shadows into open dialogue, we find during orgasm a vibratory frequency experienced by our own bodies that is at a higher rate than normal. Our ancestors, the Goddess worshippers (and the Native Americans) viewed this capacity as evidence of our link to divinity who vibrates at an even higher rate, the highest possible rate. In their view, we were able to achieve this higher vibratory frequency because of our heritage as children of the Divine Creatrix/ Great Spirit. This is reflected in a Native American genesis myth:

Originally, before any form of anything, energy of the universe was dispersed. Then the energy coagulated and polarized into positive and negative energy. When the poles of energy were united by magnetic force, the consciousness of the Great Spirit was produced. The Great Spirit could not see Itself until It decided to slow down Its energy. Slowed-down energy of the original consciousness (the Great Spirit) produced visible substances in the form of galaxies, the solar systems, the planets, and, eventually, the oceans and lands, the flora and fauna, and the humans.

All this was in order that the Great Spirit could see Itself in the creations brought about by Its slowed-down vibrations. For humans, the spiritual life that is mandated by their inception as slowed-down energy of the Great Spirit involves the practice of intentionally raising our energy to higher frequencies that are closer to that of the Great Spirit in order to manifest the sacred, divine energy of the Great Spirit in everything we think, do, and say. Praying, singing, dancing, and laughing all raise the frequency of our energy. Sexuality raises our energy to its highest vibration as a celebration of the Great Spirit in and around us.

My Native American teacher also recognized the sacredness of sexuality and its purpose to expose the divine in humans. This similarity has been an important factor in my understanding of the sacredness of the practice of sexuality in the Goddess-worshipping cultures. What I have learned in studying and comparing the two is that the function of orgasm is/was to awaken the divine place in each of us that mirrors the divine (in the form of the highest human vibration of energy) back to the Great Spirit—the great androgynous energy that cannot see Itself—and/or the Goddess.

Thus, orgasm is a means by which we celebrate the Great Spirit/ Goddess in us for the benefit not only of ourselves, but also for the benefit of the Great Spirit's/Goddess's awareness of its own nature. According to this myth, every orgasm has the potential to recreate the moment of all creation. At the same time, orgasm arranges our energy so that it is totally available to us. Sexual energy expands itself into the unknown of the unknowable, and into the deeply felt physical pleasure. Both the mystery of the unknown and the high level of physical pleasure are illuminated in the instant of orgasm, and the fact of their marriage is recognized by the celebrant. Higher level of human reality is realized in this deeply felt connection to the Great Spirit/Goddess, made fully available by high level orgasm. Continuing to dishonor our sexual natures deprives us of living in this this higher plane of life.

Most people in the United States are aware of the silencing of the Native American and the refusal to admit the sacredness of the Native Americans' connection to the Great Spirit. This is the same sort of silencing that happened to the Goddess-worshipping cultures.

In addition, the man who denies the value of women's orgasm loses for himself the huge frequency of vibration stimulated by a powerful sexual experience in the woman. The woman who denies the value of her own orgasm loses its ability to spark creativity in all aspects of her life. She cannot know the core truth of who she is; there is no spark to ignite the core; inner fire does not bring forth the force of her creativity; she cannot see the connection of herself to what she is doing, whom she is with, what she is thinking because there is no self there; she cannot speak her personal truth because there is no inner light to reveal it. The man may hold the image of himself as the sexual one, and so when and if the woman begins to know her own sexual power, she may be a threat to his image of himself.

When we are out of balance with our sexual nature and the sacredness of all life, we don't remember that we are given the capacity and the right to celebrate at the highest level of our energy through our sexuality; therefore, we do not function at our highest level, denying a gift intended to give us the energy to cope with our problems and still have energy to celebrate life. We can't solve our major problems, and we forget to celebrate. Our sexual practices do not generally include knowledge and practice of high-level orgasms that raise the vibratory frequency of climax, or the concept of orgasm as the re-enactment of creation, as our ancient ancestors believed and practiced.

Opening to the possibility that we as a people might once again become attuned to orgasm as a powerful tool for living at the highest level of awareness and celebration has become my mission in life.

Next, I want to bring your full awareness to the balance of power between women and men that existed in the Goddess-worshipping cultures before they were overrun.

❧❧❧

**My purpose here is to show the way to retrieving
the gift of sexuality.**

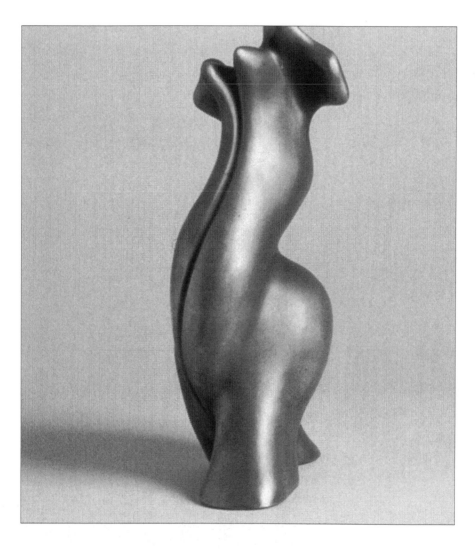

ORCHID SAYS:

It is my right and obligation to myself and life to feel the pleasure of my own beauty, to let it be fully seen, and to acknowledge recognition of it. I allow myself to be as fully beautiful as I am for the pleasure it gives me.

CHAPTER IV

WHEN THE GODDESS REIGNED

A mid my struggle to understand the root of sadness and suffering of women in the sweat lodge, and why we do not remember ourselves as equally important and powerful as our brothers, my eldest sister, who was way out in front of me in squeezing from history what is necessary to inhabit the present, invited me to attend a seminar given by Lithuanian-born anthropologist/archeologist, Marija Gimbutas.

From her I discovered what is called "pre-history," the more ancient history that has been expelled from our awareness and our educational system. Gimbutas' careful sorting and study of archeological evidence of early cultures established the foundation for a new, more inclusive history of humankind, including the ancient history of women. The male-dominated version of history has repeated itself from generation to generation for thousands of years, and until recently, no one knew any better. And women wonder why they have so much trouble achieving continued access to the resources of the planet!

Gimbutas opened a door through which my attention traveled, and with the recognition of women's history my awakening soul began to grow. Her voice directed my attention toward the Goddess and the women's roles in life enacted under Her guidance as a key to unlocking the mystery of who women are, and why they, for the most part, are not in celebration of themselves.

I began scouring Gimbutas' work for the missing parts of women's history. Devoting her life (as faculty at Harvard and then UCLA) to excavating and interpreting archeological and anthropological evidence of Goddess worship in archaic civilizations, Gimbutas brought to light the practices and beliefs of these cultures that had been overlooked for so long. Importantly, until Gimbutas' revelations, we have not known that worship of the Great Goddess in Her temple was a sacred sexual ceremony. The priestesses and the male participants celebrated the Great Goddess in the temples with high-level orgasm. The highest human vibration was offered in tribute to the even higher vibration of the creator of all things, the Goddess. The priestess' responsibility was to ceremonially enact the germinating of the seed, the nourishing of the gestating form (human or plant) and bring forth new life with her consort. The temple worship of the Great Goddess was a sacred sexual ceremony.

Tiny idols hidden in walls, many designated as incidental and trivial by earlier male researchers, were finally found and decoded by Gimbutas and others who could see outside the male-dominated paradigm. Based on carbon dating, they revealed the feminine-oriented societies that prevailed for 20,000 or 30,000 years. These artifacts from the previously unrecognized history of the Babylonians, the people of Sumer, Anatolia, Mesopotamia, and Old Europe, show powerful women engaged in acts of sacred sexuality in the places of spiritual worship.

Seeing history (as opposed to "pre-history") anew through these revelations, references in the historical writings and sacred texts of Jews, Christians, Muslims, Greeks, and Romans suddenly came into meaningful focus. They told of unwieldy women who refused to give up the idols they worshipped, the sacred groves where they gathered and danced, and the lurid sexual behavior in their temples. These were references to the Goddess worshipers who remained after She was replaced by the God. I was not taught this history!

In Sunday school, I learned of the disgrace of Adam and Eve and the terrible pagans who dared oppose God. From Greek mythology, as elucidated by the author and psychologist Jean Shinoa Bolin, we learned that male energy had the right and power to dominate the feminine. For thousands of years, the role of women in "prehistory" wasn't discussed in schools, churches, or communities, and never rose to the historical level of importance that the kings, prophets, Moses, *Muhammad*, Buddha, the Pharaoh, Caesars, Genghis Khan, and all the male leaders who took us into battle. The mostly male scribes of human history relegated women to the margins, dethroning the Goddess as the ultimate Creatrix and hiding her behind this fog of "pre-history," while offering real and symbolic powers to the male gods, kings, and prophets.

Looking at our world as it is described to us by our teachers and religious leaders, it seems that men have always been in charge, set the direction, and fought among themselves for control by whatever means necessary. We know that there was a period called Paleolithic and a period called Neolithic, but until recently all historical accounts are of the actions of a male-dominated society. But in pre-archaic societies, the Goddess was recognized and venerated as the creator of life. Gimbutas found these societies to be organized around the principles of creating, nourishing, celebrating, and regenerating life, as opposed to the organizing principles of later male-centered societies—destruction, killing, overpowering, and taking for personal gain. With the omission of the former from history, the latter violent social organization has prevailed, appearing to be how things have always been.

As I have discovered the truth and extent of the worship of the Goddess and the major role women assumed in their culture for thousands of years, I am nearly overwhelmed by the magnitude of the betrayal and continued massacres that occurred when She was overthrown and replaced by a God and male-dominated religions and cultures, and their cruel determination to accomplish this end. This sense of the horrible inequity of the latest 5,000 years of history is magnified by the realization of the huge effort to cover-up the slaughter and the removal of all traces of Goddess worshipping, discouraging any return to the ancient practices and the worship of a female deity.

Furthermore, despite the continuing archeology and anthropology bringing this truth to light, it has yet to find its way into the history books and curricula. These remain dominated by the male-oriented paradigm. Therefore, I came to understand an important truth:

If women are to re-enact our human value, return gender balance to the planet with women as full participants and regain our authentic voices, we must tell each other this ancient story of feminine preeminence and forced displacement.

So, let us take a closer look at these ancient artifacts to understand a time when each person was sacred, everything in our environment was sacred, and all the events were part of the blessing that was created when life was created, a time before the invasions of the warring Indo-Europeans, when life was a celebration.

The Goddess Worshippers and the Natural World

Thankfully, the invaders left un-noticed traces enabling us, on close inspection, to interpret who the early worshippers of the Goddess were, how they lived, and what they believed was important.

Goddess worshippers were a people closely interacting with the natural world and the natural forces influencing their daily lives. There is such an abundance of evidence showing the importance, power, and persistence of Goddess worshipping across a huge segment of the earth that it is difficult to understand why it has taken us so long to realize the disaster that occurred when women were first denied access to their sacred ways, subsequently killed for hints of remembering in much later centuries, and still today often counted as less important and capable than men.

The Goddess worshippers were consciously celebrating the fact of their lives, and developing strength and courage to enact those lives with joy from a place of understanding what was happening around them. They knew what they must do with their own energies to stay in harmony and balance with the truths of the forces of nature. In his foreword to Gimbutas' monograph, the historian and mythologist, Joseph Campbell, concurs: "The iconography of the Great Goddess arose in reflection and veneration of the laws of Nature."[1]

"The main theme of Goddess symbolism is the mystery of birth and death and the renewal of life, not only human life but all life on earth and indeed in the whole cosmos.... She was the single source of all life who took Her energy from the springs and wells, from the sun, moon, and moist earth."[2] The major types of female-centered artifacts of the Neolithic: "... the birth-giver, portrayed in a naturalistic birth-giving pose; the fertility-giver influencing growth and multiplication, portrayed as a pregnant nude; the life or nourishment-giver and protectress, portrayed as a bird-woman with breasts and protruding buttocks; and the death-wielder as a still nude ('bone') ...can all be traced back to the period when the first sculptures of bone, ivory, or stone appeared, around 25,000 B.C., and their symbols—vulvas, triangles, breasts, chevrons, zig-zags, meanders, cup-marks—to an even earlier time."[3]

The Goddess of Life, Death, and Regeneration

The Great Goddess was represented in many forms depicting her many aspects; the variations were necessary to supply the aspect needed for the situation her energy was being called to influence. "The image of the Great Goddess of Life, Death, and Regeneration in anthropomorphic form with a projection of her powers through insects, and animals—bee, butterfly, deer, bear, hare, toad, turtle, hedgehog, and dog—was the outward symbol of a community concerned with the problems of the life and death cycle."[4]

The work of maintaining health and comfort was balanced with ceremonies designed to assure the help and protection of the invisible world of the sacred. She oversaw all of life and everything that influenced living. "In making images of gods, worshippers and actors of drama, man assured the cyclic of returning and renewal of life. The pantheon reflects a society dominated by the [unseen energies]. The role of woman was not subject to that of a man, and much that was created between the inception of the Neolithic and the blossoming of the Minoan civilization was a result of that structure in which all resources of human nature, feminine and masculine, were utilized to the full as a creative force."[5]

For these early people, life was meant to be joyful, filled with all the positive emotions humans are capable of, an almost unrecognizable enactment of life when viewed from our perspective of pain, poverty, suffering, competition, and warring. "The message here is of an actual age of harmony and peace in accord with the creative energies of nature which… anteceded the (according to James Joyce) 'nightmare' (of contending tribal and national interest) from which it is now certainly time to awaken."[6]

I am proposing that we can regain the sense of wonder our ancestors knew as they engaged in life and regain our own sense of who we actually are. As human consciousness became aware of itself, it sought explanations and understandings. The big questions were asked and answered in terms of our ancestors' perception of the way nature worked to create, sustain, and regenerate life. Some symbols protected them from the gods of death. Life was insured by ideograms that provided new birth and growth of plants, animals, and human life. For these humans establishing themselves on the earth…"the historic and prehistoric Life-giver was a Mistress of mountains, stones, waters, forests and animals, an incarnation of the mysterious powers of nature."[7]

Were we to rekindle this ancient sense of wonder, our attitude toward the sacred value of water would radically change. Waters of conception, birth, hydration, and the home to major sources of food (fish and fowl) were of premium importance and warranted their own goddesses. "The primary aspect of the Goddess [is the] life-giving moisture of the Goddess's body—her breasts, eyes, mouth, and vulva."[8] By expanding that idea into their environment, our ancestors saw… "the mystery of life… in water, in oceans, deep seas, lakes, rivers."[9]

Both semen and amniotic fluid are sacred fluids, as well as milk and tears and vaginal juices. The Snake Goddess and the Bird Goddess create the world, charge it with energy, and nourish the earth and its creatures with the life-giving element conceived as water. The waters of heaven and earth were under their control. The idea of water as an elemental necessity remained significant into the times of recorded history. "Dionysus comes from water, as do… Athena, and Aphrodite… the universal snake winds around the universe like a continuous flow of water. To the poets and philosophers of ancient Greece water was the primordial element, able to produce life, stimulate its growth and nurture it with damp warmth."[10]

If we can regain their vision, we would view everything in the world surrounding us as part of our own existence. Other animals and insects also played roles in creation myths and enactments of the myths; they were honored and worshiped in the form of figurines and brought into continual association with the people as decorations on vessels and containers, some of which appear to be ceremonial objects. "The female snake, bird, eggs, and fish played parts in creation myths and the female goddess was the creative principle."[11]

These ancient people at the beginnings of civilization wanted to be sure that new life would continually be created, and that death would not be the end of the life that had already been lived, evident in the many regeneration symbols. "The goddess who was responsible for transformation from death to life became the central figure in the pantheon of gods. She, the Great Goddess, is associated with moon crescents, quadripartite designs, and bull horns, symbols of continuous creation and change. The mysterious transformation is most vividly expressed in the epiphany in the shape of a caterpillar, chrysalis and butterfly. Through this symbolism our ancestor proclaims that he believes in the beauty of young life."[12] Miracles ordained by the Great Goddess populated their environment. The bull became important in the quest to overcome the anxiety concerning death as new life began again miraculously in bees that attached themselves to the sacrificed animal.

To maintain their tenacious hold on life humans looked to their divine creator for support and protection in every moment, while we persist in our state of forgetfulness, stress, and panic with the turbulence of everyday events. Our ancient ancestors took the precaution of placing honors to the Goddess throughout their houses. The Minoans, using … "the pillar and plant… symbolizing the power of life or the power of the Goddess, created a palace (Knossos) entirely in the form of a sanctuary, with pillars to the Goddess as the source of life power and altars for [sacred sexuality] worship and bull horns of consecration."[13] Similarly, earlier peoples maintained sacred corners with miniature ovens and altars as comfort centers and shrines to particular goddesses for protection. The people were surrounded by and totally involved with their deities who were known to have the power to provide security and happiness for each day in each activity. The activities were directed by the deities to take care of the necessities of life, maintaining balance and harmony within and among the people.

For instance, spinning became an important activity as clothes began to function as everyday dress and costume. Spinning became sacred, and the objects associated with spinning were incised with symbols that would give them magic power to perform the tasks for which they were designed, indicating the attitude our ancestors maintained toward the work of each day. Imagine identifying our phones and computers as sacred providers of the information we must have to carry on.

Warring, which occupies so much of our time, attention and wealth, did not exist for the Goddess worshippers. Artifacts and tablets show no reference to warfare, in sharp contrast to modern collections such as found in the Louvre.

Humans were not isolated from the surrounding world. The Goddess was known to reside in every flower, rock, and waterfall. Symbols spoke of the drama of everyday life and the ability of the people to comprehend their environment, face their fears of the unknown and find pleasure. Symbols to fight stagnation and promote renewal of the cosmic cycle were essential in the Old European's ideology. They were concerned with representing time with their symbols, as they searched for meaning in all that unfolded around them. "The symbolic system represents cyclical, not linear, mythical time.... In art, this is manifested by the signs of dynamic motion: whirling and twisting spirals, winding and coiling snakes, circles, crescents, horns, sprouting seeds and shoots."[14] They did not hide from their problems or each other while they continued to live in celebration

We have learned to fear the snake, but for these early people the snake was a positive influence capable of providing necessary information and knowledge. "The dynamism of the serpent is a very ancient and recurring human preoccupation. The snake's energy, it was believed, was drawn from the water and the sun…the archaic metaphor that pairs the magical power of the serpent and the creative force in nature must have crystalized very early from a natural intuition. This imaginative metaphor is thoroughly integrated…. Snake coils as Divine Eyes appear singly or joined (a double spiral) as a design motif on ceramics, temples, and tombs."[15] The snake was a symbol of life energy and regeneration, a most benevolent, not an evil, creature. Can you imagine not running in fear but boldly accepting the snake as an ally?

There was a complete reversal of attitude toward black and white when the Goddess lost her power. Black was the color of fertility, of dark caves and rich soil, not death or the underworld. White was the color of death, as bones are white. What would happen in our hearts toward people of darker skin tone if we reverted to the older ways?

The moon was not an incidental occurrence. The magic of the moon created joy. Imagine how attentive these people must have been to the activity of the moon in the night sky. Imagine the records they kept from generation to generation and how the information accumulated. The moon became an important symbol for the life cycle of the plants, the rotation of the seasons, birth and growth as essential to the perpetuation of life. The relationship of the moon's cycle to women's menstrual cycle and the cessation of bleeding when pregnancy had been achieved gave added power to reference to the moon and its phases. These early people continually found ways to celebrate the possibility of new life being prepared.

We think of the compass as necessary to find our way to the grocery store. Forgotten is the power of each direction to influence our ability to live in the joy of full actualization. Four corners or cardinal directions of the world became an important symbol in our ancestors' belief that they could assure the continuance of the cosmic cycles of the moon and the changing seasons. The sun's influence gradually became apparent, and they believed that the year was a journey through the cardinal directions. All aspects of their surroundings were mined for importance for enhancing life.

Gimbutas calls it the "Language of the Goddess," and she has provided us with hundreds of examples of the symbols our ancestors created to represent their interpretation of the ordering life under the guidance of the Great Goddess before the invasions erased the traditions that had sustained the people in peace, harmony, and balance for so many thousands of years.

Bountiful Symbols Confirm the History of the Goddess Worshippers

Understanding participation with nature, not overpowering nature, and engaging in the sense of natural transitions, gave our ancestors a basis for happiness and joy in understanding and aware-ness that allowed them to choose actions in their way of life that were in harmony with the way things were.

In seeking explanations and understandings of the world around them, our ancestors devised "the symbols of 'becoming:' crescents, caterpillars and horns .... These do not depict the end result of wholeness, but rather the continuous striving toward it, the active process of life.... There is a metaphorical relationship between the bull, because of its fast-growing horns, and the waxing aspect of the moon, which is further evidence of the bull's symbolic function as invigorator. The worship of the moon and the horns is the worship of the creative and fecund powers of nature…The Great Goddess… emerges from the dead bull in the shape of a bee or a butterfly. The life process of creation and destruction is the basis for immortality."[16]

Worship and celebration of the Goddess permeated the life of the people. Their joy in life increased as they added bits of information about how and why things were as they were. The growing comprehension assuaged their fears and gave them courage to fully engage in the processes required to maintain command over their existence. We must understand the worship of the Goddess as giving representation to the entity that had power over all aspects of life. "It seems [most] appropriate to view all of these Goddess images as aspects of the one Great Goddess with her core functions—life-giving, death-wielding, regeneration, and renewal. The obvious analogy would be Nature itself: through the multiplicity of phenomena and continuing cycles of which it is made, one recognizes the fundamental and underlying unity of Nature."[17]

Worship of Her gave the people the means of explaining and engaging with all that transpired around them.

Sexuality Was Sacred to Goddess Worshippers

Most important to this topic is the evidence that our ancestors worshipped the Goddess in their temples with ceremonies of sacred sexuality in which the highest tribute was made to the Goddess by raising human energy to its highest frequency: orgasm. Orgasm was deemed a sufficiently powerful human energy to exhibit exaltation and devotion to the highest deity.

Discrimination against women after the invasions became focused on discrimination against sacred sexuality, the central form of their celebration of their Goddess. The beginnings of this discrimination, well documented in the Holy Bible 1,500 years after the first invasions and capitulations, will be thoroughly discussed in the next chapter. Returning to gender equity and joy in life requires re-establishing sexuality as a means of celebrating and experiencing the divine in life—the Creative energy of the giver of life.

I am not proposing a return to Goddess worship, but to our ancestors' sense of wonder, their recognition that all of life is meant to be a celebration in which we understand what life is about, why we are living, and then choose our actions to fully engage in our reality with no harm to ourselves or others. Renewed understanding and practice of sexuality as a sacrament will restore connection to continual celebration of life. Understanding the history that has impacted the position women hold in the culture provides a context for changing that position to one in which women once again maximize their gifts and utilize them in their full enactment of life and equal participation in the culture.

By making "pre-history" part of history and calling out the discrimination against women in the 5,000 years that we have been calling history, we can know where to begin to make our way back to equity and celebration between the genders. Thus, a major paradigm shift is needed to make the changes that are required—giving up the positions and opinions we hold in relationship to each other, women to men and men to women.

Women must know that an essential part of who they are, their sexuality, was claimed by the masculine to claim power over them. This is not awakening to something new in humanity but remembering what has always been true for humans: women are meant as equal participants in and recipients of life's blessings. A major blessing of life is the possibility of pleasure and delight in intimacy and orgasm. Sexuality is not trivial. It is a sacrament. It is not mostly for men or owned by men. High-level orgasm allows full celebration by all our molecules. Sexuality is not only the trigger for new life; it is the trigger for life filled with pleasure.

Thus, we must take back the sacredness of sexuality and orgasm. It is the means for women to reclaim their power as full participants in life, and the ability to "know."

To understand fully how the highest form of sacred being was transformed from feminine to masculine, let us now delve deeper into the painful, ruthless, and systemic ways in which the Goddess—and women—were crushed and excised from their position of importance in our world over the last five millennia.

Archeologic investigations and anthropologic studies reveal twenty to thirty thousand years of Goddess worship during which sexual unions where the highest form of tribute to the Goddess, creator of life

GWENIVIERE SAYS:

*When the masculine gives (not taking, forcing, or demanding),
the feminine can open more fully. As the woman opens, the force of life
flows through her freely without constraint. She becomes a vessel
for the life-force.*

CHAPTER V

THE UNRAVELLING OF GODDESS WORSHIP BY GOD-FEARING GROUPS

Lying among the roots of modern religions is evidence of the destruction of Goddess worship and the distortion of reality that made women the property of men and their sexuality evil, but you have to look closely. This history has been swept out of the records and purposefully made inaccessible. It has been taught in schools and through Biblical or Koranic teachings that it is self-evident that the male should be superior to the female. I have long sought clues in this hidden "pre-history" to the way women think about themselves. Why does one-half of humanity find itself in a "less-than" position and battling against discrimination? Anthropological and archeological work since about 1950 has helped me find some answers.

Who Tells the History

The framework of our reality, what we call history (what we know about how we have become who and what we are), guides our thinking and our actions. It establishes a picture of who we are based on what we have been and what we have done throughout time. More and more we are finding that this picture is dictated by who is telling the story. In the 5,000 years since the goddess traditions were overrun and dominated by the horseback riders from the North, those weapon carriers have told the history. Their stories are about the glory of their wars, their invasions, their conquests, their might, and their riches, and their God who leads the way and tells them who to fight and what to take. In the centuries that followed the brutal take over and the strong-arm subjugation of women, attempts were made to erase all traces of earlier goddess worshipping. The conquerors did not want those people to remember who they had been, and they didn't want those who came later to know that the Goddess worshippers had existed. The small pockets of Goddess worshippers that continued to go to their groves and shrines to remember and to celebrate with the cycles of the sun, moon, and seasons were gradually smashed or disbanded. All traces of songs, writings, shrines, idols, and dances were condemned, withheld, violated, and cruelly assaulted.

Just listen to this powerful passage of the Great Goddess describing herself (from The Golden Ass, written by the Roman writer Apuleius and translated by the researcher Robert Graves):

"I am nature, the universal Mother, mistress of all elements, primordial child of time, sovereign of all things spiritual, queen of the dead, queen also of the immortals, the single manifestation of all gods, and goddess of all that are. My nod governs the shinning heights of Heaven, the wholesome sea breezes, the lamentable silences of the world below. Though I am worshipped by many aspects, known by countless names, and appropriated with all manner of different rites, yet the whole round earth venerates me."[1]

The life work of pioneering researchers such as Marija Gimbutas and Merlin Stone has been to uncover the mystery of how such feminine glory and power have been erased from our collective memory. By sharing their discoveries about the participatory and responsible positions of women in the earliest cultures, and how these were violently interfered with, I hope to help awaken modern consciousness to a higher level of probability—that women have significant and unique contributions to make outside the box of securing more power and wealth. Although plenty of women have gone into action without knowledge of this ancient heritage, it is essential to expose the long and intense betrayal of women. Fundamental to the possibility of renewal and growth into the truth of who we are and our ability to maintain our sense of self-worth is knowledge of how our forefathers conspired to steal from us our connection to the Goddess and hide the practices that had sustained us throughout the initial 20,000-30,000 years of human development. With this knowledge we can move into action as authentic beings.

Likewise, it is essential that men know this history so that they might come into right relationship with themselves and with women.

Stone and Gimbutas Uncover the Goddess Tradition and Its Demise

Merlin Stone was an American author, sculptor, and professor of art and art history, best known for her 1976 book, *When God Was a Woman*. In her book, she states that she has worked to expose "the past [so that we need not] remain dependent upon interests, interpretations, translations, opinions, and pronouncements that so far have been produced... [and] remove the exclusive [male-oriented] mystique from the study of anthropology and ancient religion."[2]

Her inquiry begins where Marija Gimbutas' leaves off, telling the story of how in about 3000 B.C. Indo-European invaders from the steppes of Russia overran and dismantled the Goddess religion and its followers. Gimbutas concentrated her excavations and study of Goddess artifacts to Old Europe, particularly along the Danube. Stone found her information mostly in reference to happenings in the Near and Middle East. Both authors observe that the geographic area in which the practices of Goddess worship occurred was huge and included the areas that both had studied. "The whole of Neolithic Europe, to judge from surviving artifacts and myths, had a remarkably homogeneous system of religious ideas based on the many titled Mother Goddess... the same religion...existed... in areas known today as Iran, Iraq, India, Saudi Arabia, Lebanon, Jordan Israel, Palestine, Tunisia, Greece, Italy...Crete, Cyprus, Malta, Sicily, Sardinia."[3] More actual remains have been recovered in the Old Europe vicinity investigated by Gimbutas. Bible writers advocated for the destruction of evidence that there had ever had been a Goddess religion in the area around the fertile crescent of the Mediterranean. Much of what Stone offers about the demise of the Goddess worshippers was discovered encoded in written material, particularly the Judeo-Christian Bible. Gimbutas studied artifacts and tablets unearthed in archeologic digs. As I have accepted Gimbutas as the authority for how the religion developed and expressed itself, I have accepted Merlin Stone as the authority who best explains how and why the Goddess worshippers vanished from all except the hidden places where some devotees found it possible to continue.

Women Under the Reign of the Goddess

Looked at from the perspective of modern archeology and anthropology, evidence shows us that there was a time when women were neither second best nor considered to be merely property of their husband, true for many today even after great strides have been taken to make room for the voice of the feminine to be heard. Generally, today women are still expected to lend their voices and attention to the agenda set by men, though some women know their unique contribution which is accepted by the dominant agenda-setters. Largely, women, with their skills and education will support the agenda set down by men.

We have glimpses of the way life looked for women before the invasions by the god worshippers. By the gift of life women had had power to be themselves in their natural form and expression. According to Merlin Stone, the Roman Diodorus Siculus found women in Ethiopia carrying arms in cultures that practiced communal marriage and child rearing, and Amazon women in Libya during Roman times had authority while the men took care of the homes and did as their wives bid, never taking part in war or government. The men's children became theirs to raise the minute they were born. In these societies in Roman times the Goddess was the major deity.

Egyptian culture in most periods was matrilineal. In Egypt, while the Goddess still reigned, Isis was known as the inventor of agriculture, a great healer and physician who established laws of justice in the land among which were:

1. The Queen should have greater power and honor than the King
2. The wife has authority over the husband
3. The husband agrees to be obedient to wife in all things
4. Mother kin with preference to wives in property and inheritance lasted to Roman times
5. Women moved freely and did business while husbands stayed at home weaving

6. Daughters inherited the Royal throne
7. Brother/sister marriages allowed
8. Goddess Isis known as the throne

But women slowly lost their prestigious position. In 3000 B.C., Hathor—goddess of the sky, dance, love, beauty, joy, motherhood, foreign lands, mining, music and fertility was served by 61 priestesses and 128 priests. But by 1570-1200 B.C., in the eighteenth dynasty, women were no longer part of the religious clergy, their activity limited to being temple musicians.[4]

In early Sumer, Inanna was the Queen of Heaven and the status of woman during that period was much higher than it subsequently became when the goddesses disappeared from prominent positions. Naditu women (a group of priestesses) engaged in the business of the temple, held real estate in their own names, lent money and engaged in other economic activities—the earliest example of writing came from a Naditu meeting place. Stone attributes writing to Goddess worshipping culture. Marija Gimbutas identifies the consistency of markings on sacred objects as precursors to writing.

It is important to know these things as antidotes to the story that everything was created by and for men, as we have been told by the religious leaders through our sacred texts. We must hack away at those stories to reveal what really was happening before the invaders took over and re-wrote history to maintain dominant positions and acquire wealth.

On Crete, the Priestesses presided over religious practices as natural intermediaries with deities…with the men playing subordinate roles in the ceremonies.[5] When Stylianos Alexiou wrote about the ceremonies in Crete, he said: "Priestesses personified the Goddess 'representing an authentic epiphany of the deity to the host of authentic worshippers."[6] Further characterizing this late celebration of the Goddess, Jacuetta Hawkes noted the 'self-confidence of women and their secure place in the society was made evident [by]... the fearless and natural emphasis on sexual life that ran through all religious expression and was made obvious in the provocative dress of both sexes and their easy mingling—a spirit best understood by its opposite: total veiling and seclusion of Muslim women under a faith that denies them a soul.'"[7]

Are these the same brand of human that Yahweh (God of the Hebrews) was soon to condemn as evil and sexually obscene, admonished to remain silent in the church, and do the bidding of their husbands?

Beginning in 3000 B.C., Waves of Indo-Europeans Invade the Goddess Worshipers

Gimbutas lays down the evidence that the Goddess-wor-shipping tradition existed for 20,000-30,000 years as humanity accomplished its development into recognizable societies. Stone concentrates on how these ancient cultures were disrupted.

Into this idyllic way of life dominated by celebration for life itself, the invasions I have discussed began about 3000 B.C. as waves of horseback-riding invaders made their way across the Caucuses and upper Urartu in successive waves, discovering the bountiful lives the agriculturalists had achieved, bringing the worship of a male deity, overrunning the Goddess-worshiping communities, and establishing themselves as rulers. These animal-husbanding, meat-eating people from the North were forced by their practice of herding and pasturing animals that ate the grasses before seeding, causing the need for more and then more grazing land to push their boundaries and acquire new land. This left large expanses of desert where no grass grew and created in the human husbanders a way of being that pushed and took. That way flowed over the Caucuses, and the pushing and taking began among the Goddess worshipers.

We now know these people as the Indo-Europeans. Their continual slaughter of animals put blood on their hands and in their souls. "The pattern [of taking-over and suppression] ... in each area in which the invading Indo-Europeans made an appearance initially invading, conquering, then ruling the indigenous population of each land they entered... established in the Iranian plateau as a group called Aryans by the fourth millennium and in Anatolia by the late forth millennium. There were direct Indo-European incursions into India and into Greece. These invaders had revolutionized the art of war with horse-drawn chariots, which gave swift attack power."[8]

From Anatolia and Iran, they pushed southward into Mesopotamia and Canaan. The evidence is extensive, and the area affected huge. Merlin Stone brings this history to our awareness through her stories of invasion, conquering, and establishing rule accomplished by the God-fearing peoples over the Goddess worshippers who lived in the lands that were overrun.

These invasions sparked great turmoil between the Goddess-worshiping peoples who occupied the conquered territory and the people who brought with them a god from the volcanic mountains in the north, asserting power over the victims of their assaults. The ancient ways of the Goddess worshippers were deeply rooted in the people and did not vanish quickly or easily. In fact, the struggle continued for three thousand years until the time of Christ and beyond, into the time of the crusades and the witch hunts until now, when women must still struggle for an equal place and an equal voice in society. Concluding her extensive study, Stone declared that "there was no longer any doubt in my mind in the existence of the ancient female religion, nor that in the earliest theological systems woman was deified as the principal and supreme divine being...

That this religion preceded the male religions by thousands of years was also quite evident"[9] The over-turning of Goddess-worshipping cultures and replacing them with God-fearing ideas came about as a result of "violent aggression, brutal massacres and territorial conflicts throughout the Near and Middle East."[10]

The Gradual Shift to God Worship in the Near and Far East and Old Europe

The cultures and the religions and the languages gradually merged into each other, then emerged as male dominated. Women lost status and the male deity ascended. Reversal from female to male deity was signaled to be complete when "Murduk mythologically killed the Creator Goddess, Tiamat, to gain and secure his position."[11] The conquerors were unwilling to give up the possibility that the oracles would assist in waging war, so women did continue as oracles, the source of military and political advice. The economics of the priestesses of the temple began to decline. By the second millennium B.C., later laws of Babylonia were in effect. Married women could no longer engage in business unless directed by their husband, son, or brother-in-law.

In Anatolia, just north of Babylonia and in close political contact, the Neolithic Great Goddess was worshipped at shrines at Catal Huyuk in 6500 B.C. Those people became known as Hittites, an Indo-European group. "Records show the possibility that the Indo-Europeans married Hattian (a group of Goddess worshippers in Anatolia) priestesses in order to gain the throne."[12] The metamorphosis to masculine control of the culture and male deity was gradual, with "western sections of Anatolia maintain[ing] matrilineal descent and Goddess worship into classical time... Many Goddess-worshipping women may have fled to the

West"[13] as the Hittite portion of the Indo-European invasion occurred.

The change from Goddess to God and from matriarchal to patriarchal was very gradual, and even though the energy for change was relentless and aggressive, it was not until 380 A.D. that the "Temple of the Goddess at Ephesus was target of Paul's denunciation (Acts 19:27) and finally closed."[14] The Lyceans, who were in contact with the Greeks and Romans, were "ruled by women... Crete, as well, maintained a culture... "dominated by feminine principle [as a] matrilineal and possibly matriarchal society from Neolithic to Dorian invasion [about 1100 B.C.]."[15]

New Religious Mythologies Superimposed Over Myths of the Goddess

Stone took a courageous stand in the late '60s and early '70s. At about the same time the Women's Movement began in earnest to expose gender inequity in cultural expectation and performance, Stone looked back into history to unlock the reasons for the preposterous reality that one-half of humanity was considered less than the other half, that women could not nor would not contribute to the events and activities of their culture in an order of magnitude anywhere near that that the men could and would. Her work was probably sparked by the events and platform of the Women's Movement, but her findings did not permeate the agenda of the Movement. Little or no significance was given to the power and position women once had had or what had happened to deny women equal place and equal voice.

When God was a Woman, Stone's revelation of the demise of Goddess worship at the hand of the worshippers of a male God, was published in 1976. In this book, Stone exposes the religious mythologies that were superimposed over the stories and practices of the Goddess worshippers in the Near and Middle East. It is not true that those many thousands of years during which the Goddess was supreme were "dark and chaotic, mysterious and evil, without the light and order of reason that supposedly accompanied later male religions... it [is] archeologically confirmed that the earlier law, government, medicine, agriculture, metallurgy, wheeled vehicles, textiles, written languages were initially developed in societies that worshipped the Goddess."[16] There was an identifiable process by which the Goddess was replaced by the God in the huge area that we have been discussing that includes the Near and Middle East and Old Europe.

Changes in the Myths Tell the Tale of Progressive God-Rule Takeover

Each originally goddess-worshipping culture recorded the intermingling of the two theologies (Goddess and God worshipping) in the myths that reveal its history. The myths reveal the attitude of the Indo-European invaders that led to the suppression of Goddess worship and the rise of the influence of the God. "The prevalence of myths that explain the universe as created by a male deity or the institution of kingship, when none had existed previously strongly hints at the possibility of these myths being written by the priests of the invading tribes to justify the supremacy of the new male deity and to justify the installation of a king as a result of the relationship of that king to the male deity."[17]

Myths of the Serpent

In most of these myths in which the male deity is celebrated, "the female deity is symbolized as a serpent or dragon, most often associated with darkness and evil."[18] She was not ignored, she was deposed. The symbol of Her demise is the killing of the serpent. In Indo-European Greek myth, Hercules kills the serpent Ladon, who was said to be guarding the sacred fruit tree of the Goddess. On the main frieze of the Parthenon on the Acropolis in Athens is a mammoth warrior rearing back to thrust a spear into writhing serpent. I saw this on my first visit to Athens and knew the meaning without being told as my gaze turned from total recognition to horror. Later I will show this same serpent being battled and killed by the Hebrew god, Yahweh.

Myths of India

The myths of India show evidence of the original Goddess worship, the invasions, and the transition to a God worshipping land. "Archeological evidence...reveals that before Aryan (Indo-European) invasions the indigenous population of India revered the Goddess. The earliest inhabitants of Indus Valley had been in contact with Sumer and Elam about 3000 B.C."[19] The Indo-Europeans in India, Aryans... "came into contact with highly civilized and already ancient forms of settled society in comparison with which they were mere barbarians."[20] In the myths initiated after the invasions of the Indo-Europeans in India, Indra, Lord of the mountain (he who overthrows cities) became the God. The blinding light associated with Indra may have been a remnant of earlier volcanic association with the God the Indo-Europeans brought with them from the volcano-encircled steppes in the north.

Brahma became the supreme God whose form was light. In India, the invasions of the Indo-Europeans marked the beginnings of castes. These conquerors were larger and blonder than the people already living in India and considered themselves superior. The spread of the Indo-Aryan culture brought the beginnings of the Hindu religion and the concept of light-colored skin as better than dark-colored skin. White-skinned Aryans did not wish to mingle with dark-skinned Dravidians, and laws were created against mixed marriages. Particularly, lawlessness would mean "corruption" of women and would cause caste mixture [children of cross-cultural impregnation], definitely undesirable. The Indo-Aryan attitude toward women was made clear in two sentences attributed to Indra in the Rg Veda (Sanskrit written between 1500 and 1200 B.C.): "'The mind of woman knows no discipline. Her intellect has little weight.' An ironic statement considering the level of the culture of the patriarchal male-worshipping Indo-Aryan compared with that of the more female-oriented Goddess-worshipping people they forcibly subdued. These patriarchal invaders... saw women as inferior..."[21] or at least said they did as they asserted male superiority and capacity to accumulate wealth.

In later periods of Indian history as in many other areas where worship of the male deity was superimposed upon the female religion, many people, perhaps those who remained in more isolated areas, still retained the worship of the Goddess.

Myths of Iran

Iran is an area where the Indo-Europeans established a strong presence. "Many of the myths and customs as noted in the Rg Veda (sacred text of India) and the Avesta (sacred text in Iran) are similar, probably deriving from the same Indo-European ethnological stock established on the Iranian Plateau since the fourth millennium B.C. who were forbearers of the two cultures."[22] In Iran, the great father represents light—Ahura Mazda—referred to in the myths as the Lord of Light living on the mountain top. Good and bad as light and dark was represented everywhere, as in the myths of India. It is said in Iran that the problems of humanity are caused by mixing dark and light. The Hurians—a ruling caste of Aryans, who were in India—were also found in Iran. Most of the Hurians were not Indo-European, but their kings and rulers were—an Aryan warrior class ruling over a largely non-Aryan population.

Myths of Mesopotamia

The Tigress, Euphrates and Persian Gulf area was a major land of the Goddess worshippers where agriculture was developed. The Goddess Inanna reigned there in Sumer, but in 4000 B.C. Ubaid people (who spoke language from near Russian and Iranian border) built temple at Eridu that contained no mythological goddess references. Enki was worshipped at Eridu—mythologically, the sun god born from cosmic water. The first irrigation cannels were found there, probably the ones referred to as Inanna is informed that she knows nothing about the irrigations systems that have been developed, a reference to her growing lack of ability to rule.

As the change-over to God worshipping occurred, the myths surrounding Inanna, the Great Goddess in Sumer, evolved. Inanna gives up her royal scepter and twice asks Enki "where are my royal powers?" As if to console her, he tells her that she still has charge of the "words spoken by the young lad," words that she had established, and that the cloak, the staff, and the "wand of shepherdship" were still hers. As if in further explanation of Her loss of powers as a result of the canal building, he ends with, "Inanna, you do not know the distant wells, the fastening ropes, the inundation has come, the land is restored, the inundation of Enlil has come."[23]

A significant myth has Marduk killing the Goddess when a third male deity was introduced in Sumer: An or Anu-Sun God.

This legend, known as Enuma Elish, is similar to the legend of Indra in India when Indra agreed to kill Danu and her son Vritra. In other myths, masculine gods Enki, Enlil, Anu, Marduk were each introduced by Indo-Europeans or closely related northern groups entering the Goddess culture of Mesopotamia and usurping the position of the Goddess.

Myths of Egypt

Egyptian mythology expands to incorporate developing events of history. A Boat in Heaven brought in the male deity in an invasion just before 3000 B.C., shortly after which kingship was initiated, replacing the feminine-based ruler and religion. This myth marks the beginning of male supremacy, and it came from Mesopotamia where the Indo-Europeans were well established. In 2900 B.C. a new male deity, Hor-Wer (great Hor), was seen riding about in his boat in heaven like the horse-drawn chariot of the Sun God later in Greece and India. Upper and lower Egypt joined—the crowns worn one under the other: UaZit (north-lower Nile) cobra; Nekhebt (south-upper Nile) vulture. Ra, the new king, was a Sun God who arrived by boat from the north as the invaders of Egypt had. Ra had to fight the power of darkness, the serpent (Zet), every day, making it a difficult task for the Sun God to rise.

Egyptian contact with Sumer, already conquered by the Indo-Europeans, is evidenced in cylinder-type seals and First Dynasty tombs inspired by the new king shown as the Sun God arriving in his boat, much as Enki [in Sumer] was known a to have done. Further evidence of contact with Mesopotamia was a boat of the style found in Mesopotamia carved into a knife handle. Also, a mural from an Egyptian tomb shows a battle at sea of Egyptians engaging Mesopotamian ships.

About 3500 to 3000 B.C., followers of Horace formed a master race that ruled over Egypt. They were much bigger people, as the new rulers (descending from the Indo-Europeans) were everywhere they took over. Priests of Memphis proposed another concept of the great father God, Ptah, in which Ptah was the first created when all existence was made. "Ptah masturbated creating all the other gods, totally eliminating need for divine ancestress."[24]

Myths of Hittites in Anatolia

Hittites, a group of Indo-Europeans, were responsible for the creation of an Exclusive Caste. They entered Anatolia from the Caucuses sometime after 3000 B.C. Archeological evidence determines the incursion: "Examination of the skulls which have been found in several sites in Anatolia shows that in the third millennium B.C. the population was predominantly long-headed or dolichocephalic [Mediterranean] with only a small admixture of brachycephalic [Alpine] types. In the second millennium, the proportion of Brachycephalic skulls increased to 50 percent. The Brachycephalic of Alpine people eventually became known as the ruling class of the Hittite Empire. The earlier people were known as Hatti...they became subservient... while the Indo Europeans assumed the role of royalty and leadership much as the Shemsu Hor did in Egypt and the Aryans did in India."[25]

"The Hittite...state was the creation of an exclusive cast superimposed upon the indigenous population, the Hattians. The Indo-Europeans with their horse-drawn chariots and greater physical size (emphasized by 18- to 24-inch conical hats) possessed a military supremacy never before encountered. Compared to the copper, gold, and bronze of the Goddess cultures, iron [of the Hittites] (first smelted in the second millennium) provided more efficient weaponry. (Iron is related to word Aryan, another name for the Indo-Europeans.) They kept the process secret for centuries."[26] Hattians occupying the area conquered by the Hittites were influenced by the peoples and the temple at Catak Huyut and worshipped the Goddess. The conquered Hattians were kept in line by fear and a well-armed warrior caste. One Hittite stated: "If anyone opposes the judgment of the King, his household shall become ruin; if anyone opposes the judgment of a dignitary, his head shall be cut off.[27] Indo-European language appeared in Asia Minor in 2500 B.C. Hittites had a written language, and may have gained popular acceptance by marrying Hattian princesses who held rights to the throne by matrilineal descent. There is evidence that princesses were tools of the spread of power and influence: In Egypt, Ikhnaton's mother and wife were Hittite princesses. The change to God rule was noted in the myth of the defeat of Dragon when the young man sleeps with Goddess and gains sufficient power to help the storm god defeat the Dragon.

Myths of Greeks as Battleground for the Goddess and the God

We are often told to think of Greece as the birthplace of our culture without reference to the fact the Goddess worshippers were terminated there, as they had been in the whole region, and what we inherit from Greece is the overlaid God culture with its inherent male-superiority. We are not told and do not know about the earlier feminine deity and cultural orientation toward the Goddess. E. A. Butterworth in *Traces of the Pre-Olympian World* (1966) found evidence of the power of the female position: "...by carefully tracing lineage of royal houses that many of the greatest pre-Greek cities, that were essentially small nations, were originally matrilineal... including Argos, Thebes, Tiryns, Athens'"(Butterworth from Stone)

Then, as had occurred around the Tigress and the Euphrates, "'Greece was invaded by northern people several times... when the Dorians (a warring tribe from the north) arrived toward the end of the second millennium, patrilineal succession became the rule'"[28] "...The greatest revolution in the history of early Greece was that by which the custom was changed from matrilineal to patrilineal succession and the loyalty to the clan destroyed. The attack upon the matrilineal clans destroyed the power of the clan world itself and with it, its religion... the history of the times is penetrated through and through with the clash of patrilineal and matrilineal and the old religious dynasties were broken, swept away, and re-established... the matrilineal world was brought to an end by a number of murderous assaults upon the heart of that world, the Potma Mater (The Great Goddess) herself."[29] The new myth tells the story involves Zeus usurping Hera.

Apollo's temple at Delphi was built over the vent through which the oracle communicated with the python who brought forth the truth from the center of the earth. On my vision quest to find the underlying Goddess tradition in Greece, I performed a pipe ceremony within the ancient foundation of the Oracle's sacred site under Apollo's temple.

I found the temple to Hera on the island of Delos lost in the forest of marble monuments as treasuries built to honor war and warriors. It was unpretentious, built of stones fitted together in a style pre-dating Classical Greece by thousands of years. The birthplace of Hera in a cave on Crete became the birthplace of Zeus. (The guide who led me into the cave with a group was not aware until one of the lanterns was missing that I had stayed behind in that powerful spot to honor Hera when he led the others back to the entrance. His echoing voice called in Greek as he clambered down the steep path to fetch his lantern.) Female children turned up in trash heaps in Athens during the time of classical Greece when the honoring of women and of life had deteriorated. Zeus was given supremacy over all the gods and goddesses and is frequently portrayed as raping a goddess to serve his narcissistic needs.

Hera, whose worship appears to have survived from Mycenaean times, was thwarted in Her rebellion against Her newly assigned husband, Zeus, surely an allegorical reminder to those who struggled for primacy of the Goddess and lost.

These stories tell how the emphasis shifted from female to male. "With these northern people came the worship of the Indo-European Dyans Piar, literally God Father, eventually known in Greece as Zeus and later in Rome as Jupitar... Change from Goddess worship to the male deity [was] brought about most intensely by the Dorian invasion."[30]

Indo-Europeans Were Ancestors of the Hebrews

There seems to be no doubt that ancient Israel was connected to the Indo-European incursions and "can no longer be treated as an isolated independent object of study... its history is inseparably bound up with [the] ancient... history, political history, and culture[31] we have been discussing. Stone argues that the Indo-Europeans are in Genesis. "In about 2300 B.C., a great wave of Indo-Europeans speaking a dialect known as Luvian swept over Anatolia... their progress was marked with widespread destruction. They were perhaps a priestly caste."[32] Using linguistic clues, Stone surmises that it was the Luvites, an Indo-European group, who eventually became the Levites, leaders of the Jews.

The most ancient prophet of the Hebrews, Abraham, grew up under the influence of the Indo-Europeans. The family home of Abraham, the oldest patriarch of the Jewish tradition, father of the

Hebrew tribes, and first prophet of Yahweh, was in an area dominated by Indo-Europeans in a town named Harran near Anatolia in
what is now Turkey. He appears to have also taken residence in Ur in
Sumer. The word Yahweh may come from those people at that time
since the word yahveh means "everflowing" in the Sanskrit they used
for writing, and there are many indications that this new god was
related to the erupting and flowing volcano. When Abraham got to
Canaan he arranged with a Hittite (Indo-European) to find a burial
place for his wife, Sarah. This is evidence of the trust a Hebrew put
in a Hittite. Abraham was buried there and his grandson, Jacob,
requested that his body be returned from Egypt to be buried there
as well. In addition, marriages were arranged for Abraham's sons
and grandsons from among the Hittites and Horites in Harran
which occurred while Abraham was in Canaan and required trav-
elling the distance back to Harran. "…The repeated association of
Abraham's family with people and places we know to be connected
with Indo-European kingdoms, at the exact time of their existence,
should certainly be taken into account."[33]

Another tie between the Hebrews and the Indo-Europeans
is the practice of levirate marriage that did not exist in the Near
East until the Indo-Europeans invaded and was widely practiced by
the Hebrews. This is the law by which the widow of a dead man is
assigned to his brother or her father-in-law. It is reasonable to sup-
pose that the Hebrews continued the practice from their beginnings
as Indo-Europeans taking control of conquered lands.

The battle between Yahweh and the serpent is often referred
to in the Bible, another indication of the Hebrew tie to the
Indo-Europeans. This battle is a symbol of the battle to subdue the
Goddess, represented by the serpent, told in Indo-European tales
of overpowering the Goddess. Following the myth of the serpent
gives us clues of the demise of the value of the Goddess and her

ways. This same tale of destruction of the feminine that exists on the frieze of the Parthenon is told again and again in the Bible. "In Job 26:13 and in Psalm 104 we may still read that Yahweh destroyed the primeval serpent. In Psalm 74 we also find, 'By Thy power, Thou didst cleave the sea monster in two [just as Marduk did] and break the sea serpent's head above the waters. Thou didst crush Leviathan's many heads.'"[34] The serpent comes up in the texts of Ugarit (in northern Canaan and a few miles south of Hittite and Luvian areas where the Indo-Europeans were in control). In the foregoing myths, a direct connection of Yahweh's involvement in overpowering of the Goddess is established.

The fact that there are many similarities between Iranian and Hebrew myths to indicate that both traditions grew out of the same original religious base: Indo-European. For instance, "in the Pahlavi [Iranian] texts of 4000 B.C. ... the creation of the universe is described as having taken place in seven acts. These correlate extraordinarily closely with the Hebrew account. First the sky; second, water; third, earth; fourth, plants; fifth, cattle; sixth, man; and on the seventh day was Ohrmazd (Ahura Mazda) himself... neither was a direct loan but more likely the result of two lines of development, originally stemming from the same earlier source [presumably Indo-European]."[35]

The first woman is demonized in both Hebrew and Iranian myths, a fact that also point to beginnings in the earlier Indo-European tradition. Eve, of course, betrayed Adam by tempting him with the fruit containing knowledge of sexuality. Lilith before Eve refused to go along with the whole scheme. In the Iranian myth, the first woman, Jeh arrives at Creation with the devil and copulates him there, defiling all the women to come who in turn will defile all men.

By another joint myth, the Hebrew and Iranian traditions appear to have developed from the same earlier myth thus informing us that the Hebrew myth is not unique to the Hebrews or to their God, and that the earlier group, the Indo-Europeans, is the source of both myths. In the Iranian version, their God, Ahura, warned Yima that the world would be destroyed by floods, and he was to build a fortress into which he would bring animals and humans in pairs and all that they would need to survive. The story of the flood experienced by Noah and Yima was also experienced in the myths of Sumer. Because there are no high mountains in Sumer, this too is very likely a story brought by the Indo-Europeans, called the "mountain race."

The Indo-European influence in Egypt, created by invasions and the importation of Hittite and Hurrian priestesses to Egyptian kings to be wives, was transmitted to the Hebrews when Moses was adopted by the pharaoh's daughter and given a royal name. This is another indication of the connection between the Hebrews and the Indo-Europeans. Hebrew mingling with Indo-European influence in Egypt was also possible when Abraham went into Egypt to escape famine shortly before Moses was there. In addition, Joseph, Abraham's brother, had at about the same time developed a close relationship with the royal family in Egypt.

Identifying the connection of the Hebrews to the Indo-Europeans gives credence to the idea that the Hebrews took up the fight against the Goddess who had been in place when the Indo-European invaders arrived from the steppes of Russia. We can trace the sustained battle of the Hebrews in the Bible, but finding the roots of this hostility deeply implanted in the warring people, the Indo-Europeans, helps explain the Hebrew determination to completely eradicate the Goddess religion imposing their power over the people they found in the lands they conquered, particularly the women who sustained support for the other god who already reigned supreme in the new land: The Goddess.

The symbolism of the mountain is another connecting link between the Indo-Europeans and the Hebrews. The Indo-Europeans originated in lands with volcanoes. Both the Indians and the Iranians, who are known to have been invaded and subsequently ruled by the Indo-Europeans, declared their new God to rule from the high mountain. "Aryans of India worshipped ancestral fathers who soared to the realms of eternal light... Indra was Lord of the Mountain, his possessions described as golden... the abode of Indo-Iranian Ahura was said to be luminous and shiny, set upon the top of the mountain Hara (Hara means mountain in Iranian)."[36] Zeus, initiated in Greece by the Indo-Europeans, had thunderbolts and lived on Mt. Olympus. The Storm God of the Hitittes had lightning bolts and lived on the mountain. Among the Hebrews, Moses is associated with Mount Sinai, and he spoke with Yahweh on Mount Horeb. "We read in exod.3:1 that when Moses was in the desert alone... 'he came to [Mount] Horeb, mountain of God.' After the Exodus and the more familiar ascent of Moses on Mount Sinai we again read, 'You must never forget that the day you stood before the Lord your God on [Mount] Horeb.' (Deut.4:10) And in Deut. 4:10, 'On the day when the Lord spoke to you out of the fire on [Mount] Horeb....'"[37] Throughout the Book of Psalms Yahweh is referred to in association with a mountain or rock in Ps. 19, 28,31, 48, 62, 71, 78, 89, 94, 99. In Exod. 24:17 "The Glory of the Lord looked to the Israelites like a devouring fire on the mountaintop. And in Duet. 5:4 'The Lord spoke with you face to face on the mountain out of the fire.'"[38]

Stone challenges her reader: "Is the Hebrew Yahweh who spoke out of the fire on Mount Horeb to be considered as an image and concept much different from these Indo-European gods? Or may he also be regarded as the Indo-Aryan father who dwells in the glowing light' as portrayed in the Rig Veda?"[39] Surely the Hebrews were at one time worshipping in the awesome precincts of volcanic mountains where there was loud thundering, lightening, and dense smoke. This is a far different deity than the Goddess Creator.

The overflowing volcanic eruption with which the God of the Hebrews presents Himself is truly frightening: In Ps.18 we read, "The earth heaved and quaked, the foundations of the mountain shook; they heaved, because He was angry. Smoke rose from his nostrils, devouring fire came out of His mouth, glowing coals and searing hear... Thick clouds came out of the radiance before Him, hailstones and glowing coals... he shot forth lightning shafts and sent them echoing."[40] There is no doubt that the origins of the Hebrew God were among the high mountains as were the origins of the Indo-European. The case is made for a continuous stream of development beginning with the invasions by the Indo-Europeans, progressing through the development of the Hebrew tribes, and continuing into Christianity. This stream contains also the story of the demise of the Goddess and our inability to recognize who she had been in her 20,000-30,000 years of reigning over human development.

Now, I want to turn your attention to look more closely at how the Holy Bible has been used as a tool for repressing women, while denying that the Goddess had ever existed.

᪥᪥᪥

Male dominant invaders declared sexuality in the Goddess
worshipping temples evil and women's sexual activity sinful.

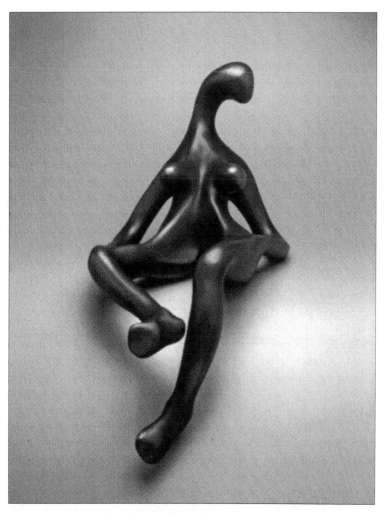

SADIE SAYS:

Our emotions tell us what is in our hearts.

CHAPTER VI

THE HOLY BIBLE AS A TOOL
OF REPRESSION

The Bible of the Hebrews and Christians can be understood as a propaganda tool used to reduce women to a secondary position with respect to men. It was intended to transform a culture oriented to the sacredness of the feminine into one in which men were given permission to have power over women and nature in their perpetual drive to acquire more power and wealth. Thus, the Bible perpetuated the myth that women were born to obey men.

The Goddess Forced to Disappear

As I have previously shown, the discontinuation of the Goddess religion was not an accident of history. Neither was it caused by the indifference of the practitioners. It was the result of an on-going, purposeful effort of invading forces to dismantle the thriving culture they invaded and impose themselves as a ruling class. The invaders' God declared Itself the creator, replacing the Goddess who was and had been the creator and sustainer of life for many thousands of years. Reviled has been "...the female divinity...deified as a direct result of the juxtaposition of ancestor worship and a female kinship system...it [had been] the mother's blood, not the father's blood that formed the original bond of kinship…if the tribal deity [had been] thought of as the parent of the stock, a goddess not a god, would necessarily have been the object of worship…".[1]

"It was the ideological inventions of the advocates of the later male deities, imposed upon that ancient worship with the intention of destroying it and its customs, that are still, through their subsequent absorption into education, law, literature, economics, philosophy, media, and general social attitudes, imposed upon even the most non-religious people of today."[2]

My purpose here is to expose the past, releasing us from the false notion that men have always been in charge and brutality is the only way of life humans know. Uncovering this long engagement in intense betrayal of women is fundamental to the possibility of renewal and growth into the truth of who we are. If we are to reclaim a sense of self-worth, we need to know how our forefathers conspired to steal from us our connection to the Goddess and hide the practices that had sustained us throughout 20,000-30,000 years of human development.

We can discover much about what happened to the Goddess religion by studying what the Bible says about "pagan" religions. From the approximate time the Biblical references began, about 3,500 years ago, the authors referred to the chaos of the Goddess worshippers and their lurid, immoral sexuality. In condemning the sexual practice of honoring the Goddess, the Bible's authors characterized all women as immoral and incompetent to manage their own lives. The Bible—as well as the Muslims' Koran—repeat these messages to each new generation of supplicants, confounding any efforts to bring the feminine to equity with the masculine. Such overwhelming and continual claims of women's sinful ways have hidden the reality of women's worth.

Why We Need to Understand This

By revealing the actual position of women in the earliest cultures—participatory and responsible — and how this was violently interfered with, I hope to awaken modern consciousness to a higher level of probability that women have significant and unique contributions to make beyond securing more power and wealth. We must create a "contemporary consciousness of the widespread veneration of the female deity as the Wise Creatress of the universe and all life and civilization…to cut through the many oppressive and falsely founded patriarchal images, stereotypes, customs, and laws that were developed as direct reactions to Goddess worship by leaders of male-worshipping religions."[3]

The effects of the "ideological inventions," such as the sin of sexuality, still affect women's ability to fully manifest themselves and establish gender balance today (women's knowledge of themselves and men's acceptance of women as full participants in life) because of distortions that have found their way into cultural institutions. By understanding the political intentions of Judeo-Christian (and Muslim) theologies and realizing the intent to diminish the position of women and take them under the control of men and the male deity by deposing the Goddess, it will be more possible to develop the means and maintain the effort to abandon those intentions. Without the oppressive condemnation of "sinful behavior"—our sexual celebrations—we will be better able to take up pursuit of the truth of who we are as sexual beings.

Why Sexuality Was Vilified

It is clear these ancient patriarchal tribes wanted to deny women the obvious blessing of pleasure, but my question is this: What creator would condemn as evil the very process by which humanity perpetuates itself?

Sexuality itself could not be erased, however. I am particularly interested here in the strident interference with the sexual practices by which Goddess worshippers honored their Goddess and maintained their energy at its highest level. Witnessing women's suffering in the Native American transformational ceremonies I was leading—women praying for healing from sexual abuses of all kinds—I have come to understand the hidden, underlying reasons for the inequity between men and women, how women were forced to be lost to themselves. This understanding and memory of sexuality as sacred can be the foundation on which women re-establish themselves as culturally significant. Restoring sexual celebration to a cultural priority will give women and men the higher level of energy with which to continually celebrate life.

Despite our present low-level practice of our sexuality, the possibility remains of raising our energy to its highest level and reclaiming ourselves through our own orgasm. To realize this possibility, we must understand how the ancient superimposed religious leaders pressed us into submission to their God and prejudiced us against the sacredness of our own sexuality. The enemy must be known so that the gift may be re-embraced.

The Levites Were a Priestly Cast of Hebrews Descended from Indo-Europeans

The Hebrews superimposed their will, their God, and their laws on the Canaanites just as the Indo-Europeans had done 1,650 years before. There is a parallel of the behavior of the Hebrews as they returned to Canaan after their time in Egypt (about 1350 B.C.) to the identical energy and its manifestation by the Indo-Europeans in the earlier wave of invasions and domination. The Levites held power over the Hebrew people much as the earlier Indo-Europeans had dominated Babylonians, Sumerians, Anatolians, and other areas of Mesopotamia. As documented in the Bible, the intention, the intensity, and the drive to overpower were all the same. In fact, evidence points to the Indo-Europeans as the ancestors of the Hebrews. The Hebrew conquering of Canaan was a continuation of the activities of the mountain God and His people of the north grabbing power and wealth from the victims of their siege. The invasions of Canaan are recorded in the Bible, giving us an account of what happened.

As leaders of the Jews, Levites may be equated with Brahmins, leaders of the (Eastern) Indians. The roles are so similar, with the Levites and Brahmins acting as priestly castes with moral and social superiority, officiating at rituals. In the early stages of the Indo-European takeover, Levites may have acquired their status by first acting as priestly figures to the Hittites. The similarity of the Hittite word "Luvite" to "Levite" indicates that the Luvites, who appear from archeological evidence to have been a priestly caste of the Hittites (Indo-Europeans), were the origins of the priestly Levites of the Hebrews. I discussed in Chapter V that the first prophet of the Jews, Abraham, had close ties to the Hittites and was born among them.

The Bible reveals the Levites as separate and superior, countless times demonstrating their priestly position, much like the Indo-European practice of entrusting authority to a priestly caste. "In Num. 8:14 we read Yahweh's words: 'You shall thus separate the Levites from the rest of the Israelites and they shall be mine.'"[4] Only Levites could be priests, first among them Moses, Aaron, and the sons of Aaron. Only Levites could enter the Tent of the Presence (where Yahweh was worshipped). Levites were to write all the laws, which were to be seen by no one else; they were to adjudicate the laws; they were to be tithed by each Hebrew male; they were to take to themselves all the offerings to Yahweh in food and jewels and coin. Moses is said to have written these laws, and the Levites themselves were responsible for the writing of the Bible, to their own reward.

The Hebrews retained memory of the myth of battle between Yahweh and Leviathan (serpent). In Job 26 and Psalm 104, Yahweh destroys the serpent: "By thy power Thou didst cleave the sea monster in two [as Murduk did] and break the serpent's head." This Biblical description of Yahweh's conquest of the primeval serpent seems to be another version of the by now familiar tale of the Indo-European male deity defeating the serpent of darkness: a symbol for the Goddess.

The Bible of the Hebrews gives testament to the vehemence with which the efforts to silence the voice of the Goddess were executed. Establishing a link between the Indo-Europeans and the Hebrews lends credence to the view that the Hebrew actions were an extension of the Indo-European's earlier and on-going efforts to eradicate the Great Goddess and all her women. The actions of the Hebrews are well documented in the Holy Bible.

As I have indicated, Babylonia, Anatolia, Sumer, and other cities of the Near and Middle East were invaded by Indo-Europeans from the north. These conquerors installed themselves as rulers in waves of invasions starting about 3000 B.C. The Bible itself tells how the Levites accomplished the takeover of the Canaanites by the Hebrews by combining brutal force and inventive lawmaking. Around the fertile crescent of the Mediterranean, the Indo-Europeans invaded culture after culture, displaced the Goddess worshippers, their sexual practices and their priestesses, and imposed the worship of one God along with the mandate to stone women who refused to do their bidding. The battles to take Canaan were a continuation of the process of subjecting the existing people.

The Hebrews knew before they arrived in the land of Canaan

that the land they intended to inhabit was already inhabited by the Canaanites. The Canaanites had a well-established culture based on the worship of the Goddess as the Great Creatrix, and their cities were well developed. But the Hebrew God, Yahweh, directed the Hebrews to invade and slaughter all the inhabitants of Canaan, as is recorded in the Old Testament.

The Slaughter of the Canaanites

About 1,500 years after the original Indo-European incursions, the brutal and bloody assault on Canaan forty years after the Hebrews came out of Egypt looking for a place to settle follows the model of those earlier invasions by the Indo-Europeans. The sinister nature of the invasions of Canaan is difficult to cast as a sacred act. Beneath the most sacred places to Jews and Christians lay the statues and other remains of the female deity who was displaced when the Hebrews took the towns of the goddess worshippers.

So many details of the invading battles are recorded in the Bible (I have noticed many kings referred to as Canaanite leaders. Perhaps this reveals the culture to be in transition from feminine to masculine domination). In Deut. 2:33, we are told about the Israelis' battle against the town of Jahaz under the leadership of Moses and Aaron: "'The Lord our God delivered him [the King Sihon] into our hands; we killed him and his sons and all his people. We captured all his cities at that time and put to death everyone in the cities, men, women, and dependents; we left no survivors.'"[5] A similar story is told about the siege of Bashan: "'So the Lord our God also delivered Og King of Bashan into our hands, with all his people. We slaughtered them and left no survivors...in all we took sixty cities. Thus, we put to death all the men, women, and dependents in every city.'"[6] The blood bath, choreographed by the God of the

Hebrews through His spokespersons, the Levites, that the arrival of the Hebrews imposed on the land of Canaan was intense and pervasive. When they entered the land of Jericho, "'everything was destroyed...they put everyone to the sword, men and women, young and old...they set fire to the city and everything in it, except they deposited the silver and gold and the vessels of copper and iron in the treasury of the Lord's house [from which it was collected by the Levites]'" (Josh. 6:21).[7] The Bible indicates that 12,000 were killed in Ai, "'The whole population...the King was left [hanged] until sunset.'" (Jos. 8:25-29). Identical tales are told in Josh. 10 about what happened in Makkedah, the Israelites being led by Joshua (son of Aaron) following the death of Moses and Aaron, and in Gezer, and in Lachish, and in Eglon, and Hebron, and in Debir. "'So Joshua massacred the population of the entire region...and all their kings. He left no survivor, destroying everything that drew breath, as the Lord the God of Israel commanded'" (Josh. 10: 28-40).[8] There is no restraint among the writers of the Bible. The bloody massacre of the Canaanites is told.

The battle by which the Hebrews overran Canaan was launched by order of the Hebrew God, by way of the Levites: "'Observe thou that which I command thee this day; Behold I drive out before thee the Amorite, and the Hittite and Perizit and the Hivite and the Jebusite. Take heed to thyself lest thou make a covenant with the inhabitants of the land whither thou goest. Lest it be for a snare in the midst of thee; But ye shall destroy their altars, break their images and cut down their groves, for thou shalt worship no other god, for the Lord whose name is jealous is a jealous God (Exod. 34:11-16).[9] The Hebrews waged the war as they were commanded and made their new home in the land of Canaan.

Apparently the violence and destruction rained over Canaan was not sufficient to destroy the Canaanite culture. In the remnants,

Hebrews found the remaining temples to the Goddess, and sneaked into them to practice the ancient sexual celebrations. Observing this, the Levites decided that the Hebrews could not dominate the region as long as there was even a trace of the Goddess tradition still in place. As long as the Goddess temples controlled the economics of any area, and there were Hebrew sons born in the temple precincts, they could not accrue the wealth to their families. Hebrew men could not bequeath their wealth to their sons if they were being born in the temples to the Goddess with no link to paternity.

The Levites were concerned with matters of patrilineal authority and inheritance leading to the establishment of a male-dominated culture and wealth. The matrilineal emphasis of the Canaanites, who continued to mix with the Hebrew people, interfered with these intentions. The Bible records that Yahweh was called into service to vehemently admonish and threaten the Hebrews for continued trafficking with the Priestesses in the temples.

When the Hebrews did not heed Yahweh's instructions (as reported by the Levites) to cease participating in the worship of the Goddess in the Canaanite temples, the Levites said that Yahweh proclaimed those sexual ceremonies as evil, and that any Hebrew woman found to be sexually active outside her home was to be stoned to death by her husband or her father. The core of what was sacred for women, sexuality, was criminalized. That incrimination has been passed down through our major religions: Judaism, Christianity, and Islam.

We know that the Goddess-worshipping Canaanites practiced sacred sexuality in their temples. Their Goddess was the Ruler of Sexuality. For eons, their women celebrated their Divinity (the Goddess) by honoring Her function as the Ruler of Sexuality with their own sexual expression. Many of the Hebrew people were returning from Egypt to the land of their family origin and familiar religious practices. Many Hebrew women returned to the temples when the Hebrew tribes returned to the area. Men were drawn to the temples to participate. All this sexual activity in the temples frustrated the Levites, who were determined to initiate and maintain patrilineal patterns of name taking and inheritance.

Children of Hebrew men born in the temples presented no problem to the Canaanites, who gave them their names and bequeathed them their property, as had long been the custom. The children of the sexual unions of celebration of the Goddess continued to be raised in the temples with the names of their mothers, the reinforcement of Goddess values and customs, and their access to matrilineal inheritance which included the massive land areas owned by the temples themselves. But the Levites were insistent that the new laws be honored in order that the men would ultimately own the land and the wealth. They could not allow the Jewish seed to be planted in the temples of the Canaanites.

That is how the trouble began. The Levites' solution to the patrilineal problem was to claim that the sexual activities in the temples were immoral, sinful, evil, and abominable. Hebrew women were forbidden to participate upon threat of death. The Bible indicates the vehemence with which the Levites—invoking the name of their God, Yahweh—continuously thrashed and flailed against their own people and the worshippers of the Canaanite Goddess who were staunchly unwilling to give up their sexual celebrations of their Goddess in the temples. Resistance to the laws forbidding sacred sexuality was strong and enduring

The Levites' new laws written in response to this problem made it a crime for a woman to lose her virginity before marriage, and she was never to have intercourse with anyone other than her husband. Disobeying these laws was punishable by stoning until death. No punishment was prescribed for the men.

Passages in the Old Testament of the Bible referring to these edicts, proclaimed by the Levites as the words of Yahweh (God), are frequent and intense. What was started by the leaders of the Hebrews was continued by the Christians and recorded also in the New Testament. Muhammadism includes in its laws recorded in the Koran the same rigid control of women's sexuality, with ownership of women belonging first to the fathers and then to the husbands.

The Old Testament is full of the stories about how the Levites, in the name of the Hebrews and their God, Yahweh, accomplished their goals. However, only fragments of earlier writing survived the devastation ordered by Yahweh through the Levites (or the Levites through Yahweh) to erase all evidence of Goddess-worshipping culture. These point to the existence of written language, but the full story the total writings would have told has been pieced together from what has been found, mostly figurines of the Goddess and plaques that tell parts of the story. Again and again, the Levites called for total crushing of all things associated with Goddess worship. As time progressed, the Levites' tolerance for this refusal of the Hebrew people to follow Levite law diminished. The means of imposition of the laws tightened. Temples were ordered to be destroyed; Goddess worshippers were slaughtered; sacred altars, sacred sycamore fig tree groves, and idols representing the Goddess and Her worship were smashed. To completely rid the area of Goddess worshipping took a sustained effort over many centuries. There remained traces of the Goddess into the time of the Christians. The continued assault by Christians is recorded in the New Testament, particularly by Paul in his lament and challenge to the Temple at Euphrates, representing the last trace of formal worship of the Goddess. By 700 A.D. that temple too was smashed.

The core of Levite law that called for the removal of everything considered sacred by the Goddess worshippers was the idea they initiated that sexuality was "immoral." There was no attempt to rectify this proclamation with the reality that sexuality was a necessary step to creating new Hebrews. They went so far as to construe that giving birth soiled not only the mother, but also the child. The sacred blood (in the Goddess tradition) of menstruation, that for the Goddess worshippers signified the wonderful potential for new life, was also condemned as evil, and the bleeding women separated from all others while they bled. I believe that one contributing factor to this radical change enforced on the Goddess-worshipping peoples was the origins of their conquerors (the Indo-Europeans) in the steppes of Siberia where their culture had been based on the slaughtering of animals, resulting in a non-sacred relationship to blood.

The evilness of sexuality manifested in the two segments of the law that did the most damage to the Goddess worshippers. They were: 1) pre-marital sexuality by women was punishable by stoning to death. Women were forbidden to take their turn as priestesses in the temples performing their sacred sexual worshiping; 2) extra-marital sexuality by women was punishable by stoning to death. Men were excluded from mention in these laws. The burden of "immorality" was entirely mounted upon the women. It was their worship of the Goddess that was the target of the laws and all Yahweh's pronouncements regarding the abomination of women's sexuality. Men continued to wed as often as they could afford.

Men were offered the prescribed daily ritual of a morning prayer thanking God that they had not been born as women, not knowing at the time that the difference between the genders belonged to the composition of one chromosome in the DNA of men. This prayer is, even today, part of what it means to be a Jewish man. (I am discovering that not all Jewish men know this prayer.)

The Bible Tells How the Hoax of Female Inferiority was Implemented

Biblical references to the Goddess (i.e. "pagan") confirm her presence and the concerted and long-lasting effort to deprive the conquered people of their sacred practices, and women of their central position in the culture

Some of that evidence is in the Old Testament. Records before that are read from artifacts and clay tablets in archeologic and anthropologic studies. I have grouped quotes from the Bible together in the Appendix. The Bible codifies what had been occurring as the domination by Indo-Europeans migrated down the eastern edge of the Mediterranean from the time of the first invasions in 3000 B.C. It is quite possible that written records preceding the Bible were destroyed in the mammoth effort to remove all evidence that there had ever been a Goddess-worshipping culture.

Religions' dominion over us has kept us from noticing how pervasive the incrimination of women is in religious texts and in the structure of the religions themselves. While we are being told to honor and subscribe to the ways of the violent god, we are not told that the ways of our ancestors were crushed along with the people of the Goddess. Assigning Goddess worshipping to "pre-history," and not teaching that history in schools, results in a questioning of whether that time of Goddess worship ever really existed, a purpose-ful result of intended actions: "push those people aside so we can install our god and control what is happening; we are the hunters who followed the animals north as the Ice Age ended; our way is law." The new rulers abolished historical reference to the Goddess in order to maintain their position of dominance unthreatened by remnants of the Goddess tradition.

At the center of the celebration of the Goddess when it was

invaded and overrun, sacred sexuality was performed in the temples as celebration of the Divine energy of the Goddess through the energy of the participants raised to its highest level: orgasm. To the invaders, this practice was the most detrimental to their purpose of bringing the Goddess cultures under their control with their God as the reigning deity. Thus, celebrating their own divinity and the divine source of life, the Great Goddess, through high-level orgasm became a sin under Hebrew law, which is confirmed in the Biblical accounts.

Women's Freedom Was Usurped by Hebrew Law

Much of what became Hebrew law was written by Moses, a Levite. The Levites' laws were written to destroy the "Divine Ancestress and the matrilineal system associated with her introduced sexuality as a sin; sexuality was made evil."[10] At the same time, black, originally the color of fertile earth and the inner space through which the magic of new life emerged, became a symbol for evil; light, the color of the newcomers skin, became the symbol for good; the serpent, for the early people the bearer of wisdom and the symbol for life-force energy, became the bringer of evil. The population was admonished in Duet. 13:6: "If your brother or son or daughter or wife or friend suggests serving other gods, you must kill him, your hard fist raised in putting him to death and all the people that follow him." "Other gods" means Goddess. Women were forbidden to take their turns as priestesses in the Goddess temples, the Levites proclaiming that all brides have an intact hymen and that all wives be faithful to their husbands. Sexuality was deemed appropriate only to replenish the tribes. Because it was so difficult to enforce mandates against involvement with the temple "whores and prostitutes," frustration among the Levites led to more and more stringent laws and enforcements. The people had strong attachments to their ancient religion and practices. Morality was invented as a weapon against the sexual practices of the Goddess worshippers, which for them were sacred. Sexuality became the worst sin, a betrayal of Yahweh.

Under these laws women became the property of their husbands. The husband could divorce but the wife could not; the wife called her husband Ba'al (master) or Adon (Lord) as the slave would his master; the wife was listed among possessions of the man; she remained a minor all her life; the wife could not inherit from the husband; her vow was invalid unless approved by her husband or father; a daughter could be sold by her father; the woman had no rights of succession; the wife had no right to money or property upon divorce; since her voice was invalid she had no business opportunities; the woman would be stoned to death for losing virginity before marriage; a single girl was forced to marry her rapist, but if already betrothed or married, she would be stoned to death; in the grave the body of the husband was placed higher than the wife; if she aborted a pregnancy a woman would be put to death.

Extreme measures were required, and force escalated over time—extending into modern history as pockets of Goddess worshippers continually popped up, and the terrible repression continued. The brutal slaughter of the Crusades, the Inquisition, and later witch hunts should all be understood as part of the determination to silence the voice of women and maintain control over their activities. This control has continued into modern times, now called "abolish the pill," "right to life," and "anti-abortion legislation."

Upside down and disconnected from all they had known, gradually the Goddess worshippers succumbed; the male god on the mountain began to rule supreme; women became the property of the men, lost to their own voice and decision. Sexuality became a bad word for something the husband had a right to impose on his wife, but the women who had once been priestesses in the temples where the Goddess was honored by sacred sexuality were stoned to death if found to be sexual outside their father's or their husband's home. "It is only as many of the tenants of the Judeo-Christian theologies are seen in the light of their political origins and the subsequent absorption of those tenants into secular lives is understood that, as women, we will be able to view ourselves as mature, self-determining human beings…The image of Eve [need not be] our image of woman."[11]

God-Fearing Dominance Must be Deposed to Regain Harmony

In historic times (meaning after writing became widespread, after the Goddess was essentially gone, and after the male-oriented religion and culture gained control), the northern invaders viewed themselves as superior people based on their ability to conquer earlier settlers, the people of the Goddess, a claim of dominance still declared by the victors in today's conflicts which I view as a continuation of the tortuous struggles inflicted on our peaceful ancestors, the Goddess worshippers. Indo-Europeans were in continual conflict, not only with the people whose land they invaded, but among themselves. This is our inheritance from those brutal ancestors who took over where our mothers had been living peacefully with neither weapons nor fortifications. We are not inherently mean and brutal in our relations to each other and to others on our planet. These ways were inflicted on us by the invaders who killed our earliest ancestors. There are traces of these early conflicts in the way we operate now, and in our belief that conflict is a necessary aspect of being human.

It is imperative to recognize the truth of our early history, this history that is not told and hidden in "pre-history." This includes the realization that if we can remove our attention from the predominant histories of war and conquest and look to times before war was introduced by the forces who invaded from the north, we find our ancestors living in peace and harmony. Out of that realization we can visualize the possibility of a future that has us standing next to each other with the intention of constructing cultural systems that maintain balance, harmony, health, and happiness for everyone. We will have found that peace as a way of life was a reality for the peoples of the Goddess and could, therefore, be a reality again.

Women have been lost to themselves since the takeover by male-oriented religions and cultures. If women are going to re-establish themselves as culturally significant, we are going to have to abandon our relationship to our religions, which have held us in bondage with lies about our behavior, particularly claiming that sexuality is evil.

The Myths of the Judeo-Christian Bible Must Be Re-imagined

The rib: We will be required to give up the idea that woman was created from the rib of Adam, an idea imposed upon the Goddess worshippers who held all humans equally sacred, men and women, as the creations of the Goddess (Creatrix). Women diminished in importance to "the rib of Adam" was the story told by the conquerors to create for women a lower tier. Men could then be in control from their exalted position in the eyes of the new creator, the invaders' "God."

The apple: We will have to give up the notion that the apple that so distracted Adam and Eve contained disallowed wisdom. Disallowed wisdom—according to the Hebrews, the Christians, and the Muslims—was what women offered through their Goddess from the 20,000 to 30,000 years of paying attention to how things worked in the Universe. This wisdom was about creating, sustaining, supporting, and re-generating the life force, which the people and their Goddess had been engaged since the dawn of time, particularly including sexuality as sacred and orgasm as the highest manifestation of human energy. Five-thousand years ago, and in the thousands of years that followed, this wisdom was what the new militant overlords wanted to claim for their own "God," the one they had brought with them from the flaming volcanos in the northern steppes.

The serpent: Who had this serpent, so maligned and feared, been? The serpent was not only the one who brought messages from deep within the earth to be interpreted by the oracle, but also the energy of the life-force as it traveled up the spine from its source in the clitoris to its full manifestation above the head in the opening to knowledge of the heavens (the Divine Source). If the influence of the Goddess was to be eliminated, Her connection to the Source of energy had to be discredited. The snake, under the new regime, became a symbol for evil to be feared. Our forefathers were relentless in their attack on the Goddess and all the symbols that were related to Her.

The tree: Why did they focus on the tree in their attack on the feminine sources of power? The Tree of Life was sacred to the Goddess worshippers. The tree was part of the sacred grove that connected the life force coming into the roots in the earth to the sustainer of life as it reached for the sun. The sacred groves were cut down by the God worshippers who were imposing their will, intent on removing all traces of the Goddess and the worship of Her. The Tree in the myth of Adam and Eve held the forbidden fruit that tempted the lovers and caused their fall from grace, a totally negative symbol superimposed over the symbol positive to the Goddess worshippers.

The garden: Why was it necessary for Adam and Eve to leave the Garden of Eden—the garden as symbol for all of nature? This garden was the home of the Goddess worshippers who stayed in harmony with all of nature and felt at ease, blessed by all the gifts of life given with the blessing of their own lives. Comfort in this home had to be destroyed to make room for the violent God the Indo-Europeans had brought with them.

The lovers: Why in Genesis is doubt cast on the lovers, Adam and Eve, who consummated their love in the Garden with the wisdom offered by the serpent? The God of these Indo-European invaders wanted His triumph over the previous inhabitants of that Garden to prevail. All stops were out in the campaign to eradicate everything that had been sacred to the Goddess worshippers. And, sexuality as a sacred celebration of the Goddess, attracted Hebrew men who themselves or their ancestors had performed those ceremonies. Sons of the God worshippers born in those temples eliminated the possibility of inheritance of their fathers' wealth in the patrilineal structure being imposed.

Shyla-no-gigs. Shyla-no-gigs, carved in stone, were squat female figures composed with 70 percent vulva. They were symbols of the Goddess's capacity to create new life and were placed as a sign of where to worship Her. Still, in the 14th Century, cathedrals in Great Britain were built where Shyla-no-gigs were found, with the idea that people would be drawn to the new sacred that was being imposed over the old. The same objective was also true for the cathedrals in other parts of Europe that were erected under the name "Notre Dame" to attract into the Church pockets of Goddess worshippers that remained even 3,000 years after the original invasions and slaughter of Goddess worshippers. "All cathedrals give a name of Our Lady, the Holy Mother to give form to retained worship of the ancient Goddess."[12]

The Teachings of Jesus Did Not Influence the Church to Honor Women

The 2,000 years since Christ have been wasted by women who accepted the tenants of Christianity. With no access to knowledge of their importance, or power to be part of the forming energy of their cultures, they largely obeyed the will of their religion, the threat of being labeled a witch held over their heads. They were taught: do not be too smart, too energetic, too opinionated, too lusty, too out of control, too individual. Jesus, on the other hand, was a strong proponent of gender equity and women as the sacred source of life. He taught that no spiritual intermediary is needed since we are God as He was God. The Gnostics, who wanted to include women in the highest positions of their faith, were pushed out of Christianity, losing their struggle to provide prominent positions for women in Christianity.

Religions of today, as they began and have perpetuated themselves, hide who women were, are, and what they are to become. The Bible tells us (and the Koran re-states—Mohammad converted many legends and attitudes of the Old and New Testaments into the Muslim Koran) that the man is wiser than the woman; that she is to submit to her husband, that she is to be silent in the Church. "Men have authority over women because God has made the one superior to the other and because they spend their wealth to maintain them so good women are obedient, guarding the unseen parts as god has guarded them."[13]

The strongest condemnation has been of the sexual practices. The vacuum created by the male denial of women's sexual power, while at the same time the men were given unrestrained, unlimited access to their own sexual expression, causes the imbalance, the distortion of reality, the confusion, and lack of access to the natural source of empowerment and enlightenment among the women: orgasm. Reconnecting the legitimacy of women's claim to their own orgasm will reinstate women to their natural place of wisdom and knowledge within themselves and among the people. Orgasm is a gift of life that has not been (and cannot be) usurped (even with continual suppression over 5,000 years), and it allows each of us access to the highest vibration of our molecules, a vibrant place of full awareness. For women and "for men interested in achieving [the] goal (of gender equality), exploring the past offers a deeper and more realistic understanding of today's sexual stereotypes by placing them in perspective of their historical beginnings and evolution."[14]

We have been pushed off the track to fulfillment of the blessings of life. We cannot live the perfection of our lives so long as our sexuality is not integrated and honored.

We Must Look Again at the Idea of Sin

Most significant is the sin of overt sexual practice, a sin created by the imposed religions to condemn the most sacred celebrations in the temples of the Goddess worshippers: priestesses performing the highest tribute to their Goddess with their male partners as they achieved high-level orgasms. Sacrament became sin, an evil enactment, condemned and punished by stoning women to death, not because it was evil but because it was necessary to halt the sacred practice so that the male-dominated religion and culture could be thoroughly instituted.

Because these leaders wanted to initiate and preserve the practice of patrilineal inheritance, they used this ruse to finally keep men from participating in intercourse in the Goddess-worshipping temples These proclamations were political and economic, ensuring more political power to the surging male religion, and more wealth accumulated to the men as the father's bequests to the son would no longer be lost to him among all the children born to the priestesses in the Goddess worshiping temples whose fathers could not be determined. The idea of the sacredness of sexuality was lost in the proclamations of the new deity. In the construction of new sacraments for the new deity, sexuality was left out, condemned and lost as a sacrament to all subsequent worshippers.

I am writing in order that we may all retrieve our brilliance from the ashes of the Goddess and shine as life intends us to shine. By reconnecting to sexuality as a sacrament, women will regain access to their inner knowing and the true power of their unique life-force.

Orgasm must regain its rightful place in the life of each woman as the energy source of inner wisdom and power. No amount of propaganda or violence against women over all these 5,000 years has had the power to change our physiology: our orgasms remain our own; we have but to remember their sacredness, the height of their vibration, and the means of achieving that pinnacle from which our true ancestors, the Goddess worshippers, viewed inner wisdom.

Now let's take a deeper look at how the legacy of terror from Biblical times affects our world today.

అఅఅ

Women have significant and unique contributions to make beyond securing more power and wealth.

MAGDELENA SAYS:

Women must remember themselves as a source of knowledge in order to be open to it.

CHAPTER VII

WOMEN ASLEEP TO THEMSELVES ARE UNAVAILABLE FOR SOLVING CULTURAL PROBLEMS

A culture made lopsided by suppression of the natural voice of women has lots of problems, and our efforts to regain balance and harmony are inadequate. For instance:

- Of course, black lives matter. Most probably black people are ancestors to us all. Black boys and men are regularly gunned down without cause in the United States, or they are thrown in prison for long periods for trifles, sometimes because they have no money for bail. There are more than two million black men in American prisons today. The war on drugs that began this massive increase in the 1970s has been a failure—prisons are bursting with overcrowding, and we have seen a horrendous escalation in drug use. And yet there are men in office today who believe we should continue such failed policies, even though there are more black men in our prisons today than there were slaves before 1850, and they are now enslaved to perform tasks for corporate interests. If the voices of more mothers were heard on this subject, our prisons would go out of business.

- Since the water source was switched in Flint, Michigan in April 2014, the population has been poisoned by lead and other toxins flowing from their taps. Even with proven elevated levels of brain-attacking lead in the blood of children, the problem has yet to be solved in September 2017. As that situation evolved, the majority of those decision-makers had no sympathy for the families that would suffer.
- The United States continues to sell arms to Saudi Arabia and refuel their bombers mid-air regardless of proof that the Saudis are killing citizens in Yemen with bombs manufactured in the United States. If women were making these decisions, would they enable the slaughter of other women's children? The Saudi Monarchy also has used its vast wealth to spread Wahhabism, a radical and austere form of Islam, throughout Europe and the Middle East. Wahhabism teaches that all those who don't practice their form of Islam are heathens and enemies. Osama bin Laden, Al Qaeda, and the Taliban are all considered to be adherents of Wahhabism. The decision-makers of the royal family in Saudi Arabia are men.
- Despite the consensus of scientists that human activity is warming the planet and will lead to truly terrible problems, the current U.S. administration, led almost exclusively by men, denies global warming is due to the burning of fossil fuels. Meanwhile, each hurricane is stronger and more damaging than the last; fires raged in the Western United States for months during 2016 and 2017; one-half of the giant pines in the Sierra Nevada are dead (observed with mourning tears during the summer of 2016); the world's oceans are warming, releasing more carbon dioxide into the atmosphere, and their inhabitants, which sustain our lives,

are and being decimated by pollutants. In 2017, the city
of Chicago saw less than one inch of snow in January or
February for the first time in recorded history. In September
2017, we saw unprecedented weather events throughout the
world—two massive hurricanes hitting the Caribbean and
the southern U.S. within a week of each other; successive
deadly earthquakes in Mexico, the worst wildfires ever
seen in Montana, the northeast U.S., and Canada; massive,
deadly flooding in Bangladesh. The situation is obvious, and
it goes on and on. Many of the protesters are women, but
too many of the decision-makers are male.

- In many parts of the world girls are sold by their parents
  into the sex-trafficking market. Lured by promises of jobs
  and U.S. citizenship, girls are sold into sexual slavery in the
  United States. In many cultures, female genital excision/
  mutilation persists, robbing millions of girls of any hope of
  sexual pleasure in the future by removing the clitoris. All of
  this is dehumanizing the feminine. And, at last, the barriers
  are down to pulling back the shields that have protected
  powerful American men while they fondled and abused
  women they encounter in the workplace.
- Legislative bodies across the U.S. continue their assault on
  women's control of their own body, homosexual equality,
  and social safety nets for less-fortunate Americans. President Trump has made numerous disparaging comments
  about women's looks, and their bodily functions, such as
  menstruating, breast feeding, and going to the toilet, calling
  them "disgusting." These are views shared by all patriarchal
  societies in the world, especially those controlled by religion,
  such as Muslims and orthodox Jews.
- Perhaps worst of all, the Americans have elected to their

highest office a man who cannot govern; who aggravates problems instead of solving them; who makes himself obnoxious to Americans and all the rest of the world; who is making a twisted mess of the American Government.

This nightmarish list could go on and on. These realities cloud the beauty of life for all of us, and beyond these atrocities, multitudes of women are not fully experiencing the blessing of their lives. This lack of full participation by one-half of its people is damaging to culture.

Throwing another bomb at the situation is not working. Fundamentally, something must change to bring back living as a celebration. This is where the feminine has something to offer.

By Mid-Twentieth Century the Long Slumber Began to End

In the mid-twentieth century women began awakening from the trance induced by lack of information about the centuries of systemic oppression of the feminine. Somewhat dazed, they emerged from their homes to replace their brothers, husbands, and fathers who left their jobs to go to war. They found, to their surprise and the surprise of almost everyone, that they could perfectly perform the tasks that had been ascribed as "men only." Sisters before them had wondered about their subservient position in society. Many had already fought for more equity again and again and very strongly from about 1850 on, despite ignorance of their true history, but, overall, women remained in second place in the home.

Then, in 1949, during the time of confusion after the Second World War when women were being pushed out of their places of war-time societal contribution to make jobs for returning soldiers, the French writer, existentialist philosopher, and feminist, Simone de Beauvoir published her famous book, *The Second Sex*. She spoke from deep within the paradigm with no knowledge of the history of women as powerful. Women's feet were dragging on the return path to the kitchen sink, and *The Second Sex* provided context for the suppression women were experiencing and confirmed the nature of the shackles to which they would be re-submitting. She brought forth the reality of the culture, shining a light on the relationship of men to women. She spoke about how much men continued to (and still do today):

- Believe themselves to be "sovereign beings" whose truths are revealed in comparison to other men. The woman carries what he lacks in his heart. He seeks to be made whole through her for his full realization of self. He loves her to the extent that she is his; he fears her in so far as she remains the other.
- Believe that man's true victory, whether he is liberator or conqueror, lies in this: that woman freely recognized him as her destiny.
- Enslave woman; but in the same degree he has deprived her of what made her possession desirable.
- Believe women to be difficult yet consumable as they mold them to their desire as possessions.
- Believe that to have woman is to conquer her; he penetrates her as the plow-share into the furrow; he makes her his own as he makes his land he works; he labors, he plants, he sows.
- Be afraid of being in the power of uncontrollable forces. He makes up the story of Virgin Birth.
- Believe there is a serpent in the vagina which would bite the husband just as the hymen is broken.
- Believe that the feminine is un-clean and men have the

right to take over all that is sacred for women and destroy worship of the essence of the feminine.

- Believe women accept men's sovereignty willingly since man came from Adam. She was destined by Him for man. She is the earth raised to keep men company.
- Believe that he fulfills himself as a carnal being by carnally possessing a being but at the same time confirming his sense of freedom by the docility of the free person.
- Believe that she is privileged prey, a privileged object through which man subdues Nature.
- Believe that the little girl not yet in puberty, carries no menace, she is under no taboo and has no sacred character. (Author's note: This pure feminine must be pretext for incest.)
- Believe that woman is at times the blessing of mother and wife and at other times a blight to be avoided.
- Believe his curse is to be fallen from a bright and ordered heaven into the chaotic shadows of his mother's womb. This fire, this impure and active exaltation in which he likes to recognize himself is imprisoned by the woman in the mud of earth. Through the fact of his birth Nature has a murderous hold on him.
- Believe that menstruation and blood are evil (especially blood which equals the capacity to create new life, something men cannot do). Through menstrual blood is expressed the horror inspired in men by woman's fecundity. It has been supposed that masculine energy and vitality would be destroyed because the feminine principle is then at its maximum force…man finds it repugnant to come upon the dreaded essence of the mother in the woman he possesses; he is determined to dissociate these two aspects of femininity.

- Believe that all that is sacred is unclean and seek to destroy the worship of the essence of the feminine with myths such as the one that meat spoils when it is touched by a menstruating woman
- Ornament the woman to hide the animal crudity of her flesh, her odor. In woman dressed and adorned, nature is present but under restraint, by human will re-molded nearer to man's desire. A woman is rendered more desirable to the extent that nature is more highly developed in her and more rigorously confined; it is the "sophisticated" woman who has always been the ideal erotic object.
- Believe in the glories of the phallus when he thinks of it as transcendence... a means for taking possession of the other; but he is ashamed of it when he sees it as merely passive flesh through which he is the plaything of the dark forces of Life.
- Believe that no man would consent to be a woman, but every man wants women to exist.
- Believe that original sin makes of the body the enemy of the soul; all ties of the flesh seem evil... Evil is an absolute reality; and his flesh is sin... the flesh that is for the Christian the hostile Other is precisely woman. In her the Christian finds incarnated the temptations of the world, the flesh, and the devil.
- Believe that woman causes fright not because she gives venereal diseases; the truth is that the diseases seem abominable because they come from women.
- Believe that marriage and the wish to have children are protective against the bad effects of eroticism.
- Believe that baptism is required to wash child from the sin of conception and the filth of birth. (Author's note: For

many of our ancestors, creating babies and sexual pleasure
have been immoral.)

- Believe that if society can persuade mothers to yield up their
  sons to death, then it feels it has the right to kill them off.
  Because the influence the mother has over her sons, it is
  advantageous for society to have her in hand: that is why the
  mother is surrounded with so many marks of respect, she is
  endowed with all virtues, a religion is created with special
  reference to her, from which it is forbidden to depart at the
  risk of committing sacrilege and blasphemy.
- Believe that as servant woman is entitled to the most
  splendid deification.[1]

How much of what de Beauvoir exposed has been put to rest?
How much do women still dream through the dreams of men as
they asserted they were still doing when she wrote—how much are
male gods still women's gods, representing the sacred in the world
offered by men as the world itself is defined by men. I suspect there
are potent traces under the illusion of content: women now wary of
suggesting that all is not well, that they still experience discrimination and lack of respect, that they really do not know what the truth
of the feminine is, and men afraid to admit that they resist giving
up their positions of supremacy and their right to sexually use and
abuse women.

News Alert: As I am finishing the editing of this book in January 2018, Hollywood celebrities used the Globe Awards to make a
stand against the multiple accounts of sexual abuse in their industry.
I applaud this development and pray that it does not eventually
amount to another black mark against sexuality itself.

Are we aware of the minimizing of the vagina, which caused
the Sheela-na-gigs (figurative carvings of naked women displaying

an exaggerated vulva) to be wiped out of Great Britain? Once an important symbol for the power of the feminine to create new life, these squat figures composed of 70 percent vagina were almost entirely scratched out and replaced by cathedrals to the God. [I found two She-la-no-gigs during my 2003 vision-quest to Avebury, a still-standing ceremonial circle of huge stones in Great Britain.]

Revelations of the Feminine Mystique Inspire Women to Leave the Safety of Their Homes

Following the deep penetration of Simone de Beauvoir into the psyches of men and women, their relation to each other and their attitudes regarding hierarchy, and following the return of women to their homes as the center of their universes after the war, Betty Friedan, a journalist and writer who identified and recounted the situation of women in the late 1950s and early '60s, recognized their deep dissatisfaction with the myth they had told themselves in an effort to assuage their discomfort in conforming to the role of "housewife." Friedan called her book, *The Feminine Mystique.* This myth made it seem okay to confine their participation in life to the requirements of their homes, camouflaging their true yearnings for greater use of their gifts and their humanity.

Confusion arose in young women who were the daughters of "Rosie the Riveter" because they could not take cues from their own mothers who were pushed back into their homes or were well-edu-cated and prepared to enter the larger world but refused entry. These mothers, squished in their homes, demonstrated resentment and vacuousness to their daughters as they played cards and drank coffee together in the suburbs. Tied to their homes, mothers could only tell their daughters that what they themselves had made of their lives was not enough. Their daughters responded to the discomfort of their confined mothers and prepared for their own release into the larger world with college educations, but they faltered at the threshold and took the easy way: look beautiful, be very "popular," find a man, buckle down and let him make the hard decisions about growing up and taking responsibility.

It would have been a tremendous paradigm shift if they had been able to accomplish the move into the larger world. Instead, they wrapped themselves in the myth of the feminine mystique and their own fear of making a commitment to find the energy and the courage to declare their position and their goal, to choose their human identity, and to take responsibility for their own lives. They too fell back into the kitchen under the banner of the feminine mystique, which convinced them of their appropriate place in the home as it created in them the motivation to buy the post-war economy required.

Friedan's feminine mystique was an identity that women accepted that made achieving their life ambitions within the home palatable. It was a socio-economic ruse that kept women away from the work of men where they were a distraction and a competition. It confined them to the home where they would express their uniqueness through purchase of goods the marketplace created for their consumption. The GPA required their attention to consumption. Post-war development and production needed an adequate supply of buyers to keep its machinery moving. Women had their marching orders: back to the kitchen to buy new mixers and washing-machines.

By accepting that their first goal was to find the right man, young women, side-stepping the difficult questions of who they were, what their gifts were, and how they were meant to actualize themselves in their lives in a situation that gave them free choice to take paths that had not been taken by women ever, as far as they knew. They lost themselves to babies and housework instead of making a choice from all the available possibilities and taking a stand for themselves. They did not ask what they desired beyond being taken care of by the man they would trap. With the new hair products and eye make-up provided by the marketplace, they pursued their goal paying no attention to their own movement into life or what unique contributions they might make. Popular women's magazines played their roles. All advertising and writing was required by the new male editors to conform to the idea of women's legitimate role in the home as consumers. University courses in Marriage and the Family portrayed women as the subjects of their husband's work requirements: dressed and coiffed with high-heels and perfume, the children fed and bathed, and a roast ready to pop out of the oven when he and his client appeared for dinner. Their job was to be alluring and available so that their husband's sexual needs would always be met, cementing for these women the illusion of caring and love for the intimacy of the bedroom. For them and for their men sexuality had more to do with function than desire.

The sexuality in these homes largely became perfunctory, unstimulating, and un-rewarding. Both the man and the woman believed they were performing correctly; both were dismayed that their proximity in the bed left them stressed and unsatisfied; they either began to search for gratification with other partners or suffered in sexual anxiety. Women's frustration mounted as the life plan dependent on life-blood from marriage betrayed their hopes and expectations. Freudian thought re-emerged in the 1950s in the United States to explain the difficulty arising in the homes of woman who had accepted home and family as their entire life purpose. "Freudian thought [became the] ... ideological birthmark of the counter-revolution in America. Without Freud's dysfunction of women's sexual nature to give the (then) conventional image of femininity new authority I do not think several generations of educated, spirited American women would have been so easily diverted from the dawning of realization of who they were..." said Friedan. "Victorian era—was seized in this country in the 1940s as the literal explanation of all that was wrong with American women after it was long ago refuted in Europe"[2] where hysteria and sexual dysfunction were characteristic of some middle-class men and women, not a product of universal human nature with biological and instinctual causes.

The mistake, says the mystique, the root of women's troubles in the past is that women envied men. Women tried to be like men, instead of accepting their own nature, which can find fulfillment only in sexual passivity, male domination, and nurturing maternal love... [the truth is, according to the feminine mystique] Betty Friedan tells us that men determine women's role. The feminine mystique as envisioned by Friedan glorifies domestic activities of cooking, washing, cleaning, and bearing children as functions of all women to be lived if their femininity is not to be denied. The young woman seeking to be a heroine must have lots of babies. She loses herself in babies and housework instead of making a choice and taking a stand for herself. In the *Feminine Mystique* Betty Friedan claims that "the end of the road" for women is "togetherness" in which she has renounced her independence in order to experience her life through her husband and her children with no account for her own being. She cannot have freedom of human existence or "a voice in her own destiny." In America the woman cannot tell us "who she is, or can be, or wants to be." Cloaked in the mystique but knowing somewhere inside that they were more than the role they were playing, women in their homes began to show signs of discontent that the purchase of one more pair of gloves or microwave oven did not satisfy.

She knew her mother had been unhappy but believed that the tenants of the feminine mystique glorifying the homemaker and perfect mother would protect her from her mother's depression only to find herself mired in a similar malaise. "[The problem of women today is] a problem of identity, a stunting or evasion of growth that is perpetuated by the feminine mystique. It is my thesis that as the Victorian culture did not permit women to accept or gratify their basic sexual needs, our culture does not permit women to accept or gratify their basic need to grow and fulfill potentialities as human beings, a role that is not solely defined by their sexual role."[5] It was this condition in women of wanting more that greeted the idea of finding identity within the Civil Rights and the anti-Viet Nam war movements with a stampede of enthusiasm. Not redeemed by those out-of-house involvements, they segued over to the Women's Movement, as I will discuss in the following chapter.

Freidan and de Beauvoir painted pictures of the problem women were experiencing without the knowledge that there had once been a reality of women in full glory of themselves participating authentically. These two accounts of the situation women found themselves in did not reveal that women had long been deprived of their authentic self.

Their writings provided the backdrop against which the Women's Movement of the late 1960s, '70s and '80s took place, and laid the groundwork. The discomfort many women felt locked away in their homes, devising importance for trivial pursuits was acknowledged. Their disquiet received a label and therefore could be given more credence by them. Growing awareness among women that their feeling of being only partially alive and little fulfilled was not unique, that others felt the vacuous hole in the center of their being that they were sensing finally brought them out of their homes, first into the Civil rights and anti-war movements, then into the consciousness-raising gatherings of the Women's Movement.

Breaking the shackles of the feminine mystique, women

opened the doors of their homes and stepped into a wider reality eventually accepting the tenants of the Women's Movement that more education, a job or career, and equal pay would project women into full acknowledgment of themselves.

Since neither writer was aware of the restrictions placed on the being and activities of vibrant woman in 3000 BC, they were looking at the result of 5,000 years of repression without identifying the cause. Their offered solutions were directed at the results they were seeing: women in inadequate roles in society. Not getting to the cause meant that the offered solutions were off the mark, ineffectual in releasing women to the truth of who they are. What we got was additional foot-soldiers for the war against our planet; more taking and accumulating; more hostilities; more competition and separation. Not looking for the truth of who women are, that truth was not found.

The result was that the power women are now experiencing in their more active roles in society, made possible by the Women's Movement, is not the power that would be released by their true nature. More education, better jobs, and higher pay do not function as recognition of the offerings women would make from their true nature. In general, women are functioning in the system that denies the truth of who they are and does not allow them to contribute authentic insights into the plan and activities of the culture that remains oriented to the dominant ideas of lust and greed.

Thus, out-of-balance culture persists, with women as active participants in destabilizing natural systems. Next, let us look at the underlying reasons that modern women's movements have not achieved the hoped-for liberation of women's true potential.

ઢૹ ઢૹ ઢૹ

I applaud the stand against the multiple accounts of sexual abuse in the movie industry and pray that it does not eventually amount to another black mark against sexuality itself.

CLAIRE SAYS:

Healing of ourselves and our planet is not possible as long as sexuality is ignored as an element of what must be healed.

CHAPTER VIII

HOW THE WOMEN'S
MOVEMENTS FAILED

In modern eras, sufficient healing has taken place to enable women to notice the gender imbalance in the culture and attempt to adjust the scales. The 1850s produced the women's rights movement; the 1920s saw the fight for the vote waged by the suffragettes; a long struggle was waged to enact an equal rights amendment to the Constitution; and in the latest women's movement in the 1960s, women awoke to their situation again and clamored for justice.

When our most recent women's movement petered out, women believed that their position had finally been guaranteed, and men hoped that the threat to their positions would subside. Women today have more college degrees including lots of PhDs, better and more responsible jobs, and more equity in pay. But it is in these very times that women in the purification lodges I led cried in pain at the abuses they had been forced to endure. Those tears and distress have brought me to my belief that the battle for women's rights has not been won. Women are still on the fringes of wages earned and wealth accrued; they remain the subject of male domination—more subtle, perhaps hidden—seen in the overall plan for what we as a society are doing and seeking and how we go about it; seen in disrespect for women; seen in the number of rapes, incidents of incest, harassment, and molestation; seen in low energy and low life expectation among women; seen in molestation of the earth, the water, and the air; seen in jammed freeways; seen in war and strife as constant societal involvements; and seen in a low level of love and celebration among the people. We have endured these major women's movements, but the problem still exists.

I have taken a closer look at the various modern women's movements and considered what has been overlooked, why true gender equity has not been achieved.

Women's Rights Movement of 1850

In 1850, women began participating in the anti-slavery movement, in which they found their power and the issue of their own enslavement. Women saw the need to overcome their "helpless gentility." They began to understand the possibility of asking for experience of a full life. The Women's Rights Movement of 1850 rallied around Elizabeth Stanton Cady in Seneca Falls, New York, her home, to which she retreated when she and the other women who had traveled to London to address the issue of slavery were hidden behind a curtain and not allowed to participate. They thought at the time, and Betty Friedan thought one hundred years later, that "the problem of identity was new for women then, truly new. The women were pioneering on the front edge of women's evolution."[1]

When they came forward in 1850, "the feminists had only one model, one image, one vision of a full and free human: MAN... only men [had] the freedom and the education necessary to realize their full abilities, to pioneer and create and discover, and map new trails for future generations. Only men had the vote: the freedom to shape major decisions of society. Only men had the freedom to love, and enjoy love, and decide for themselves in the eyes of their God the problems of right and wrong. Did women want these freedoms because they wanted to be men? Or did women want them because they wanted to be human?"[2]

Grievances expressed at Seneca Falls:

1. "He has compelled her to submit to laws in the formation of which she has no voice

2. He has made her if married, in the eyes of the law, civilly dead

3. He has taken from her all right to property, even the wages she earns

4. In the covenant of marriage, she is compelled to promise obedience to her husband, he becoming to all intents and purposes her master—the law giving him power to deprive her of her liberty, and to administer chastisement

5. He closes to her all the avenues of wealth and distinction which he considers more honorable to himself

6. As a teacher of theology, medicine or law, she is not known

7. He denies her the facilities for obtaining a thorough education, all colleges being closed against her

8. He has created a false public sentiment by giving to the world a different code of morals for men and women by which moral delinquencies which exclude women from society are not only tolerated, but deemed to be of little account to men

9. He has usurped the prerogative of Jehovah himself, claiming it his right to assign her a sphere of action, when that belongs to her conscience and to her God

10. He has endeavored in every way that he could to destroy her confidence in her own powers, to lessen her

self-respect, and to make her willing to lead a dependent and abject life."[3]

It is interesting, isn't it, that this list very closely resembles exactly what had been eliminated from the realm of women by the Indo-European invaders who usurped the land and the place women had occupied during the thousands of years in which they had laid the groundwork for the development of humankind's civilization? But the women in Seneca Falls did not know this.

Many women came forward with a passion knowing that something was dreadfully wrong with a situation that had one-half of humankind corseted and bound, weighted down by many petticoats and imprisoned in the homes as fixtures in their husbands' lives, show-places for the emeralds and sapphires that signaled his success. (These feminists briefly substituted "bloomers" for their uncomfortable, con-straining clothing.) Even though the religions taught that the women were the property of their husbands and their voices were not to be heard, these women courageously set out into the unknown territory of speaking their minds and finding ways to be heard. They were intel-ligent, many educated by members of their families. "It is a strangely unquestioned perversion of history that the passion and fire of the feminist movement came from man-hating, embittered, sex-starved spinsters, unsexed non-women who burned with such envy for the male organ that they wanted to take it away from all men, or destroy them, demanding rights only because they lacked the power to love as women. Mary Wollstonecraft, Angelina Grimke, Ernestine Rose, Margaret Fuller, Elizabeth Cady Stanton, Julia ward Howe, Margaret Stoner all loved, were loved, and married; many seem to have been as passionate in their relations with lover and husband, in an age when passion in women was as forbidden as intelligence, as they were in their battle for women's chance to grow to full human stature."[4]

Women travelled as many as 50 miles to hear what the feminists had to say about a new environment for women in which they would own property, keep their own wages, and generally emerge from the dark as humans with access to their own minds, bodies, and connection to spirit (God, in this case), even the right to become full participants in their sexual experience. "Running like a bright and sometimes dangerous thread through the history of the feminist movement was... the idea that equality for women was necessary to free both men and women for true sexual fulfillment... the degradation of women degraded love, marriage, and all relations between men and women."[5] They saw the ground floor of the sexual reality the Goddess worshippers had known and accessed to attain their highest powers.

Clearly our great-great-grandmothers were seeing through the veil, but their way was blocked by the power of the fear and resistance of the men who had the power and positions to refute them. Men rose up in one voice to restrain the efforts to change the system over which they had all the control, power and wealth. "At every step of the way, the feminists had to fight the conception that they were violating the God-given nature of women."[6] Neither the women nor their ministers understood that the original writers of the Bible made up the idea of who women were and how they were to live in relation to men in order to take control of women and constrain the worshipping of the Goddess. In their ignorance and fear, "clergy shouted and raved and showed the Bible's opposition to equality...the prohibition of women's full participation written in the Bible was tossed at women as reprimand for their efforts to gain freedom."[7] The women did not know that those biblical constraints had put them in the straightjackets they were in.

In 1886, when the property rights petition was presented, a "NY State Assembly roared with laughter ... it had 6,000 signatures...

one Assemblyman said it was not legitimate since women get choice tidbits at table, best seats in carriage, their choice of the side of the bed. If there is any inequity or oppression, gentlemen are the sufferers."[8] When the petition was turned down, "an assemblyman said: They do not appear to be satisfied to have unsexed themselves, but they desire to unsex every female in the land…since God created man as the representative of the race…then took from his side the material for woman's creation (returning to his side in matrimony) one flesh, one being… a higher power than that which emanates legislative enactments has given forth the mandate that men and women shall not be equal."[9] Hiding in the mandates of the Holy Bible, the legislator disguised his fear and the real issue of women's right to seek equal place and equal power with men. "The myth that these women were 'un-natural monsters' was based on the belief that to destroy the God-given subservience of women would destroy the home and make slaves of men."[10]

Suffragettes of 1920

In 1920, women struggled against the refusal to allow them to participate in the selection of governance. They recognized that without voting rights they had no power to make real change in their situation. They "could not get any political party to take them seriously"[11] as they sought to improve their positions in life.

Particularly fearful of women's vote were:

1. Brewers
2. Saloon owners who feared they would be shut down
3. Those who underpaid women and children
4. Machine politicians who feared they could not control the women's vote. Women did not accept bribes[12]

Friedan reports that the "final battles were waged by college educated women, some of whom chained themselves to the White House fence: were beaten, arrested, force-fed when they went on hunger strike… [they] were not the monsters of the myth of man-eaters…[in fact]many [were] Quakers and pacifists."[13]

When the vote was finally granted to women, it was a giant step into self-realization. But still, the true nature of women had not been found; the idea that the restrictions on sexuality played a significant part in subduing women had not been targeted for change.

The Influence of Sigmund Freud

At this point, it is important to understand how Sigmund Freud, the Austrian neurologist and the founder of psychoanalysis, and a product of Victorian times, came to vastly influence thinking about women in the late 19th and early 20th century, and the march of American women back to the confines of their homes. Just as more and more women gained college degrees and were otherwise prepared to take part outside of the home, his writings were used after World War II in America to explain and justify the diminished image of woman as inadequate to participate in the world. Freud's thinking became a major justification for keeping women in the homes buying the products of post-war recovery; it was not informed by knowledge of the thousands of years in which the Goddess reigned. He had a low opinion of women's intrinsic nature. The Indo-Europeans and their offspring had done a good job of erasing the position of women in the society.

In her groundbreaking book of 1963, *The Feminine Mystique*, Friedan, revealed that, "The feminine mystique derived its power from Freudian thought; for it was the idea born of Freud which led women and those who studied with them to misinterpret their mothers' frustration and their fathers,' brothers' and husbands' resentments and inadequacies, and their own emotions and choices in life...the feminine mystique, elevated by Freudian theory into a scientific religion, sounded a single, overprotective, life-restricting, future-denying note for women...they were told by the most advanced thinkers of our time to go back [from your advanced education] and live their lives as if they were Noras, [of Ibsen's play] restricted to the doll's house of Victorian prejudice. And their own respect for science...kept them from questioning the feminine mystique."[14]

While Freud made irrefutably important contributions to the culture and to effective healing of mental disturbance, Freudian thought, well regarded and influential, buried women in his low opinion of their infantile natures, their lack of intelligence, and their inability to accomplish anything. They were, in his opinion, meant to be ornaments to the lives of their husband as childlike dolls, taking care of his needs and helping him project himself through his acts.

Paradoxically, "Freud's concept of super-ego helped free men of the tyranny of 'should' ... which prevents the child from becoming an adult, the human he is meant to be. Yet Freudian thought helped create a new superego that paralyze[d] educated modern American women—a new tyranny of the "should" which chain[ed] women to an old image, prohibit[ed] choice and growth, and deni[ed] them individual identity."[15]

Studies of Freud, the man, have found that his sexual development was arrested by an early glimpse of his parents copulating. Despite the importance of sex in Freud's theory, one gets from his words the impression that "the sex act appears degrading to him; if women themselves were so degraded in the eyes of men, how could sex appear in any other light?"[16] As an adult he had little interest in sexuality. "The real injustices life held for women a century ago, compared to men, were dismissed as mere rationalizations of penis envy. And the real opportunities life offered women now, compared to women then, were forbidden in the name of penis envy...scientists who have separated themselves from Freud's interpretations believe that the neurosis Freud was observing in women he called 'hysterical' would as well have been produced by constraint on the human need to grow...though Freud saw only "penis envy."[17] The distorted thinking evolved: "Followers of Freud wanted to help women find sexual fulfillment as women by affirming their natural inferiority."[18]

"Freudian theory about women is obsolescent, an obstacle to the truth for women in America today [1960], and a major cause of the pervasive problem that has no name (the malaise caused by women's imprisonment made possible by the 'feminine mystique.')."[19] So much of what Freud discovered and taught was so valuable in straightening out the distortion of the human mind that his mistake about women was effectively hidden. Now behavioral scientists believe that the need to grow is the basic human need... and that interference with this need leads to psychological trouble.

Equal Rights for Women as a Constitutional Amendment

The next big battle our foremothers waged was for full equal rights as a Constitutional Amendment. The amendment as it was put forth finally by the Congress needed to be ratified by 38 states, and only 36 states did ratify the amendment before the deadline in 1956. That issue has not been revisited.

Rosie the Riveter and the Great Setback

Friedan exposed the post-World War II phenomenon of chasing Rosie the riveter, and all the women who had come forward to make the war effort successful, back to their homes and the plotting to keep them there as buyers of the products that were taking the place of rifles in an economy that was righting itself and putting the returning soldiers back to work. The mind-set of "the feminine mystique" allowed young women in the late '40s and '50s to bypass the places won for them in society by their grandmothers and great-grandmothers.

There was a purposeful reconstruction of the lives of women as the soldiers came back from WWII, wanting their jobs back. It became culturally desirable for the women to return to the home. The economy depended on this emigration: women could be convinced to buy for their homes what industry wanted to produce. The media, including particularly women's magazines that began to be published and edited by men, promoted a myth that it was women and only women who could tend to the needs of the home and family. This story was promoted to young women, especially brides to be, and accompanied by accouterments of beautiful furniture, lavish carpets, fine china, crystal, and silverware. The quintessential picture of the young women's perfect future was of the happy housewife, dressed in high-heels, dresses from Saks (covered by hand-embroidered aprons), fully made-up, greeting her tired and expectant husband as he returned from the city ... right after she returned in the station wagon from picking up the kids at baseball practice as the roast neared perfect tenderness in the oven to be placed in a moment on the table, linen covered and set with silver, china, and crystal. These young women bought the story. It solved the question of what they were going to do—try to enter careers and suffer the disappointment their mothers had; make the effort and not succeed in the huge, unknown, and frightening world. There were very few role models or encouragement. The male-created world did not want women to accommodate in the workplace. Men wanted their women at home as symbols of their success and backup for the kind of lives they thought they deserved, to say nothing about fulfilling their requirements in bed. The idea of women at home as consumers and bedmate was a lot less confrontational than trying to figure out how to integrate the weaker, more ignorant sex into the workplace.

Then, in the late 1960s the new cry was for equal work and equal pay, a lament that erupted as women began to take their university educations seriously, giving up their prejudice against "career women," and finding the courage to step out of their homes and view themselves as possible contributors in the larger world. The latest Women's Movement had begun.

Friedan was influential in opening the door, by revealing the plight of women held prisoner in their homes by the doctrines that limited their own sense of their abilities to participate in the culture in which Freudian thought played a part. Friedan made an urgent plea for women to climb out of the trap they had made for themselves out of fear of confronting the effort and courage required to find their own dream and become part of it. She saw this fear born of the extreme difficulty young women of her timeframe (1947 to 1957) were confronted with as they launched their lives: the image of womanhood their anxious and unhappy mothers set before them, women who had been largely disillusioned by their efforts to use their educations in a broader world context. Even though the doors of education were open to this new batch of young women in even greater numbers, they were taught to be fearful of exposing their true selves to view. They sought excuses to "ignore the question of their identity,"[20] and accepted instead the principles of the "feminine mystique," secure in the protection of their husbands in the home that took all their attention to maintain in perfect order and cleanliness embracing and projecting the perfect children who reflected there perfect mothering. "Women [grew] up no longer knowing that they [had] desires and capabilities the mystique forbade...[they] no longer [had] private images to tell them who they [were], or [could] be, or want[ed] to be."[21] Within the "feminine mystique" the young women became truly "feminine" when she gave up her uniqueness and her own goals and accepted as her own fulfillment the achievements of her husband or son.

The editors and the writers of women's magazines were among the plotters ramping down intellectual content and increasing the volume on expression of ideas that women belonged in the home buying products— the same products that appeared on their advertising pages that supported the magazine industry—to make their homes perfect as evidence of the homemakers' high value. "New editors [of women's magazines] were men returning from the war with nostalgic desire for home and hearth—they established printed images of what they wanted."[22] Friedan begged her readers in the '60s to "consider as a symptom the increasing emphasis on glamor in the women's magazines: the housewife wearing eye makeup as she vacuums the floor...McCall's Magazine, published for more than 5,000,000 American women, almost all of whom [had] been through High School and nearly half to college, contained almost no mention of the world beyond the home."[23] She saw this trend in another major women's magazine: "In the 1950s [The Ladies Home Journal] published only articles that serviced women as housewives, or described women as housewives, or permitted a purely feminine identification like the Duchess of Windsor or Princess Margaret. 'If we get an article about any women that does something adventurous, out of the way, something by herself... we figure she must be terribly aggressive, neurotic.'"[24]

Education was still a priority for women, but increasingly young women were channeled to marriage and the family courses where their role as wife, mother, and homemaker was emphasized as the most appropriate for them. Their innate or developed skills, their interests and desires, all other possibilities of enacting their humanity were put aside. Science, math, philosophy were not encouraged. "They learned that truly feminine women do not want careers, higher education, political rights—the independence and opportunity the old-fashioned feminists had fought for ... a thousand expert voices applauded their femininity, their adjustments, and their new maturity. All they had to do was devote their lives from earliest girlhood to finding a husband and bearing children [a clear picture of the 'feminine mystique']... A century before women had fought for higher education; now girls went to college to find a husband. By the mid- 1950s, 60 percent dropped out of college to marry, or because they believed that too much education would be a marriage barrier."[25]

A new science was created by the industrialists and their supporters: the psychology of advertising. Since women were the main buyers, they were studied for weakness that could be catered to and strengths to be satisfied by convincing them that the newest products would bring them satisfaction and happiness. Advertising was developed as a means of showing women what they needed and making buyers of them. (This was the beginning of a culture of buyers of things that satiated illusions of hungers, random things that ultimately added volume to trash heaps after doing time in storage lockers.) Advertisers were taught to tap into women's sexual appetites and frustrations by showing how their products would make adequate substitutes for the real thing. The prized husbands were not, after all, at home all day with their wives in the suburbs.

Young women accepted blocks to their entry into larger roles in their adult lives, even welcoming them. These impediments satisfied their own resistance to do the work and effort required to grow up and face responsibility for fully enacting themselves. They were afraid. They had seen their miserable mothers who had found so much resistance when they took positions next to men who were threatened by the entry of even more competition into their workplaces, their mothers who had come home to languish inside the four safe walls of their homes. The new entries into adulthood after the war were easily distracted from bigger goals. They accepted the "feminine mystique" that said they would find full satisfaction in being perfect wives, mothers, and house-keepers. Career woman gained bad-name status.

Gradually, as lives developed around the decisions to avoid a larger context to their lives, the women who had retreated into the homes that their husbands provided began to feel the lackluster boredom of claiming the brightest shine on their floors, the cleanest windows and curtains, the most perfect children as their finest achievements. Stretching the household duties into longer and longer time frames, buying the newest and best appliance and cleaning product, volunteering for another community project did not alter the underlying sense of worthlessness. Signs of dissatisfaction began to show in extra-marital affairs, alcohol and drug addictions, physical illness, and psychiatrist's intervention. Tranquilizers became the solution for many women who had begun to wonder what being alive was about. The homes that were their castles became their prisons; these women became as dull and uninspired as Nazi concentration camp victims. They were miserable, engulfed in a malaise caused by insufficient demand on their life-force, by the question of what it meant to be a woman, and by the haunting memory of their early refusal to make the effort to step into a bigger picture of themselves. They became ashamed and unable to admit their mistake, never knowing that there were so many others ensnared in the same trap.

And yet, a tiny voice deep within could be heard: "I want something more than my husband, my children, and my home."[26]

When feminists opened the kitchen door in the '60s, they shed light on what they found there: Women chained to a tradition that did not challenge them to all that they were; depressed; tied to their husband's needs and demands; often unaware of the world around them with no way to engage—cut off. I was a young adult in the 1960s as the Women's Movement began, a mother with children, whose husband was drafted into the Vietnam conflict the minute his deferment was terminated as he finished his studies. I noticed the Women's Movement but participated minimally. The frustrations and confusions of that time were part of my awareness even as three children demanded my attention and loyalty, but I had little time and no willingness to become involved in hating men.

The Women's Movement grew out of the combined energy of Viet Nam War protest and the Civil Rights' Movement. In the '60s the U.S. culture heated up over the Viet Nam war, a camouflage for actively (with great risk and cost of life and dollar) in response to our fear of Communism while actually functioning as an American thrust to position itself in an advantageous position of power and access to oil in that area. Our homeland erupted in protest. Women came forward to support the men who did not want to go and felt the wrongness of the conflict.

A second great struggle also erupted at the same time (was that because black people were being called up once again while still languishing in poverty and discrimination in the culture at large?). Black people in this country, led by many, but particularly Martin Luther King Jr., looked around at their condition and their prospects and saw inequity. They began to protest with real intent to set their lives on equal footing with the white people who were no longer their masters but were living much more balanced and abundant lives with their needs addressed and satisfied. Women entered these struggles hoping to make a difference, but soon realized that they were not equal partners in plotting and executing the revolutions. Their tasks were being defined by the men as subservient. Women were seen as background, serving the men's needs so that the men could do the real work. Women made sandwiches, served coffee, and bedded with the men,[27] but their own needs to be relevant were not met. When they asked for more prominent positions and acceptance of their voices and ideas, they were greeted with laughter and ridicule. Stokely Carmichael famously said, "the position for women in the movement was prone." It was out of the restless need of the women to be part of what was transforming their lives and their desire to be honored for the wisdom of their contributions that led them to withdraw and gather separately in what became the Women's Movement.

Women's Movements of the Late '60s, '70s, and '80s

The country was engulfed in another struggle for freedom: women's. Mostly in New York, but across the country as well, women gathered to express their will to have equal voice, equal opportunity, and equal pay. Encounter groups sprang up everywhere bringing thousands of women into the process of gaining access to their voices and their self-esteem. In Los Angeles, Judy Chicago drew attention to powerful women throughout history by leading artists in the construction of a table set with plates decorated with luscious three-dimensional vaginas. I was part of demonstrations at the Los Angeles County Museum of Art calling out the director (Maurice Tuchman) for the meager representation of women artists in the collection and in the museum's special exhibitions. There was a hopeful turbulence of brave women stepping out into the unknown of new possibility. Little by little women began to believe that they had a right to a piece of the pie, and could locate that piece by their own efforts. Today, fifty years after these efforts began, the image of women and what they expect and obtain in their lives is far different. There are only small traces of the "feminine mystique." Women bustle about in their own BMWs that they paid for themselves doing work that they feel honors them and benefits the culture.

However, I believe the opportunity offered by the Women's Movement missed its mark. The efforts to achieve parity involved women taking on the characteristics of men that allowed them success in obtaining power and wealth, but did not address the underlying problem for women: that they had been denied access to natural growth into their true natures. It was assumed that "success" was what women desired in the same forms that men had achieved. The root of the problem for women, that their true voices and natures had been robbed from them, was neither part of the purpose of the Women's Movement nor part of what the Women's Movement achieved. Blinded by their own ignorance and lack of knowledge, the women of the Movement proceeded along the same track their brothers had followed for 5,000 years, believing power and wealth were their objectives and the source of possible contentment. A successful life for women was defined in the exact terms that success for men had been defined for 5,000 years. With this definition in place, the objectives of the Women's Movement appear to have been achieved, and the polarization between women and men remains hidden and little talked about.

My search led me to another problem with the outcome of the Women's Movement. Understanding that the most recent Women's Movement was terminated before the equality in the expression of the life-force between men and women was achieved clarifies where we are right now. Ruth Rosen (Provost of Yale University, President of the University of Pennsylvania, and President of the Rockefeller Foundation) and author of *The World Split Open*, makes it clear that the Movement was diverted by an interior takeover. According to Rosen, the Lesbian women who joined the original Women's Movement added so much raw energy, voice, and intense drive to push men aside that many women of the Women's Movement silently went back to their kitchens. More was being stated in their names than they had agreed to. Women in the movement shied from leadership roles and from having leaders of their groups, fearful that power over individuals would reoccur as it had existed in the earlier leftist groups they had fled in order to hear their own voices, decide their own priorities and actions. They were suspicious of loud voices and pushy people. These were the very traits the lesbians had used to gain their sense of power and they were not timid about using them in their interactions with the women of the women's movement. It did not take long for the lesbian invasion to take full root and for early spokeswomen for the movement to become outraged by what was happening within their own groups. Trashing of the important women within the women's liberation movement began as a way of bringing everyone down to the lowest common denominator. Truthful spokespeople such as Erica Jong and Gloria Steinem were chased out for their brilliance.

The general population of women did not know that The Movement was co-opted by this takeover by the already well-organized Lesbian women. The natural development of ideas that might have taken place within the Movement did not happen. What emerged was hate for men and the insistence that women receive equal pay for equal work. What did not happen was a long look at history and the reality of how women had come to a lesser role in society over the last 5,000 years from the first invasions by Indo-Europeans entering the fertile crescent of the Mediterranean from the north riding horses, carrying weapons, and slaughtering the peaceful Goddess worshippers. Merlin Stone and others told that story, but too few were listening. Marija Gimbutas was hard at work deciphering and publishing her archeological findings that support the existence of the Goddess worshippers for 20,000-30,000 years before those invasions began, but no one in the Movement noticed.

The Women's Movement is not dead or over. It folded its tent until another time.

How Things Could Have Been Different

It is now more that 30 years since the Women's Movement petered out. There are many women pulling in six-digit salaries in major positions in major companies. Many women live happy and fulfilled lives becoming doctors, lawyers, business executives, politicians, and military officials. But men continue to dominate important American institutions. Women are moving into situations that have been dominated by men, but they cannot achieve complete access. There is unfinished business in the transition into a full sense of well-being. The men are afraid and the women do not thoroughly trust themselves. If the truth of how women found themselves in the position of the servants to men's desires and intentions while submerging their own had been given the full voice of the Movement, a solution based on the reality of the problem might have been found by the millions of women who took part, making an urgent appeal to set matters right. That truth would include the fact that women have been denied an equal share in the activity and the benefits of the culture on purpose for 5,000 years, and that decisions to limit full participation were made and implemented in order to effect change from a matrilineal to patrilineal inheritance. This is the reality that still must be faced.

The four modern movements to return women to full status in the culture (1850, 1920, effort to pass the Equal Rights Amendment to the Constitution, and 1960-80) have not succeeded because the context and cause of women's subjection has not been made clear. Understanding the cause of gender imbalance and women pushed into the background gives us a means of righting these wrongs. The truth must be exposed in the history that is being uncovered: women as expressions of themselves have been thwarted, denied, dishonored, ignored, and killed for 5,000 years, and women's knowledge of this reality has been withheld, hidden, subverted, and denied.

There were those who knew and those who said, but their voices were not loud enough to be heard. As I have mentioned, Marija Gimbutas was toiling away and teaching at UCLA, but not enough attention was given to her work. Gimbutas' archeology and anthropology are the foundation for knowledge of the Goddess-worshiping tradition that she indicates had its beginnings as far back as 30,000 years in Paleolithic times. Women were writing about the goddesses and the ancient history of Goddess worship, but the connection had not been made by the women in the '70s and '80s in the United States of what the facts were revealing about the killing of the identity of women as celebrants of the Goddess and the invasions and warring that dismantled Goddess-worshipping cultures.

The actions of the Women's Movement were not guided by clarity of vision. Understanding of what was required to achieve parity with men was shallow: equal pay for equal work. The Women's Movement of the last quarter of the twentieth century acted as if taking the scab off a wound and calling it healed without any disinfectant for the wound itself would take care of the problem.

The Curse of Our Cultural Trance

The means to get to the root of the problem were deeply submerged in the psyches of the women in the Movement, and remains so for nearly everyone. For 5,000 years women have been called evil for the natural gift of their sexuality. Sexuality, orgasm, masturbation are words that women have not even used among themselves. They had no access to the vocabulary required to understand the true nature of their problem: 5,000 years of restricting, shaping, and disallowing the natural form given to each of us as means of revealing, experiencing, and celebrating our true inner natures. Sexuality had been made a male prerogative with woman as subjects of their whims, which sometimes included desire, sometimes respect, sometimes out-of-control abandon, sometimes reckless will, sometimes total disrespect and dishonoring, and often casual neglect in service of self-interest.

The topic of sexuality was not a well-known by-product of the Women's Movement. Women did feel that permission had been gained for more abundant sexual lives, but the form became as profane as that of their brothers. I am arguing for sex as a sacrament for honoring the highest level of our own life-force energy and the Creator, who gave us the life and the means to celebrate, referring to our ancestors, the Goddess worshippers, who celebrated their Goddess with sacred sexuality and were cast aside by those who wrote the history. For the Goddess worshipers, the Creator was a female deity. For Native Americans, the Great Spirit is androgynous. Only those who believe in a male God and His power to punish can be forced to attribute the creation of life to a male.

Finishing the Work of the Women's Movement

The problem is that there are so many problems. The problem is that women, unaware of their ancient history as the creators of life have come to share the helm as a result of the Women's Movement without knowing where they are going or what ship they are on.

They do not know their history or the truth of who they are as unique from men. As much as women have not identified their own purpose and the truth of their own energy and insight, they have gotten on the ship that was already loaded and they are engaged in steering toward the existing goals they did not put in place and of which they would not approve if they applied their inner knowing to the questions of what must be done.

The opportunity offered by the Women's Movement was lost because the true nature of women was not looked at or grasped as important, nor was the history of the true identity of women and their ancient power revealed. Women have taken up positions as the servants of men's goals without asking what their own might be, without knowing the reality of 20,000 to 30,000 years of history in which the Creatrix was a Goddess, and the ability to create and sustain life was known to be sacred and inherent in their nature (now known as DNA). We must look at this history in order to establish what the women are and what they are meant to do to support and sustain life—their own and all of life.

It is not about returning to that time in history when the Goddess was alive and active, but of recognizing from that history, as we come to know it, the truth of women's potential to perform on an equal level with men in their own way providing the insight and context that cannot be known by the masculine. The idea that women cannot perform in the interest of the culture at large must be eliminated. It was never true. Women had been in charge, not only of their own lives, but as cultural leaders as well for much of the total history of humankind.

Why have efforts to achieve equality failed for so many women? The true nature of the problem has not been known. The magnitude of the resistance to women taking their place in the truth of who they are, what they have to offer, and the power of their sexuality to direct us all to harmony and balance has not been identified from the time it was cruelly eliminated. We must face 5,000 years of lies, suppression, denial, and slaughter to know that these violations occurred in a continuous effort (still going on today) to conceal the power that women had once had in their celebration of themselves as they celebrated the Goddess (creator of all things) by means of the sexuality that gave them and Her that power. Fear of the disturbance as a new balance is found is one factor in the long delay, as is the reluctance among the dominating male deciders to give up their positions of power and wealth to a more equitable system that includes women as full participants, contributing from the truth of their real natures. The underlying wisdom of women at the core of cultural reality is their natural role as the creators and sustainers of life. For us today, this function goes beyond motherhood to women's energy applied to the re-birth of the means to sustain all of life in health, harmony, and happiness. Birth of all life into its capacity to celebrate life is the function of the feminine when given the space and acknowledgement to be itself.

I see the magnitude of the problem in the fact that the women of the Women's Movement did not know that there had been a time of female supremacy, causing their appeal for power to become a hollow whine that they be given more instead of a bold assertion of inherent life-giving-and-sustaining human qualities; and I see the magnitude of the problem in the ongoing suspicions, hate, and fear among men. As for this fear among men, we are only seeing the tip if the iceberg. Each woman who is dealing with one man does not know how deep his ignorance and fear are or how far back it goes, how deeply the problem is hidden in his own psyche and in the psyche of all the men. It was not known in 1850, in 1920, or in 1960-80 how much work was needed to make appropriate room for women at the table of life or how sustained the effort had to be, or even what the work really was—like dealing with an iceberg, or a boulder of granite in the earth, or crab-grass in the garden, or an ant's nest. You do not know what is there until you start working at it.

The history of the demise of the Goddess worshippers was emerging in the 1970s, but did not find a way to integrate and direct the actions of those in the Women's Movement. Even today, when I speak about this history, there is resistance, denial, and disbelief. Twenty to thirty thousand years of history has been wiped off the slate, and not integrated into the story of humankind. This is a huge story that must be revealed and integrated. The Goddess as creator and sustainer of life must be reckoned with. The job of the Women's Movement was incomplete as was the attempt to pass the Equal Rights Amendment, and for the same reasons: lack of understanding among the women of the enormous boulder they were rolling back, and the enormous effort among many men to disallow women an equal voice or a place at the table.

We all must understand that "the way things are" has grown out of a time in history that has been hidden so that the order that we now know could move forward. "The order that we now know" did not want us to know about the order that had preceded it.

So, what is the means of regaining what was lost?

Orgasm as Sacrament

Taking back the sacredness of sexuality and the ability to "know" made possible in our highest vibration is the means for women to reclaim their power as full participants in life. Sexuality was historically an ancient tool of empowerment. Awakening to our sexuality will spark women into memory of themselves and their capacity to fully celebrate their lives. The loss of access to sexuality as a blessing and a sacrament as a major cause of women's low-level of functioning in the society has not been recognized or addressed in the efforts to raise women's estimation of themselves and to create gender equity.

Worship of the Goddess at its highest level involved high-level orgasm: orgasm with great wave-lengths and frequencies of vibration. This sacrament was performed in the temples to raise the celebrants' energy as high as that of the Goddess Herself. We have missed the discussion of this reality in our attempt to establish a place for the true feminine in our culture. Sexuality was integral to the sacredness of all life for the Goddess worshippers. We must re-integrate sexuality to its place of sanctity if we are to find our way together to the place where life for all is once again a celebration: "the Garden of Eden in the Promised Land!" We must talk about and reclaim our knowledge of ourselves and our experience of pleasure in our own highest energy if we are to find our way back into life as celebrants of who we, aware of all of life around us, and prepared to celebrate each moment as a blessing.

My purpose as a sculptor of women in full celebration of themselves, and, now, putting this issue on paper, is to awaken women to the possibility that their offerings to the culture are beyond equal pay for equal work, that the issues of "what work" and "what money" do not touch the essence of what is possible. These are questions and answers that rise out of the male-dominated culture that worships work and money. When women begin to ask their own questions, those will be in the realm of "What is important about life and living?" "What are the special gifts given to me that I may offer to assure abundance, satisfaction, and happiness for everyone?" "What are the things around here that I can do something about that will serve us all?" "What are the blessings of life?" "How does the love of and for all beings find expression in what I do?" "Who are the people who know that life is about loving, about giving, about receiving gifts?" "How can I support their efforts?" "How can my life make a difference in the possibility of life being a celebration for everyone?" Finding our way to the next step in recovery of the feminine to itself, we must take into account the imposition of restraints that have been in place for 5,000 years, and we must revoke them in order that the feminine might act from the core of what it is.

Women still must do the work of claiming the truth of who they are and proclaiming it in their words and actions, turning the culture to the truth of what it must be to re-establish harmony and balance with all that is.

The Women's Movement is not over. It is delayed.

❧❧❧

The power women are now experiencing in their more active roles in society, made possible by the Women's Movement, is not all the power that would be released by their true nature.

DAISY SAYS:

Our sexuality makes possible the highest level of our energy.
The spark of orgasm is an explosion into life.
It is given as a blessing in order to express love.

CHAPTER IX

THE SHAM OF GENDER EQUITY

As noted in the previous chapter, many people assume that women have attained equality with men, or at least near equality. After all, at least women in Western culture have better jobs and better pay. Some have been elected to office, some are heading up corporations. However, there is tension of unfinished business hidden under the portrait of well-being. Men's fears and women's limitations still exist.

Even though in the early part of the twentieth century, the eruption of feminine energy brought pressure to the male-dominated government to allow women to vote, and in 1920 suffrage was granted to women in the United States, and in 1928 the women of Great Britain achieved the same goal, women have not yet achieved the power to meaningfully set the goals of society, nor the wealth to make the needed changes.

Certainly, things have changed. The situation is much different than it was in the childhood of my grandmother, my mother, and even my own childhood. While my two choices were teaching or nursing with a back-up in shorthand and typing, just in case, today women have abundant choices and possibilities for high degrees of success in expressing themselves through the way that they live. Women today own property, sign their own checks and credit charges, get loans for new automobiles, graduate from undergraduate and graduate schools in large numbers with high achievement, hold responsible jobs, become CEOs, and achieve closer and closer salary parody. The election of 2018 demonstrates a stronger voice of the feminine.

However, consider this: The equal Rights Amendment to the Constitution finally adopted by Congress went down to defeat in the states after a hard-fought battle. In 1982, time expired for ratification by 38 states with approval by 36, certainly a strong indicator of remaining resistance to women occupying their full position in the culture. Hillary Clinton's defeat for the highest office in the land illuminates that we are not yet there. It did not matter that Trump was exposed as an abuser of women and a denier of the climate trouble our planet is in. Resentment and resistance took the front seat. For 5,000 years since the systemic destruction of the Goddess-worshipping societies, women have yet to break through the barricades set up to surround their energy and activity.

The Same, Old Agenda

The old agenda, the daily pursuit of wealth and power is still being served, selectively ignoring human-caused climate change, the rapidly escalating extinction of thousands of Earth's species, the dire situation of millions fleeing from war-torn homes, millions of homeless human beings, and starving children. In far too many women's lives, sexual abuse remains a destructive element. We have failed to eliminate racism, and misogyny in our society. Indeed, these appear to be getting worse. Instead of building a society in which pursuit of the common good is a virtue, our leaders (including some women in leadership positions) are under the sway of campaign donors who seek only a greater accumulation of wealth and power for a tiny minority of elites.

Despite women's increased contributions to the culture we remain ensnared in the limitations of a framework imposed upon us by 5,000 years of the repression of women's voices and values, of women's energy, and what women find important in life and how it is lived. I am deeply disturbed by the choices women make to fit in to the way things are.

I am concerned by our focus on getting ahead in a system that is known to be harming the planet and everything on it. After all, women hold at least half of the wisdom and energy available for solving problems, setting goals, and designing a way of living that allows joy and abundance for everyone. Do we really want to fit into a system that puts celebration of life in a third or fourth or fifth position behind acquiring wealth and power?

The Path to True Gender Equality

What will it take for gender balance to become a reality? How do we achieve balance and harmony within, between, and among women and men in a celebration of life? A first step is to understand the truth of history that has been suppressed for millennia. It is why I have spent so many years and the previous chapters revealing the deception we have been living under, that women are naturally inferior and unable to participate in the creation of peaceful, working societies. In modern times, we have been unaware of the moment in history when the curtailment of women and their sexuality occurred, or even that there was such a moment when limitations were imposed on our being or the nature of that being.

Another important step: we must call out the pretend balance that has been established following the major women's movements of the 19th and 20th centuries. The problem is not solved by women accepting the tenants of their captors and finding their way out into the world using the means and methods of their dominators. It is the woman true to her own instincts and sources that will allow the planet to settle into sustainable patterns once again.

The women's movement of the '70s and '80s brought awareness to everyone that women could participate more profoundly in their own lives and in life around them. The men moved over a little bit. They harnessed their fears and shut their mouths and gave a little.

OK, we will not open doors for you.

OK, we will not stand back and let you go first.

OK, we will not lay our coats in the gutter to keep the filth off your dress (and we will clean those gutters).

We might listen to what you have to say.

We will raise your pay.

We might vote for you if you run for political office.

But we will not give you all the secrets that we have hoarded for 5,000 years. We will not let you into our inner world, and we will not share the greater wealth. We will pretend that you are one of us, but we will continue to incest our grandchildren and rape your daughters. We will act kindly, but we will know that we are still in charge and you have little hope of rising to the top of our system.

This sham of equality bothers me. Women's willingness to accept only one piece of their own pie forces me to speak out. The lack of courage among women to address the real and lasting pain of their own betrayals, and the hands ruined in ineffectual hammering on the door to possibility cry for attention. The problem of women being fully alive in their own lives is not solved. Would we be more effective in finding solutions if women were more prominent in identifying the major questions?

You may not think there is a problem. Maybe you have beaten

the odds and risen to a very high level in the activity of life. Maybe it doesn't take much to allow you to feel happy. Maybe you haven't noticed sisters languishing, or the ones who are hiding because their uncle incested them or their schoolmate raped them. Maybe you are satisfied with your minimum piece of the pie. Maybe you think that is all there is.

But I am not satisfied. I know that so much more is possible, and that something truthful and abundant is missing. This wonderful planet is a paradise within which to celebrate, and we are given all the means to enact a totally joyous life. We have the place, the potential energy, and the gifts of imagination and physical abilities, even, often, the insight into what must be done. Why isn't life a continuous enactment of joy for all of us?

Male-owned corporations drive the boat. Halting global warming, stopping the manufacture of plastic, Styrofoam, harmful agricultural chemicals, reducing the amount of atmospheric carbon that is acidifying our oceans and killing coral reefs, these are not priorities for most of them.

More than twenty years of leading Native American transformational ceremonies, hearing women pray in the purification lodge and recount vision-quest discoveries showed me that women suffer from injuries of incest, rape, harassment, and molestation, and that these wounds are signs of the imbalance that remains between men and women. Women are not full participants, and one important way they are kept in their "place" is by sexual injustices.

What Energy Do We Require?

Women must make changes. Our energy has been curtailed. When women discover the appropriate shifts, it will be apparent what men must do to achieve and maintain the outcome of gender balance. The long history of domination and control may come to an end as men witness the life-supporting contributions of women who are awake and aware of their uniquely feminine biases. I am not talking about lipstick color or corset style. It's more like breast milk and fresh air, clean water, a keen interest in the ideas and activities of children, and time spent relaxing.

What must women do to make a shift occur? How is it that we are to be women living in the truth of ourselves? How are we to discover our true natures and our appropriate behaviors? How do we remove the restraints? How do we draw a new picture of cultural form and practice that takes into account the authentic contribution of women? How do we bring into focus the faint image that has begun to appear as women have taken the brave steps of breaking out of the cocoons built around them to keep them in check? What is the role for men as women re-awaken to their ancient roots and their innate power and worth?

Our minds may not know the answers, but our sexuality at its highest vibration has the capacity to access the unknown realms of spirit. Our path to healing, to knowledge, and to our total abundance of human energy resides in opening to the full power of our sexuality that informs the truth of our energy.

I am afraid that the round of revelations at the end of 2017 will drive our understanding of sexuality into deep hiding as we are overwhelmed by witnessing aggressive misuse.

Where does the energy come from that will make change happen, and how does fighting back bring to life a better picture in which everyone regains the right to find the joy in their own lives?

I believe that the energy called for is radically different from the energy existing all around us forging the way into wealth and power. It will be found as women lift themselves from the cocoons of restraint and identify their own true natures. Women acting as women have potential to access answers that have long been hidden while their energy and voices have been repressed in many ways including resistance to unwanted sexual advances. Unleashed, this energy holds the potential to alter the course of action of human-kind and bring us back to balance and health. When women have the courage to choose to be themselves and function in a reality that nourishes them, they will find that energy.

Our ancestors, the Goddess worshippers, knew that this energy already exists in our sexuality as it is naturally given to us. The very act that we have been taught to hide and fear holds the potential to heal us. Sexual energy already exists in our physical bodies, but we have been disconnected from its availability and its power to inform and direct us by the declarations of immorality made by leaders in ancient times who eradicated the Goddess cultures in which sexuality was the way of celebrating the Divine and illuminating the divine in humans. The fear and denial surrounding sexual activity is a learned trait imposed by religious leaders installing their own God-centered religions, establishing control over women in their Goddess-centered societies.

Reclaiming of memory and accessing the power of sexuality to inform, empower, and enhance the quality of our lives will be no small task. The major religions hold tightly to the principle of women as fundamentally evil and immoral, especially concerning their sexual nature at the very same time that men use their positions of power to harass and harm women sexually. Because sexuality was the major means of celebrating and worshipping the Goddess in the temples, and because the fathers of children born of this worship could not be identified, sexuality was attacked by the new, male-oriented culture that sought dominance.

Resistance to Righting the Wrong

So, even though access to the source of energy that will return women to their former knowledge of their own wisdom and power and their potential to bring light to the problems we currently face already exists, there are strong forces acting against this memory and behavior modification. We must find the way to break out of this cultural trance and remember the legitimate place our sexuality holds in the five aspects that make us human—mind, body, emotions, spiritual, and sexual—and reinstall it there overcoming strong resistance by religious leaders. It will take all of us being aware together to set a new course and hold to it.

We can expect a backlash, which we are seeing today in the resurgence of piety represented in the political right, Christian evangelicals, the vehement interference with women's sexual freedom by laws about when life begins, and the widespread attempts by legislators to limit what women can do about unwanted pregnancy. At its roots is the same old war of overpowering the feminine to maintain male control.

While we continue to be taught in our current houses of worship that pleasure in the sexual experience is evil, we must awaken and begin again to practice the fact that the pleasure and magnified energy of our sexual experience identifies us as human as much as our opposing thumb that allows us to hold and use tools, our conscious mind that does math problems and tells stories, our emotions that direct our attention to significant events, insights, and actions, and our ability to identify the sacredness of life.

The higher vibration you experience in the moments of orgasm is energy. Think of the alignment of molecules you know has occurred in the instant of climax. That is energy free of kinks and barriers: totally available. We have been taught to trivialize this blessing while advancing the importance of the other aspects of life: mind, emotions, physical body, and spirituality. Too often we profane this sacred event after dark in hidden places, often with people we do not know or have any feelings for. This is not the sexuality I am speaking of. This perversion has developed as we have remained in hiding from the essence of our own being and the power released by the spark of orgasm. To heal from this perversion, we must pay attention to what emerges in our awareness at the height of orgasm. Our own experience will refute the tyranny of the religious leaders and their ancient manuscripts.

Love, desire, pleasure, joy, and all the ways they are expressed are the best of what it means to be human. We must remember not to push them aside in our pursuit of what—something better? What would that be? It is the dominant ethic that makes us slaves to work, the one that eliminated women's access to themselves and continues to suppress total sexual expression and power as it goes about solving the problems it creates with bigger and bigger, more and more threatening and destructive weapons and new and more complex problems.

Memory, Not Blame, Will Redeem Us

This is not about blame. Men and women are all suppressed under the warped myth of male dominance. We must understand that something did happen to us about 5,000 years ago, and we are all still living under the heavy weight of the results of that event. This history that is rarely taught, and the myth that the world and the wealth belong to men endures.

Knowing of the events of 5,000 years ago gives us the chance to put the matter right and bring forth the truth. Some may still believe that the Goddess is a fiction. She is not, even less than God is a fiction. Of course, you could argue that both Gods and Goddesses are fiction. The point here is that a male image of Divine was constructed to elevate men to a higher stature than women who, at the time, were celebrating the female face of God and whose civilizations were organized around the Goddess as the central figure. It is hard to deny the feminine as the creator of life.

These ancestors looked toward a feminine deity for help from the realm of the sacred in their efforts. In their temples, they performed sacred sexuality with the belief that the prerequisite for human reproduction would celebrate and influence the outcome of cultivating and planting in the soil. They believed that sexuality was overseen by Divine energy; it was itself a celebration of the Divine, and their enactment of sacred sexuality insured divine intervention in the growth of their seeds and the magnitude of their harvest.

Today, women do not know or remember the sacredness of sexuality. Especially, women do not remember that their Divine Creatrix was celebrated in their temples by the practice of sacred sexuality, raising the human body to its highest level of vibration, orgasm, that was deemed most appropriate for their celebration of the Divine energy. Forgetting the sacredness of sexuality and all that it had been during the time of the Goddess worshippers has meant that as women during the Women's Movement gave themselves permission to be more sexual like their brothers, they did not take up the more reverent practice of their sexuality as a sacred task, through which they could celebrate at a higher level who they are, witness their own highest potentials, and see clearly what cannot be seen with the eyes. Tortured by the conundrum that their churches forbade sexual pleasure and their bosses demanded it, while their teachers forgot to tell them of the ancient sexual celebrations, women have been lost in a sea of confusion and miss-information.

Women must know this part of our history. We cannot regain

the balance that was lost if we never look at what happened and admit that we supported and gave credence with our acceptance of the laws of the Bible and the Koran and were willing to bring our children to the perpetrators for continued indoctrination. We cannot eradicate the injustice to women and the inappropriate power handed to men if we refuse to look at the whole picture of overpowering and prescribed dominance that has ruled our reality for 5,000 years. For men, this means facing that what was done created a male-dominated culture and then owning the possibility that there could be a way to be a man without the need to take over, be in charge, and punish resisters. For women, this means owning the power demonstrated by their foremothers and reclaiming the truth of who they are.

We must know not only that there was a Goddess in the areas of the planet where women were in charge and the principles of the feminine valued, but also that the idea of one God is not the only way to witness the Divine and the sacredness of life. There is no threat here, only an opening to another way. If we will allow ourselves to open to this possibility, we can be on our way to finding balance and harmony. As long as the Goddess worshippers' ways remain hidden, buried, and feared, we will not be able to find our way to equity. We remain lopsided, struggling for footing, and ignorant of the possibilities available when everyone is participating.

The mechanism for this joining resides in sexual intimacy and the powerful energy of orgasm, and it already exists in our lives. We have forgotten the identification of sexuality as sacred with the fundamental purpose of activating and aligning our energy to our own purpose and the purpose of life. Since the Goddess-worshipping cultures were destroyed, we have not been aligned with the infusion of sexual energy as power to accomplish our lives that the orgasm provides, robbed from us by the Indo-Europeans and their descendants, the Hebrews (who invented morality and wrote the laws to insure it), the Christians, and the Muslims.

With the Bible, the Koran, and other religious texts, denigration of women and sexuality have implanted themselves deeply within the membranes of human life. It remains unthinkable among great throngs of the people that either women or sexuality be considered sacred. Good Jews, Christians, and Muslims have believed the dictates of their religions. Women have been stoned to death for sexual breaches, often by the lovers who shared the transgression and/or by their own fathers. The laws governing women's sexuality made no mention of male control over their actions. While women have been under strict control of their fathers and then their husbands, male sexuality has been out of control, spreading overwhelming psychological warfare among molested and incested children, among raped young women, and among abused wives.

Our Fathers, Brothers, Husbands Did Not Do It

The enemy for women now isn't this individual man or this individual law or custom. It is the whole system and the ideas that permeate it that women are not as strong, as smart, as deserving, that sexuality belongs to men, that wealth naturally accrues to the masculine. Barriers to women's full participation have come down, but many remain. Essentially both men and women still believe that the men call the shots, lay down the goals, and have the largest say in who succeeds. The game is still who achieves with the strongest, most violent approach, the most competitive, aggressive strategy to win. Few of us know any other way. If we do not feel up to the "battle," then we are not "winners." The idea that there is a less macho and overpowering way to "succeed" is foreign to us. That life could be engaged as a natural encounter with natural forces to find the way to balance and harmony with everything that is seems weak to us, shying away from achievement, not coming up to bat.

Raised under moral standards of our religions, the attitudes of Goddess worshippers may seem "disturbing, shocking, or even sacreligious." This response is a "result of teaching and conditioning of religious attitudes present in our society which are themselves based on ideologies of those who initially and repetitively condemned the sexual customs of the Goddess."[1] Our Bibles say these practices are immoral. Without knowing the history, we are taught to be good little Christians, Jews, or Muslims and we accept that these teachings are sacred. No one has ever told us how desperate the Levites were to get the Hebrew men out of the Goddess temples. We believe that when Yahweh says what is going on in there is evil, He must know. And it is blasphemy to refute the word of God.

We must forgive what each individual man did not himself do, acknowledging that men have lived under the negative influence of the Levite Laws as much as women, robbed of access to women as divine and sexuality as sacred, as well as the full participation of women in addressing the issues of life and living. Leading the way to balance and harmony in all things, women can return to their sacred function of honoring and caring for all life. An uprising against or simply dismissing as absurd the laws laid down by the Levites to gain control over the Canaanites will be all that is needed to find our way back to a functional society in which all people and all energy share in the efforts and the gifts. It will not be easy, but we must begin by redirecting our thinking.

We Could Remain in Ignorance

We could remain in ignorance and continue to forget who we are. But, why? Since the evidence of Goddess worshipping and its takeover has been revealed there is no more reason to cower and refuse to carry our portion of the burden of enacting life, as well as the celebration of all the gifts inherent in living. Full and truthful history already tells the story of our power to be purposeful in our integration with life. Women must come forward, claim the past and the future and restore the balance of human nature that requires the insight and the action of all people, both those ruled by testosterone and those ruled by estrogen.

It is understandable that we are inclined to give in and give up. These forces have been in charge since the feminine-based cultures were overpowered. Our ancestors stopped believing in their own strength and forgot about the power of the Goddess. They no longer taught their daughters and their grand-daughters the sacred practices that honored women and the Goddess. Today, mention of the Goddess prompts blank stares and revelation of meager knowledge. For women, it is like stepping off a cliff into the unknown. For men, it is like jumping into a tumultuous sea. The matter is mostly left alone while we are distracted by the newest technological trinket.

Nonetheless, it is incumbent on us to fully face up to the challenge and act before the destructive forces unleashed by gender imbalance destroy any hope of saving ourselves and our planet.

Recognizing the Power of Sexuality

Like some pioneers of the Women's Movements, even without having the knowledge of ancient Goddess-worshipping cultures and their sexual practices, pioneers of psychology began peeling away the layers of indoctrination that suppress human sexuality and come to some startling conclusions about how this has negatively affected our world. In the next chapter, I will highlight the findings of Sigmund

Freud and Wilhelm Reich, and the consequences the latter suffered by revealing the violent underbelly of modern society.

ॐ ॐ ॐ

Women crying in the purification lodges in pain at the abuses they had been forced to endure revealed that the battle for women's rights has not been won.

FUCHSIA SAYS:

I am nourished by love and grow in self-awareness, self-pleasure, self-appreciation, self-love, and self-acceptance: into full understanding of spirit in me and my mandate to celebrate life.

CHAPTER X

FREUD AND REICH PRICK THE BALLOON OF SEXUAL IGNORANCE IN THE EARLY 1900's

There have been moments in history when discrimination against women and their role in society has risen to the surface. I have already mentioned the women's rights movement of the 1850s, the suffragists of the 1920s, the drive toward adaptation of the women's rights amendment to the Constitution ending in 1982, and the Women's Movement of the '60s, '70s, and '80s were eruptions of the broiling turmoil in the lives of women who knew, without knowing, that they were legitimate members of the human race with rights to an equal place and an equal voice to that of men.

It is part of our history that pioneering psychoanalysts Sigmund Freud and Wilhelm Reich, also knowing without knowing, began in the late 1800s and early 1900s to recognize that there was a prevalent, buried dis-ease among the population: our true sexual natures. They began to recognize in their patients, both women and men, mental disturbances arising from sexual imbalances. I call your attention to them here because, although their work is widely known (especially that of Freud), for the most part we remain trapped in our sexual inadequacies. As I have noted, the former movements made no reference to sexuality as an underlying causal phenomenon.

In the beginning of the twentieth century, Sigmund Freud and Wilhelm Reich were engaged in the study of what made people psychically imbalanced. Unknown to them, they were on the trail to discovering the psychic impediments caused by sexual imbalance begun 5,000 years ago.

Freud first, and then Reich, were engaged in the birth of psychoanalysis as a means of assisting mentally imbalanced people back to health. Freud first proposed (then Reich supported) the idea that sexuality was at the root of the psychic problems their patients were experiencing. Freud "put the 'incest fantasy' on the fear of being injured in one's genitals at the core of every psychosis and psychoneurosis."[1] As their work progressed and their practice of psychoanalysis was perfected, their relationship to the core problem diverged. Reich discovered that sexual tension that had been dammed by lack of sexual expression and confusion regarding sexual natures, was released by sexual gratification. At first, he and Freud agreed that this dis-ease had been brought about by early childhood or adolescent sexual discomfort and trauma. Reich believed he saw in his patients the urgent but hidden drive toward happiness and their ability to achieve happiness as they unraveled the sexual repressions that had been part of their early authoritarian upbringing. As Reich approached the solution to the problem Freud had proposed, Freud balked. Reich went on to study the electrical functions of the body that allowed energy to be manifest in orgasm and proved sexuality to be a natural function of man's physical nature. His many years of working with patients confirmed for him that dialogue and dream work inadequately disposed of what was causing neuroses, and that "complete and repeated genital gratification"[2] resolved the issue. His patients recovered, while the unravelling of dream imagery that was Freud's method often failed to relieve patients of symptoms. (Note: Reich denies he took part in his patient's sexual gratification, but he did develop a massage therapy to reduce armoring.)

Reich's work eventually appalled Freud. Freud was not prepared to take on the cultural backlash he believed he would face if he began to speak openly about sexual gratification, let alone the means of achieving it, and that this would mean the deterioration of his dominant position in the field of psychoanalysis. Freud's introduction of ego, id, and libido [after all, had] offered an alternative to the uncomfortable talk about sexual energy. Beyond that, his statements began to contradict his earlier discoveries. He began to voice the idea of the death wish and man's inability to achieve happiness, saying that man had a biological striving for suffering and death. Freud's new position was that: "anxiety [was] no longer to be understood as the result of sexual repression but its actual cause."[3] "Life as we find it, is too hard for us [Freud wrote]; it brings us too many pains, disappointments, and impossible tasks. In order to bear it we cannot dispense with palliative measures...There are perhaps three such measures: powerful deflections, which cause us to make light of our misery; substitute satisfactions, which diminish it; and intoxicating substances which make us insensitive to it. Something of the kind is indispensable."[4]

Freud was resigned to humankind's acceptance of dependence on the God as creator and sustainer of life and separated himself from politics. Reich believed you betrayed humankind by acquiescing to the forms of its delusion and denial. Freud became resigned to happiness as a fantastic vision—he saw that humankind sought happiness, but said, "there is no possibility at all of its being carried through; all the regulations of the universe run counter to it; one feels inclined to say that the intention that man should be happy is not included in the plan for 'creation,'" to which Reich responded: "to have admitted the possibility of human happiness would have been tantamount to admitting the incorrectness of the theory of repetition compulsion and the theory of the death instinct."[5]

Maybe Freud held on to his new position because it complemented Hitler's idea that authoritarian households and sexual denial were cultural necessities—Freud because he seemed unwilling to admit the influence of his own upbringing on his theories and, perhaps, his own discomfort with his own sexuality, and Hitler because he was initiating an authoritarian state that required participants who would stay in line and perform as told. This was achieved initially by the authoritarian child-rearing methods of "killing spontaneous life impulses" (sexuality) in the interest of questionable refinement when adolescents began to show signs of independence by engaging in sexual activity.

Reich could not accept much of what Freud ultimately maintained. For instance, "while Freud admitted that the striving for pleasure is ineradicable, he claimed that it is not the social chaos but the drive for happiness that should be influenced [altered in psychotherapy]."[6] Also at variance with what Reich was discovering from his patients was Freud's position that "by influencing the instinctual impulses, not the world which forces people to live in want, one could hope to free oneself from a certain amount of suffering-kill the instincts."[7] Also at variance with Reich's position, "Freud maintained that human structure and the condition of human existence were unchangeable...He assumed sexual gratification was a right unattainable because of social mores."[8] Particularly counter to the path Reich was taking was Freud's suggestion that narcotics would help achieve happiness, this without mentioning the problem of addiction. It took some time for Reich to accept that the man who had established the fact of child sexual repression—the first dim awareness that the sexual renunciation that had been going on for thousands of years was a root of mental instability—was willing to turn away so dramatically from his own thesis.

Reich hardened his position, believing himself to be in the right because he saw so much improvement in his patients as soon as they were able to begin to overcome their resistance to sexual fulfillment. His position intensified as he declared that "hate develops as a result of the exclusion of the original goal of love [and that the] hate [was] most intense when the act of love or being loved is blocked,"[9] and because he believed in "the overwhelming and fundamentally correct role of human striving for happiness."[10]

Reich did suffer discrimination by the psychoanalytic world in which he held a prominent position, and his relationship to Freud was severely damaged by his position that mental illness could be cured by sexual gratification. But he remained undaunted in the belief in the importance of his work, that it was revolutionary, and that the health of the culture required him to continue in his efforts to unlock the sexual suppression he had discovered with the key he knew fit the lock. He said that at the time "it was clear to me that the sole function of psychiatric science was to divert attention from the true elucidation of the sexual content of existence."[11] Reich was determined to overturn this prejudice.

As I became familiar with this feud, I recognized in it my own gradual awakening to the underlying problem, cracked open to my awareness by praying women in the purification lodge, by the lack of awareness or willingness to discuss this situation I encountered, by the difficulty many (most?) men and women had engaging with my sculptural expression of women in full ecstatic celebration of themselves. I have maintained a solitary effort to bring awareness of the reality of goddess worshipping destroyed by a patriarchal system that continues to repress the real nature of women, and the necessity for feminine awareness and influence to rise to importance in our culture.

The differences between these two pioneers of psychoanalysis is an indication of our resistance to admitting that sexuality must hold a central place in our enactment of life. Freud's theories of sexual distortion being at the root of mental confusion have been much repeated with little knowledge that he held up the problem to our awareness then retreated from it. Reich did not have the same prominence when he began his work in support of Freud's idea, and he met with resistance among his colleagues (even at the top level of his field) but continued his efforts to determine the method of release from turmoil he witnessed in his patients. He devoted his life to this revelation, continuing his research in the United States after retreating from Austria, Germany, and Scandinavia. He died in prison when his employee shipped the orgone machine (Reich's device in which patients sat for health benefits) across state lines, in violation of interstate commerce in 1957.

Words such as "sexuality," "orgasm," and "intercourse" burned the ears of Americans in perhaps a slightly different way than Freud's had been singed. Considering ourselves advanced, we resisted Reich's message and actively thwarted his attempt to bring to us his awareness. We continue, even now to abandon our children on the subject of sexuality and allow them to grow up believing the most important thing about sexuality is that it has the potential to give them AIDS, herpes, syphilis, or gonorrhea, not to mention the horror of pregnancy. We continue to believe our expenditures in fighting for oil, control, and power over others are more important than any movement toward celebrating life. Sexuality has a low and hidden importance and is definitely not considered to be a sacrament. We have a long way to go.

Freud discovered and engaged Reich in the study of the residual internal accumulation of crude and twisted distortions caused by the discrediting and undermining of natural sexual drives and un-released sexual tensions without knowing the history of Goddess-worshipping cultures that prevailed for 20,000-30,000 years, or their custom of celebrating their own divinity and the Great Goddess with their sacred sexual ceremonies in their temples, without knowing about the Indo-European invasions and the assaults on the Goddess-worshipping cultures that eventually destroyed them and their practices, without knowing that declaring their sacred sexual ceremonies amoral and the women participants evil was the ultimate means of wiping these people out. They began to glimpse the problem without knowing its cause.

Now it is time to put all these pieces of understanding and awareness together and reclaim the healthy sexual practices that will allow us to celebrate life at the highest level, while honing our bodies and psyches to perceive and preserve all the goodness around us—right now. It is not too late.

Emotional Plague Prevents Happiness

Reich wrote in 1942: "According to the prevailing view of life, 'sexuality' is an offensive term. It is very tempting to wipe out its importance for human life altogether."[12] For many Americans this statement is still true today. His decades of investigation led him to believe that "psychic health depends on orgasmic potency, i.e. upon the degree to which one can surrender to and experience the climax or excitation in the natural sex act... [with a] healthy character attitude of the individual's capacity to love."[13] Reich concluded that the psychic illnesses he was treating grew out of interference with the natural ability to love. He believed that most people suffered from orgasmic impotence, which was causing dammed up energy leading to irrational actions. Without knowing that he was excavating an ancient tomb where sexuality had been buried by the Indo-Europeans and their descendants, Reich continued his quest.

He called it an "emotional plague," and warned that it had to be wiped out if we were to make people well and restore pleasure to life, especially for young children and adolescents who took the brunt of the authoritarian family's social conditioning. Reich identified "sexual chaos" in the culture caused by the forced internalization of "external mechanisms of life," by which he meant rousing sexual orgasms. Reich felt that "Man has alienated himself from, and grown hostile to, life."[14] Glimpsing the truth without knowing the actual history, Reich believed that the patriarchy had stolen man's freedom in demanding obedience to authority, alienating him from himself and making him hostile to life. He believed that blind obedience was achieved by the authoritarian family that exerted its power over the sexuality of young children and adolescents, achieving control by denying natural pleasure and making it sinful.

It is amazing to realize that this man conducted his fervent intentions and efforts at exactly the same place and time that the most distorted view of appropriate life and power was growing right around him. Was Hitler's rise to power part of the same disturbance that compelled Freud to contradict his own findings that sexual tensions caused psychic distortions? What would the outcome have been if Freud had used his prominent position to further the cause of sexual liberation by working with Reich instead of turning against the idea that sexual gratification was freeing patients of their distortions and mental imbalances? There is still a tremendous weeding required to finish the work that Reich began after Freud first intuited the sexual undercurrent of mental anxiety and disease, and Reich found a solution in the release of sexual tension. The "emotional plague" continues its scourge in slightly different forms even as we now claim so much greater sexual freedom. From his many years of studying the issue and assisting patients to overcome their sexual distortions, Reich came to believe that "the unity and congruity of culture and nature, work and love, morality and sexuality longed for from time immemorial, will remain a dream as long as man continues to condemn the biological demand for natural (orgasmic) sexual gratification."[15] What he did not know—and I am now repeating from the work of Marija Gimbutas, Merlin Stone, Riane Eisler and others—is that that longing has not been "from time immemorial," but since the invasions of the Indo-Europeans disrupted cultures that did live in unity, loving work and love, with sexuality as a foundation of their pleasure with and in life.

Reich saw the family as the source of the problem and of the solution. "To master the psychic plague, it is necessary to draw a clear-cut distinction between the natural love which exists between parents and children and every form of familial compulsion."[16] Reich recognized that "the child's love grows out of the love parents feel for each other, not joined merely by the sacrament they received, but by the love they feel."[17] He witnessed most families as suffering from an illness that "destroys everything which honest human strivings are attempting to achieve...resorting to the compulsive morality that goes hand in hand with pathological sexuality."[18]

Thus, from 1923-1957, Reich was giving voice to the methods used to carry out the repression that had begun as the warring forces of Indo-Europeans invaded and overran the peaceful, pleasure-loving Goddess worshippers. Observing the families of his culture in Vienna, Germany, Scandinavia, and finally the United States, he concluded that "it is easier to demand discipline and enforce it authoritatively than it is to bring up children to take pleasure in doing independent work and to have a natural attitude to sexuality...it is easier to insist on legal fulfilment of respect and love than to win friendship through humane behavior,"[19] which had become the standard for families of his time and place, promoting the distorted attitude toward sexuality that had been put in place 5,000 years ago. Unable to develop freely, especially in relation to their natural sexual interest and investigation such as touching the sexual organs or masturbating, children develop distortions and fear in the place of pleasure.

Pleasure as the Enemy

The entire tangle of deprived and contorted sexual needs is a result of the disruption of natural sexual practices that occurred when the Goddess was overrun. By the 20th century it had become the accepted normal state of humankind's relationship to sexuality. Pleasure was not on the road map.

As his investigation progressed, Reich was convinced that "patients do not improve when the content of the unconscious is revealed [which was the focus of Freud's psychoanalysis]... there must be a force of unconscious ego...which prevents the patient from getting well...this force revealed itself as the physiological fear of pleasure and the organic incapacity to experience pleasure."[20] Lifting the veil of history as he continued to question the relationship of sexuality to mental imbalance, Reich observed that "the destructiveness bound in the character is nothing but the rage the person feels owing to his frustration in life and his lack of sexual gratification."[21] He went even further, declaring "if a person encounters insurmountable obstacles in his efforts to experience love or gratification of sexual urges, he begins to hate."[22]

Looking around him as the Nazis gained power, he noted that "the sadistic pleasure of destruction so evident in our times can be traced to the general inhibition of natural sexuality,"[23] which he saw as "the demand for asceticism for adolescents [that had] ...the intent of making adolescents amenable and marriageable—it [did]—and in the process...produces the very sexual impotence which...destroys marriages and heightens marriage crises."[24]

Reich came to firmly believe that "the pleasure of living and the pleasure of orgasm are identical," and that "extreme orgasm anxiety forms the basis for the general fear of life."[25] What had begun 5,000 years ago as an effort to replace the Goddess with the God and reserve power and wealth to the male rulers had become a fortress of distress, confusion, and unhappiness built on the ancient foundation of assault and slaughter constructed of the stones of deprivation. Pleasure as a right of life had been long buried and forgotten.

Invented by Indo-Europeans, Morality Has Become the Behavioral Standard

Morality was a political invention to make the pleasures experienced in the Goddess's temples bad, and force Hebrew men to give up that habit. For Reich's patients, the moral stance against natural sexual behavior had become rigid over 5,000 years and created mental disease. As discussed in chapter 5, morality was invented to discredit the sacred sexuality of the Goddess worshippers and force the men to return to their homes, impregnate their wives, and welcome their sons into their homes as their natural descendants, in line to inherit and accrue their fathers' wealth, thus benefiting the Hebrew nation's ability to accumulate wealth.

History whispered in his ear when Reich knew what he did not know, and he revealed "Morality function[ing] as an obligation... incompatible with the natural gratification of instinct...produc[ing] conflicts that are often hidden and from an underground unknown position caus[ing] distortion...creat[ing] sharp irreconcilable psychic contradictions."[26] By asking: "Why has the concept of a sharp antithesis between nature and culture, instinct and morality, body and spirit, devil and God, love and work, become one of the most salient characteristics of our culture and life?"[27] Reich introduced the subject of this book without actual knowledge of it: the overpowering of the natural way of the Goddess so that the invaders could be in charge with their God.

Reich envisioned another kind of morality, one more in keeping with what our foremothers would have advocated. This other "form of morality was not governed by 'Thou shalt' or 'Thou shalt not;' it develops spontaneously from the [natural] demands of genital gratification...one refrains from an ungratifying action not out of fear, but because one values sexual happiness...moralistic injunctions had been totally dispensed with and replaced by better and more tangible guarantees against antisocial behavior. They were guarantees which were not incompatible with natural needs; indeed, they were based precisely on principles that fostered joy in life...Actions were carried out in accordance with self-regulating principles...which brought about a certain amount of harmony because it eliminated and obviated the struggle against instinct which, though inhibited, was constantly obtruding itself."[28]

Sexual Potency Relieves Symptoms

Our ancestors, the Goddess worshippers, had not studied sexuality or orgasm. Reich, and others have. Their findings support the idea that those ancients were keeping themselves in alignment with life as a joy through their free and open sexuality, and are in keeping with what I learned in the Deertribe. The culture has been so far from paying attention to sexuality that the term "orgasm" was not coined until 1923, and then it referred only to ejaculations and erective potency, the only activities sexologists and psychoanalysts desired to name.

Reich defined orgasmic potency as "the capacity to surrender to the flow of energy free of any inhibitions; the capacity to discharge completely the dammed up sexual excitation through involuntary pleasurable convulsions of the body," and noted that "it is the complete release of the excitation from the genitals to the entire body that constitutes the gratification."[29] He learned from his experience with his patients that affection played a significant role as did the focus of the patient on the importance and energy source of orgasm.

Ultimately, Reich concluded from his decades of investigation that, "due to universal sexual suppression, men and women have lost the ability to experience the ultimate surrender to the involuntary, which is sexual potency."[30] This is what I consider to be humankind's dis-ease taking us again and again to war instead of dancing and singing with our neighbors.

Children's and Adolescents' First Signs of Sexual Exploration Must Be Supported

I have devoted a later chapter to the responsibility we must begin to take to ensure that our children do not continue to fall into the trap of sexual discomfort, and worse, sexual armoring that prevents them from becoming fully actualized humans. Reich said "safe-guarding the sexual happiness of maturing adolescents is a central point in the prophylaxis (action taken to prevent disease) of neurosis.... The typical adolescent rebellion against the parental home is not a neurotic manifestation of puberty, but a preparation for the social function these young people will have to perform as adults. They have to fight their way to progress...they must find their way into real life and work; they must make their own imprint on life, which may contradict what their parents have done.[31]

Reich warns that "pre-marital abstinence is supposed to prepare a person for marriage. But this very abstinence creates sexual disturbances thereby undermining the marriage."[32] He also encourages masturbation for young children as the foreplay to healthy adult sexuality.

To make his point that an approach to sexual maturing in children that does not involve hostile deprivation, Reich pointed to the aboriginal Trobrianders, occupants of the Trobiand Island off the east coast of New Guinea, who "freely expressed sexuality throughout life and exhibited no sexual perversion, functional mental illness, psychoneurosis, sexual murder—confirming the theory that natural sexual maturity occurs from a very early age—refuting Freud's claim that there was a latency period between 6 and 12."[33] The Trobrianders' approach to adolescent sexuality supported Reich's claim that restrictions on pubescent young people were a result of unnatural societal requirements; "for the Trobrianders intercourse began when puberty demands it." He diagnosed the situation in European culture by stating that "in our sexual education, we are not faced with the alienation of sexual activity or asceticism, but with the alienation of natural and healthy, or perverse and neurotic sexuality."[34]

War as a Talisman of Sexual Impotence

After the horrors of World War II we said, "NEVER AGAIN." But we have gone to war, again and again, finding reasons that do not mention our thirst for oil and wealth, and the allure of arms sales.

Our tendency toward war continues, representing the most obvious proof that we have lost our ability to celebrate life. It has become incidental and commonplace for families to be blasted apart, their homes destroyed, their towns desecrated, themselves forced to flee into the unknown, desperate to survive. This continued warring is the ultimate symptom of the dis-ease with which we have been infected for 5,000 years. In this light, it would seem that the flower children of the '60s had it right—make love, not war—but we never really paid attention.

The work of Freud and Reich intensified after the First World War. Reich saw that "the death of millions of people in the war was a result of overt, social negation of life."[35] I believe our continued "anxious contractions" propel us into the next war and the next war after that because we are caught in the anxiety that lack of gratification manufactures in us, unable to access the pleasure also housed there, lost to us because of our profane relationship to our sexuality and inability to talk about it. Reich devoted his efforts to uncovering the possibility of expanding the natural source of pleasure, hidden from us in the burial of sexuality as a sacrament, so that all lives could be productive and people could live in harmony with themselves and each other.

The life process, which is inherently "rational" becomes distorted and grotesque when it is not allowed to freely develop. "When the life process is disturbed (here I am speaking about natural sexual exploration in children), it can only engender fear. Only knowledge of life processes can dispel fear. It has become one of man's essential characteristics that he is only too happy to shift this [responsibility of regulation or lack of regulation of biological energy] from himself to some Fuhrer or politician, since he no longer comprehends and indeed fears himself and his institutions. He is helpless, incapable of freedom, and he craves authority because he cannot act spontaneously; he is armored and wants to be told what to do, for he is full of contradictions and cannot rely on himself."[36]

Many of us were not alive during either World War, but we have all witnessed the insanity of war: man creating weapons that can delete rival fractions, cause death and destruction of whole populations and terrible disruption of whole societies that find it nearly impossible to repair the dissolution of their lives. Reich refers to the wars of his time and the kinds of imbalances that made those wars possible. I maintain that we continue to be at the effect of the sexual imbalances perpetrated upon us 5,000 years ago, and that these imbalances hide from us the possibility of seeking pleasure always. We have been so encased in our fear and ignorance about sexuality as a sacred mandate that we have not been willing to look at how our sexual distortions rule us. We have heard none of Reich's warnings, and we will go on using war to fix everything until we look at how our unwillingness to reassess sexuality as a profound requirement, preventing us from finding pleasure and happiness as our rightful means of living.

As we have seen, sexual repression began with the advent of the Indo-Europeans and was codified and pushed forward in history by our major religions. From its powerful position in the lives of many Germans, the Church, as well as much of the rest of the developed world, insisted that happiness depended on the elimination of sin, sexuality being among the worst, and making the population dependent on a supernatural, omnipresent being who was in charge and who judged their sins. "Hitler appeared and called himself the supernatural, omnipresent figure who would remove mundane misery—an earthly God who could be seen and could hear their appeal for help."[37]

Europeans were engulfed by the need for freedom and impeded by subhuman forces of repression that had been going on for hundreds of years. "The fact that the masses of people had always been taught to acknowledge traditional political authority instead of authority based on factual knowledge constituted the bases on which the fascistic demand for obedience could operate." They longed for freedom but lacked the ability to sustain it for themselves. Instead, masses of people affirmed and concretely implemented their own suppression, "the need for authority stronger than the will to independence."[38] This is what had become of humankind under 5,000 years of patriarchal rule.

Reich came to believe that the tragedy of World War II could be explained by the sexual disturbance that had robbed humankind of experiencing life as a pleasure, and in their misery seeking freedom by ascribing to the authority of the Fuhrer who would make their life decisions for them, becoming responsible for their happiness and freeing them from making the choices needed to achieve that result themselves. As much as we have looked at and tried to analyze the dynamics of World War II, this is an aspect that I have not seen recognized: "Illusionary freedom relieved them of all individual responsibility."[39]

Hitler's promise of male supremacy and women in the kitchen was how Germans saw themselves based on the ancient tainted images. Women backed Hitler strongly. The people were "willing... to surrender self to an authoritarian father figure," a reversal of the concept that freedom comes with assuming responsibility for one's daily life. Hitler's promise to eliminate birth control and other manifestations of the sexual-reform movement accompanied cranking up the forces of repression on sexuality itself. Exploiting human ignorance and fear of happiness, Hitler, a pathological genius, plunged Europe into the abys with the slogan of the "heroic renunciation of happiness." Hitler was very successful in his youth movement because democratic society had not educated the youth to lead a free and responsible life. "Schools [and families] had already instilled in students fear of authority."[40]

The people were persuaded to vote for Hitler, creating their own entrapment. Workers voted for him because he promised employment. The masses voted for him because he promised protection.

They had been raised in compulsive authoritarian families, and "Hitler exploited absolute obedience to the authority of the family espousing loyalty to family while drawing children into youth groups…by stressing emotional ties to family, nation-state fascism made possible a smooth transition from the structure of family to the structure of the fascist state… Mother Germany and Father God Hitler became the symbols of deeply rooted infantile emotions."[41]

Hitler's Germany was a manifestation of the people, robbed of their individual dignity and right to pleasure as represented by their sexual repression. They were willing to be led into atrocities against other humans because they had forgotten that life was meant to be celebrated among all the children. "When the fascist says Jew he means money-maker, insurer, capitalist, deeper, dirtier, sensually bestially sexual, shylock, murderer."[42] Thus the perpetrators of the anti-sexuality hoax became the subject of their own propaganda. The Jews became a target of Hitler's perversity, the result of their own imposed 5,000 years earlier. "Since the fear of natural sexuality [had become] as deeply rooted as the fear of perverse sexuality, it is easily understood that the skillfully executed persecution of the Jews stirred the deepest sexual defense function of people brought up in sexually aberrant ways… unconscious longing for sexual joy in life and sexual purity coupled with fear of natural sexuality and horror of perverse sexuality produces fascist, sadistic anti-Semitism."[43]

Because we have never come to terms with exactly what led us into World War I, and soon after into World War II, we continue to flirt with the idea that war will solve our problems, and we blindly allow ourselves to be led by forces that benefit from continual war: the arms industry, the oil industry, the military, and the government. If we were people convinced of our right to happiness we would be looking more closely at where our leaders are leading us. These crises, including the now almost global invasion of Isis, can and must be avoided. We can do it if we find our way to love each other, our sexuality, and our capacity to find joy in living.

Perhaps we should measure the distance we have already come by the fact that even in Freud's time it was still believed that procreation and sexuality were regarded as one and the same thing, even though the Goddess worshippers had known the difference thousands of years ago. The edition of Grey's Anatomy, from which my medical-student husband was learning anatomy in 1960, had no reference to the clitoris.

Reich Lifted the Edge of History and Did Not Know It

Because he did not know the history of interference with natural sexuality as it had occurred in 3,000 B.C., Reich was confused by his findings. He saw that "the life process and the sexual process are one in the same...sexual vegetative energy is active in everything alive...he asked, "If the attitudes of genital character are so self-evident and desirable, why are the intimate relations between sociality and orgasmic potency overlooked?"[44] He felt that the entire official world fought against his hypothesis. He found in male patients the ability to brag about sexual potency while experiencing no pleasure or ejaculation, and even reporting disgust and unpleasantness while viewing sexual intercourse as piercing, overpowering, or conquering the woman. Why would this be the case when pleasure was so eminently possible? Some of these same patients referred to the sex act as "fucking." "Fucking" is defilement. No sensitive woman wants "to let herself be fucked." What Reich was talking about when he spoke of "sex [was] not... "fucking" but the embrace prompted by genuine love; not urinating into the woman but making her happy.

Reich Saw the Magnitude of the Problem

In his work with his patients, Reich understood that "to be able to cope with this world, people had to suppress what was most beautiful and true, what was most basic in themselves; they had to strive to annihilate it, to surround it with the thick wall of character armor."[45] These patients pursued wealth and possessions as their goals, willing to exist without feelings. Education forced this condition on them and put them in life conditions that supported denial of emotions. Compulsive mechanisms for dealing with life issues buried natural self-regulating behaviors. He viewed his culture as "based on sexual repression," and "genital sexuality...looked on as something low and dirty...with the father look[ing] on the sexual activity of daughter as defilement...and for the average man, the sexual act is merely an evacuation or a proof of conquest.... Under poor internal and external conditions, the above contradiction leads to resignation.... Sexual partnership and human friendship are replaced by fatherliness and motherliness-mutual slavish dependency-disguised incest.... Compulsive marriage and the compulsive family reproduce the human structure of the economically and psychically mechanized era."[46]

These are the long-term products of Indo-European interference with sexuality as a natural and sacred element of living. Reich uncovered the root of the cultural disaster that had been occurring for 5,000 years, presaging the point of this book. The goddess worshippers knew pleasure as the core of their lives. Even Freud saw that happiness should be a goal, and "that sexual love was the strongest sensation of pleasure, but there was a weak side, otherwise it would never have occurred to anyone to leave this path in favor of another."[47] He could not conceive the brutal means by which we were forced off the path of sexuality as sacred.

Reich does not say how, but history certainly caught up with his ideas. He learned of the sexual repression that had been imposed on society for thousands of years. Late in his career he began to reference the primeval period of mankind that adhered to natural laws, which established the foundation for natural society. "Sexual repression is of a socio-economic and not a biological origin. Its function is to lay the foundation for authoritarian, patriarchal culture and economic sharing."[48] He understood that "patriarchal laws pertaining to religion, culture, and marriage were predominantly laws against sexuality, that all education suffers from the fact that social adjustment requires the repression of natural sexuality, and that that repression makes people sick and asocial."[49] Here, buried in the work of Reich who had been so discredited, I find what Gimbutas, Eisler, and Stone had taught me: "Using the energy of suppressed sexuality, the intermediary period of authoritarian patriarchal society for some four or six thousand years has produced the secondary, perverse, disturbed sexuality of modern man …the natural laws of sexuality must be reclaimed." Reich wanted to see humankind return to "natural socially and sexually spontaneous joy in work, the capacity for love. This is the biological core of the unconscious, and it is feared. It is at variance with every aspect of authoritarian education and control... but the only real hope man has of one day mastering social misery."[50]

Reich Suggests Recovery

It is only the liberation of man's capacity for love that can vanquish sadistic destructiveness. Loving our children, we will refrain from severely suppressing their sexuality in order to continually reproduce patriarchal dominance and make them easier to handle. Reich was certain that "sexual suppression has the function of making man amenable to authority, serving their purpose of the existing social system—molding of a negative sexual character structure was the purpose of education...just as castration of stallions and bulls makes them willing draft animals"[51] (Indo-Europeans surely had knowledge of this.) He believed that this authority, "the moral and social assessment of man's most important biological function was in the hands of sexually frustrated ladies and dignified, vegetatively inert privy councilors,"[52] who made and enforced the laws.

"A single thread stretching from childhood practice of holding the breath in order to not masturbate, to the muscular block of patients, to the stiff posture of militarism, to the destructive artificial techniques of self-control of entire cultural circle. The 'rigid military attitude' stomach in, chest out...sexually suppressive intent of military techniques the exact opposite of the natural, lose, agile attitude—make those people incapable of experiencing natural vegetative impulses and responses. It destroys the joy of life."[53]

Eventually he ascribed the impulse of orgasm to the electromagnetic function of the body. "Bioelectrically—orgasm is electrical discharge—an electric response of contraction in the muscle is transmitted to other muscles—so the strong electrical release in contractions of the genitals travels to other muscles throughout the body (Bladder contracts when it is full)."[54] Making sexuality not in the service of procreation, rather procreation is an incidental result of the tension-charge process of the genitals."[55] The intensity of pleasure sensation corresponds with the magnitude of charge. Orgasmic "gratification is a bioelectric discharge and the sexual drive occurs when there is a congestion of electrical impulses in the genitals." The armoring of children helped them repress the forbidden impulses creates the tension that as adults prevents the movement of the electrical impulses that would lead to gratification. "A deflection in the natural course of bioelectric energy lies at the basis of disturbances [we have been discussing]."[56] This was Reich's final proof that sexuality is natural and must not be curtailed. The time has come to respond to these teachings and recover the sacred in our sexual practices.

Peter Redgrove, the British poet and author, illuminates further the function of bioelectricity as confirmation of sexuality as a physiological necessity provided for in our body's electromagnetic capacities. The overruling of sexuality as an ongoing function of humankind by the Indo-Europeans was not simply a political and economic reformation, but a distortion of how we are made up and meant to live. Their history of slaughtering animals had left them insensitive to life. In the next chapter, I will discuss how Redgrove reveals the nature of sexual experience and its value in opening awareness to invisible properties of living. He does not address the history of why we lost our ability to access this huge realm of life through our natural sexuality, but he illuminates the core functioning biological reality in which sexual orgasm sparks the totality of our energy.

ও ও ও

Freud is the name we know, but his contemporary, Reich, told us that hate develops when love is excluded and the act of love is blocked.

ALEJANRA SAYS:

Sexuality activates the creative force.

CHAPTER XI

ELECTROMAGNETISM AS A CONFIRMATION OF SEXUALITY AS ENERGY

My journey toward the awakening of feminine energy led me to *The Black Goddess* by Peter Redgrove, a poet and philosopher who, like me, began to believe in the possibility of women awakening to a higher level of their own reality. His inquiry highlighted electromagnetic energy, which is also the basis for the Native American genesis story. In this myth, it is the conscious slowing down of this energy by the Great Spirit from which all manifestations of life are created. Each aspect of the created realities of the universe, therefore, contain that same magnetic energy.

These ideas interested me. Redgrove's investigation points to a scientific confirmation of the idea I am proposing: sexual orgasm is a climactic electrical energy that awakens a higher consciousness in humans, and that the termination of that enactment by women, along with the enforcement of a second-rate position, has led to women's reduced function in society.

Our ancestors knew how to open themselves to all of the invisible energy around them. They trusted what they could not see as having the ability to inform them. In their efforts to fully enact the gift that had been given when life was given, to understand what life was all about and to live it fully, they accepted all forms of input, including unseen but felt energies.

The overruling of sexuality by the Indo-Europeans as an ongoing function and celebration of our humanity was not simply a political and economic reformation, but a distortion of how we are made up and meant to live. Their history of slaughtering animals had left them insensitive to life, and worshipping blood was a sign of power achieved by killing, not a blessing that confers life. For me, Redgrove's revelation of the nature of sexual experience as a property of our electromagnetic makeup, and its value in opening awareness to invisible properties of living, increases the urgency to recognize the history of how and why we lost our ability to access this huge realm of life through our natural sexuality. His revelations show modern science lending credence to the phenomenon of sexual awakening.

Sciences have now recognized the geomagnetic field traced by the magnetic core of the earth, synchronized with the magnetic fields of the sun, the moon, and the planets. Surely it was the influence of these "pulls" that galvanized the Goddess worshippers to recognize sexual energy as worship and celebration. They were open to all ways that life was instructing them. *Our bodies are made to synchronize with the electromagnetic wave lengths of the earth. Our full participation in the electromagnetic discharges of our orgasm provides us with access to all the revelations of electromagnetic energy of creation.*

Other Evidence of Electromagnetic Transfer of Information:

- Helen Keller knew who was approaching because she could feel the way her companion held herself, and "hear" through the vibration of her companion's hand
- The symphony was transmitted to the deaf and blind "listener" by the vibration of a sheet of paper
- A fly trusts its ability to get to the meat, guided electromagnetically

- Birds have been found to have tiny concentrations of iron in their inner ear that aids navigation using the earth's magnetic field
- Butterflies navigate thousands of miles of migration by the electromagnetic energy of the planet
- Other animals use Earth's magnetic field to travel inherited migratory routes
- Pheromones act to attract a moth's mate, and may be more important than we remember in attracting a human mate

The Goddess was rescinded and hidden for 5,000 years, but the electromagnetic energy within our bodies that she manifested in her total engagement with everything that is continues as ever. Science, without wanting to invest in the sacred, is the companion and the champion of the reawakening of the sacred within and around us as it reveals the comprehensive activity of electromagnetic energy in living and non-living substances. Science confirms that what we see around us is only one percent of what is there. The remaining ninety-nine percent exists and communicates with us and everything else by electromagnetic impulses (electromagnetic waves: oscillating electric and magnetic fields).

With the confirmation of the electromagnetic transfer of information came clarity on human ability to know without know-ing—our unconscious senses electrically providing information and understanding. I am directing your attention to these thoughts and studies to confirm the power of high-level sexual experience to reveal what cannot be assessed by our senses. It might have been "magic" to our ancestors, but we know it today as electromagnetic energy animating our organism, and the basis for our whole body acting as a unit. We continue to refer to this realm as the unconscious since we are, for the most part, unconscious of its stimuli.

Redgrove describes the composition of our bodies scientifically: "Protoplasm is not a mere chemical jelly, but a semi-fluid electrical crystal which, like its mineral counterpoints in rocks, radio transistors, and light meters, possesses properties which include semi-conductivity (which directs and rectifies currents), photo-conductors (which generates and switches currents when light shines on the crystal), and piezoelectricity (which generates currents when pressure is applied, or causes a crystal to move when an electric current is applied)."[1] We are made of these crystals, and there is an electrical flow transmitting signals within lattices of electric potentials in and around and through us. Our bodies harmonize with the 10H2 frequencies emitted from the earth, making our bodies sensitive and accurate instruments of the earth's electromagnetic energies which we perceive in our feelings and our sense of reality. He defines "the sexual act is a celebration of the mystery of being."[2]

Our foremothers lived in a reality that allowed these "undercurrents" of reality to be present in their lives. The reality for Paleolithic and Neolithic people included all of nature connected in an electromagnetic web (not their name for it) that kept communication open and actively aligned among all things. Their senses were awakened to broader frequencies. They looked for meaning in all input from all realms. The oracle at Delphi, reading the currents emitted from the earth's vents, is an example that lived on because the male-dominated culture required its directives for its battles. "The energy being read by the oracle (physiologically active vapors) carried data."[3] The energy of the earth was symbolized by the snake.

We must remember our own involvement in electromagnetics in order to access the much bigger reality of our heritage. Nature communicates among all of its manifestations by electromagnetic impulses, and we can know all that surrounds us as we allow our senses to provide available information at higher and lower frequencies of electromagnetics. We were robbed of this deeper knowledge and communication by the masculine-dominated, warring tribes that came over the Caucuses and systematically wiped out the Goddess cultures, depriving women access to the full reality of who they are and ignoring the deep reality of nature's offerings to everyone outside and beyond the quest for wealth and power.

Electromagnetic Energy Connects Us with Insect and Animal Worlds, and Everything

What we are recognizing here is that, along with the suppression and discrediting of the feminine aspects of life, the place of humans within the natural world was lost as the male-dominated society pushed boundaries into more and more consumption and acquisitions, with no regard for the requirements of other species or the planet itself. This attitude of self-importance took the dominators farther and farther away from the offerings of the natural world that serve to support and preserve life itself. In acting continually to aggrandize themselves, they moved away from what it means to be alive. Gradually humans lost their awareness of basic realities: life is dominated by the presence of the sun that gives us light and warmth; the moon exerts a pull on the earth, and that pull is strongest when the moon is full; Earth itself is composed of the nutrients necessary to support life; gravity is our ally as it keeps us connected to the earth, but we struggle against it to remain upright; air and water are fundamental requirements for life and growth; all things are connected by their electromagnetic properties.

And now, disconnected from everything around us by our ignorance and greed, we find ourselves in trouble and struggling to re-establish a method of living that does not destroy us and the planet we inhabit. We must begin to remember the truth of our fundamental nature as electromagnetic entities aligning us with all other living and non-living inhabitants of this earth. We can look to the insect and animal worlds for clues for transformation and rebirth into the more balanced ways our earliest ancestors managed their lives in harmony with all inhabitants of the earth. I found in Redgrove's work a road map for the awakening of the human spirit made possible by remembering our electromagnetic composition as identical to everything that exists on the planet. He offered proof for the electromagnetic reality of living things by recounting the first indications of electrical response when Galvani's frog leg twitched when its exposed spinal column was touched by a metal rod; the discovery that seagulls fly in perfect coordination next to each other by their electromagnetic exchange; by how small insects manage their performances with little or no brain; how male moths respond to fragrances they cannot "smell," and travel great distances to the female who is emitting pheromones and flapping her wings to propel them into her surroundings in electromagnetic waves that can travel great distances through vegetative and atmospheric obstacles. And, of course, our own brain is accepting and responding to electromagnetic impulses.

Humans need this great big brain because there is so much "deciding" in our activity. The fly does without deciding. The insect brain has no meaning—these tiny creatures are thoroughly equipped to be in life the way they are, electrically. They carry on their wings a conductive film that keeps them informed. That female moth emitting pheromones takes on an infra-red electromagnetic glow that a male can track for long distances. Human women unconsciously apply perfumes that mask their true odors and their effect, one of the many ways we, out of ignorance, defy nature's contribution to the wonders of our lives. The study of electromagnetic energy allows us to reconnect with all that was lost in connection to nature and the ways of nature when women and their knowledge were suppressed.

Continuing on a path not aligned with the basic truth of our connectedness with everything that it is unsustainable. The interconnection of all things makes this planet function for all things, including humans.

Sexual Energy Raises Electromagnetic Frequency and Connects Us to the Unseen World

Now we come to the reason I feel it is important to understand that all of life is a manifestation of electromagnetic energy. We are speaking of sexuality as a form of human energy, and high-level orgasms as the most intense or highest-frequency vibration of that energy. Recognizing our natures as electric gives us a context within which to speak of "raising our energy" to its highest vibration.

Our knowledge of this part of natural life and our place in it was lost when we were wrenched from the Goddess and put under the protection and control of the all-knowing God, who knew nothing of life, the deep connection among living things, or their need for co-relation in order to sustain the level of celebration of each other that the Goddess worshippers knew and practiced.

Our insistence that nothing was true or existed that we did not have the instruments to measure, limited us to the minuscule range our limited intelligence has found for us. The ways of knowing that had evolved in all the preceding 20,000 or 30,000 years were thrown out over the 5,000 years since. The Goddess concept gave us the capacity to know all things knowable, but since then we have been at the effect of those who do not know and do not want us to remember our knowing. However, we now have instruments that measure electromagnetic energy, and have proven the web of lattices that connect us to everything.

The science of electromagnetism is difficult to penetrate, even though its use dominates our technical reality, as well as our physicality. Our Goddess-worshipping ancestors had no science. They witnessed and accepted. Let's remember that their practice of celebrating themselves and their Goddess with sacred sexuality meant that they were functioning at a high level of vibration themselves. The denial of sexuality as a legitimate expression robbed these foremothers and their progeny of their sensitive perception of all that surrounded them. Revealing this travesty has been impeded by the 5,000-year-old cultural taboos to considering the importance and role of sexuality. As I have mentioned, for many years anthropologists and archeologists (encased in their "chauvinistic cocoons") were indifferent to the images of the Goddess religion that were being excavated. Mostly men, they were products of a culture that had grown out of the Indo-European invasions, which produced a culture that cannot use the word "sex" except as a profanity or a dirty secret, and parents who cannot prepare their children for the wonders their hormones will entitle them to.

The accumulation of electrical energy in the erogenous zones that Reich predicted has been confirmed; the dispersal of these electrical impulses back throughout the body in a blast of energy when climax is achieved is also now a known fact. The expansion of energy involves the whole skin, and body, and the surroundings as well. The possibility that our senses are catalyzed to awareness of unseen information by the super sensibility of sexual climax must now be believed. It is the current that flows through all things, ch'i (the Chinese word for the natural energy of the universe), that bio-electrically flows through the whole body during orgasm. Immediately after love-making, new truths may be perceived and old confusions resolved. Couples have reported seeing a green glow outlining each other's body after simply lying together for an hour.

The erotic state, according to Redgrove, is "probably the most powerful kind that we are capable of experiencing," when love reveals itself is an "electric-moment" arrived at by concentration and spontaneity. It is a "hypnoidal" state in which what feels like magic happens, and "unexpected regions of the self are revealed."[5] When this union is with an enlightened woman, it is horasis, a name given to the sacred women of the Goddess temples. Heightened awareness in mind and body—sex for the illumination of partners—was a culturally integrated practice for the Goddess worshipers and remains so in isolated sexual/spiritual practices around the world. Most religions today limit sexuality to procreation and claim any other function to be evil. Illumination became the function of their God, disallowed in the sexual experience. Sex during a woman's menstruation has been especially forbidden by religions, even though the breaking up of the ovum, according to the Tao, contributes additional power to the woman during coitus.

Author Barbara Walker compiled The Women's Encyclopedia of Myths and Secrets, and Redgrove explains that her reintroduction of the concept of "horasis closes the gap between sexual and religious [I would say "sacred"] ...or revelatory experiences...of infinite natural wonders...the joy and pleasure...like that experienced by a person who drinks good vintage wine... [we are taken] into the marvels of the commonplace."[6]

Now we know that, "When humans kiss, semi-hormonal 'semi-chemicals' are exchanged whose effect is so powerful as to be almost psychedelic, and also somewhat addictive."[7] The kiss is a major player in the buildup of electromagnetic influence in the human. For animals, magic stuff is already there, immersed as they are in their natural continuum of electromagnetic sensitivity of hearing, touch, extended vision, profound olfactory sensitivity, and such synaethesias (more than one sense responding to a stimulus) as the free-floating pheromone maser (microwave amplification of stimulated emission of radiation).

Redgrove reveals electromagnetic energy as a source of understanding and subconscious reality, especially perceived in heightened awareness of orgasm when "a million sources of delight merged into one and streamed to the skin—seeing the bioelectrical field of the lover,"[8] which may occur at its highest peak for higher primates during menstruation when no child will be produced. The experience of this peak, during which humans access their higher consciousness, has been outlawed by religions that limit sexual experience to procreation.

Intermittent Spotlights on the Power of the Feminine to Reveal Unseen Realities

Throughout the latest five millennia of history, there have been individuals and groups who have seen through the veil of deception lowered by the God worshippers, who gave up their power to their God and no longer had depth of recognition of what the individual life experience could be when it was open to the unseen realities available to the Goddess worshippers. The God worshippers exercised the power of their weapons in ignorance of the deeper reality of life their subjects had been experiencing. The subjugation that occurred 5,000 years ago remained in place, with women forced to participate in their own denial. Despite this, there is much evidence—the Gnostics, the Troubadours, Dante's Divine Comedy, the work of St. Thomas Aquinas, poets and artists—that shows how the celebration of love and life through women continually arose even as it was being suppressed.

The Gnostics

Gnostics attempted to resurrect the value and the power of women, as had Christ. They maintained that Mary Magdalene was the companion of Jesus, "and there was no grace that He refused her, nor any mark of affection that he withheld from her."[9] It was an unfortunate reality for the Church that Jesus was intimate with Mary Magdalene, since the denial of the value of the feminine had so long been their dictate. The Church called her "whore" in a negative sense, and contorted her relationship with Jesus. The Gnostics included Mary Magdalene in their version of Christianity, and gave women positions of influence. Gnosis is a common Greek word for knowledge—mystical enlightenment or insight—self-knowledge needed first on path to enlightenment. The Gnostics knew that Jesus knew, and Redgrove confirms for our time with the inclusion of electromagnetic energy exchange, that there is an awakening of human spirit possible from remembering connection to each other, the world at large, and the electromagnetic sources.

The Troubadours

The troubadours of the latter part of the 12th century, in their romantic poems and erotic trysts, reawakened attention to love and the illuminations manufactured in lovemaking. They represent an eruption of memory among men that circumvented the dictates of religion to experience the raised energy of being in love, an increase in the vibration of electromagnetic energy. "The experience of being in love totally altered their perception of the world…as they were driven to explore the essence of their sexual being they experienced ever higher levels of consciousness in instantaneous but ever memorable moments of illumination."[10] Redgrove, a poet himself, believed that the celebrated poet, William Blake, had indicated a similar rise in energy "in a dreamy, postcoital state found an unusual effervescence of ideas, and this is what he meant by passing into the World of Poetic Imagination by the Fifth Window...a privileged moment opened to everyone especially in sexual embrace."[11]

St. Thomas Aquinas

St. Thomas Aquinas lived from 1225 to 1275, and proposed a natural theology that gave much power of knowing to human interpretation without denying God's ultimate wisdom. He attempted to synthesize Aristotle's pagan ideas with Christianity. He believed humans could know many things without divine intervention, particularly what they could know through their God-given senses. "There was a passing of invisible spirits through the medium of visible light when a man fell in love and, when these spirits passed from the eyes of the lady and entered the man's nature, a process could be set in motion that led to intellect d'amore: this process would seem to involve a transformation of sexual energy through which the love of the lady's exterior form would dissolve into love of the miraculous revelation of her soul. The invisible thus became sensible by the operation of spirits dependent on the physiological workings of the body."[12]

Dante

In another break in the massive condemnation of women and their role in humanity, one hundred years later, Dante Alighieri, the famed Italian poet worked on the Divine Comedy from 1308 to 1320, a poetic journey from the binding of hell to the illumination of paradise. He envisioned the power of the woman's imagination and perception as open to illumination of Sapientia (wisdom). She was the initiator "expressing in words not simply the ineffable experience of mystical illumination, but that illumination experienced through women, in whom divine and earthly love were united as one."[13]

Rainer Maria Rilke

The Austrian poet, Rainer Maria Rilke (1875-1926), was inspired to tell us that "the world must pass into invisibility before it can be felt...Earth do you not wish this: to arise invisibly within us? Is this not your dream, to be invisible too one day?"[14]

The Africans

Africans might have inspired us to allow women to lead us to look within the unknown for the cause of our depression (not knowing), if we had given them sufficient status to bridge our arrogance. Once again, we threw away access to knowledge when we took Africans out of their context and subordinated them to our economic needs without ever recognizing them as people with significant cultural realities of their own. (Americans have had a practice of indifference to peoples of another culture in their treatment of the Native Americans, who occupied our country long before us.) In the 1700s, the sacred had been repressed for 4,700 years, and we did not know that our random actions of war, suppression, and building towns and wealth were contrary to the wisdom of nature and disengaged from the knowledge and power of women. We were so locked in our superiority and quest for greater wealth that it never occurred to us to inquire into the truth of who these black people (or the Native Americans) were. They were inferior in our minds because we had subdued them and were able to bend their will to our own, and use their strength to help us in our blind and ignorant quest for more of what we could get in life, even though we were not recognizing life's gifts.

Three hundred years later, Redgrove proposed that black contains the secret to the unlocking of life's energies to their proper place in our consciousness, becoming attuned to the unconscious and its awareness of the other invisible ninety-nine percent of the life that surrounds us. We might have learned this from the African slaves who brought this awareness with them, but we remain indifferent or afraid of what their dark knowledge is—and what the black people in our midst could have taught us about standing in our own lives, knowing ourselves as relatives of all that is, trusting our perceptions and emotional responses to transmit the truth to our awareness. The Africans themselves have lost much of this knowledge.

Redgrove proposed that we could learn about the enactment of electromagnetic energy from more primitive Africans who were naturally in touch with the energies that surrounded them as they totally submerged in the magical energies of life. They had recognition of personal participation in all the energies of the universe that our most ancient ancestors had had. Things were not separate: everything was accepted as energy. They knew the mind as a barrier between the sacred and the profane. By their dance they participated in the energy that is everything. Redgrove remembers the African: "Black skin like primordial night...unites all in feeling... he does not start out by distinguishing himself from stone, tree, man, animal, or social event...he takes it like a blind man into his hands, he fingers it. Such a pure sensory field like the insect discovers all with its feeling... The black man is moved to his bowels...beauty strikes him at the root of his belly and gives rise to sexual feeling...[it is raised]in dance and music...beating of the heart, breathing, making love...ebb and flow...succession of days, seasons, cosmos...African spirituality is rooted in… sensuality…know[ing] the act of love bears the fruits of knowledge…the African does not kill the other life but strengthens his own with it."[15] Some black people still reflect the value of emotions as revelations of higher consciousness and see the white person as a bird of prey ready to devour even its allies. "For the Yoruba, Dahomen, and Benin people, Oduda is the Black One, personification of the serpent current [chief Goddess] … in arousal she is seen by subliminal senses of electrical structure of body."[16] We could have learned from these brothers and sisters that "the sex act to Black people [was] the celebration of the mystery of being."[17] Instead, we have drained ourselves of spirit and taken our hollow hunk back to Africa (out of which we all most probably emerged) and drained the Africans calling our forefathers and foremothers there ignorant because we no longer could see in their way. We have wasted the influence black people could have provided to deepen our relationship to all of life.

The Black Goddess

The Black Goddess emerged in France as recognition of Mary Magdalene's importance to Christ and a subversive (from the point of view of the Church) reclamation of woman's place in the family of man. Black may be a reference to "the black Moon or Lilith, the redemptive anima and the estranged part…'the inexhaustible source of creativity' for creative men who have found their inspiration here in 'the disruptive and magical feminine.'"[18] Blackness is also "that satisfactory completeness that is achieved in relaxation and meditation, the 'ese,' the postcoital state, the valley, the 'happiness orgasm' when the heart, mind, and chest will feel open and free, the 'lightness,' the relaxation response. Such a state allows the 'common sense' of all senses together—synesthesia—to operate and proceed to intuition."[19] In both cases, the Black Goddess is a symbol for the resurrection of the power of the feminine to see within the unknown ninety-nine percent of what it is to access the knowledge and wisdom that has been lost in her repression.

This Goddess symbol is black because "Hope-in-love is represented in black...because she is the symbol and gateway to everything we could know in the apparent blackness beyond visible sight; because she represents all those forces that surround us which are not perceived in the eyes, but which extend from the visible spectrum into unexplored modes of being to which animals seem closer than we are, at the crossroads of the senses... she is Isis [Egyptian Goddess] in her temple of dream incubation. She is goddess of the vision of night, the dream, the marvels we see by inner light...because she is goddess of pure light—clairvoyance, clear-seeing, second sight, truth of first sight (that loved touch in bed), dark light of touch in womb, Goddess of Intimacy, the fifth-window (skin)... because she lives in the darkness men have create in their blindness...[because she is the] blind Shekhina who has wept her eyes out in exile to which men have consigned her...[and because she is]Salome... blind because she does not see the meaning of things."[20] She has been hidden in the dark of electromagnetic energy in which the Goddess worshippers had participated. Remember the early reference in this writing to the sacredness of "black" as the entrance to the vagina.

Lilith

Lilith was an early form of the Black Goddess. She was "to the respectable and self-regarding...dangerous... [and] particularly shunned in Mesopotamian Semitic mythology, which anathematized all erotic experience except that which led to the conception of children."[21]The cover-up of the usurping of women's position in the culture has been so complete that many modern people have not heard of Lilith, the predecessor of Eva. Lilith refused to succumb to the power of the God, who was trying to make the case for His creation of Her. For the most part, we have accepted that Adam's rib was the initiation of woman's being in Eve, while Adam himself was created in the image of this new God. Black is the color of Lilith returning from the depth where she was hidden away.

Jungian analyst Barbara Black Koltuv, in The Book of Lilith, maintains that "it appears that the whole Judeo-Christianity was built on the repression of this figure, the putting down to the lowest depths of exile this wonderful magical part of women."[22] Lilith took with her our consciousness of the relationship of the moon's ebb and flow to the menstrual cycle; the sense of the body's aliveness to subliminal senses that animals have not forgotten; "prophetic inner logic" experienced as "direct sensuous intuition of reality; God's other half, the qualities of the Creatrix."[23] Instead, we kicked Lilith out of the Garden of Eden.

The Surrealists

I identified with surrealist artists before I knew the direction my art would take: toward the recovery of women's energy in the cultural milieu. My sculpture of ecstatic women is part of the surrealist heritage, since my method of working is to ask the unformed clay to reveal the forgotten nature of women in full sexually exotic manifestations. Essentially, I am following the surrealist mandate to explore in the unknown for pertinent truths: the artist's energy engaged to reveal unknown energies.

Surrealism was another form through which humanity sought to right itself from the distortions inherent in trivializing and/ or ignoring one-half of humanity. In desiring to work in states of heightened awareness beyond ordinary reality, creating art from inner sources the surrealists reached back (probably without knowing the source) to the ways of their ancestors, the Goddess worshippers. They approached their work by attending to the imagination in order to experience a state of unknowing, which they found charged with knowledge.

Andre Breton, who invented the idea of surrealism, "practiced the art of visualizing sensations." For surrealists, women were necessary to humanize men, and called upon as the muse to excite the creative process. Breton is said to have stated that "the woman is endowed with two special gifts: the inspiration of lucid frenzy and the power of parthenogenesis or 'unaided conception.'" [24] He was speaking as an artist himself, but not of the woman as an artist. He saw women as the core of nature, having the forbidden mysteries needed by the artist to inspire creation. Breton believed "erotic love was the way man's creative powers could be brought once again into close contact with the transforming energies that were the basis of the universe, and love was the means by which man moved into the circle of woman's magic powers." [25] Another example is Melusine, a female water spirit of French folklore, who had been transformed into a serpent and remained hidden. She concentrates telluric energy (low-level frequency near the surface of the earth) in her being and holds the key to mysteries not available to men, but which are needed in the creative process. Melusine, then, identifies women with the core of nature. The French novelist and playwright, Honoré de Balzac (1845), believed his "healing came from direct contact with healing Powers of Mother Earth...the only idea which remained was terra mater. I felt her [Mother Earth] plainly caressing and pitying and warming her wounded child." [26]

One woman surrealist artist, Whitney Chadwick, "in recognizing her intuitive connection with the magic realm of experience that governed creation, [saw that] surrealism offered the woman artist a self-image that united her role as woman and creator in a way that neither the concept of the femme-enfant nor that of the erotic muse could.[27] Another woman surrealist, Méret Oppenheim, revealed through her work her belief that nature is the dwelling place of the female creative spirit....she could imagine that the first state was matriarchal... [and that] Eve [had] been condemned and the snake with her...by men."[28] The surrealist path to art was different for men and women. Women had to find the feminine gnosis for themselves.

The surrealists were finding their way back to the earliest graphic expressions when painting was magic, a key to the invisible world and the magic of animals attempting to re-establish connections to their primordial nature.

During the ages since the Goddess was forced to retreat, there have been continual eruptions of memory of her and her way of knowing. The science of electromagnetism is not refutable. Access to invisible realities has now been proven. It can no longer be denied that the human's "charge" is increased by orgasm, nor that this increased charge is available to increased connection to the electromagnetism that surrounds us all, availing us of information in the unseen realm.

In the next chapter I offer means by which we can once again engage in the miracles apprehensible in the deepest bliss of sexual awakening.

ॐॐॐ

Orgasm creates the highest rate of electromagnetic charge available to the human body by which we know ourselves as most fully alive.

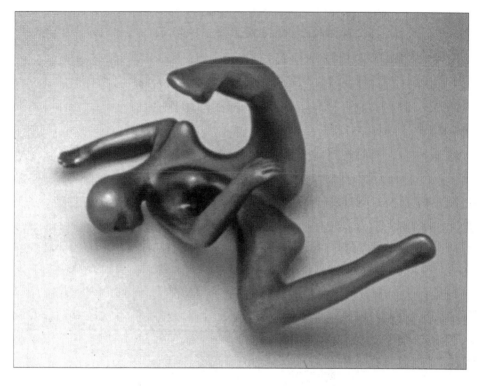

SHAYLA SAYS:

In some Native American tribes there were phoenix-fire people (an older man for the young girl and an older women for the young man) to show adolescents how to proceed so that both achieved full pleasure and explosive release of orgasm in their sexual encounters.

CHAPTER XII

TECHNIQUES FOR ACHIEVING HIGH-LEVEL ORGASMS

It is time for me to share some of what I have discovered that allowed me to move along to reclaiming sexuality as sacred, with powerful orgasms that opened me to a higher awareness.

I believe a spiritual practice is necessary to allow a transition from the mundane reality of job, family, and survival to a larger reality beyond the physical and visible world. This larger world is where our souls are at home and at peace, where we gain understanding and awareness of life with a bigger mission in life than what is apparent when we limit our focus to the next step, the next task, or the next computer keyboard in maintaining our presence in the visible world around us.

Spiritual awareness opens us to life as participants in a holy experiment manifest in all that is seen, engaged with all that is unseen. We encounter ourselves as having a larger purpose than acquiring wealth and status during the time we are alive. Our spiritual selves align with the Creator of all things to celebrate life and all that is possible.

Our ancestors knew this, but we have been robbed of our memories. If you are interested in finding a way of living within a surrounding of abundant JOY, you will need to make a commitment to finding a way to erase the impediments that have ensnared you. Awareness and practice of the sacredness and power of sexuality can help. The greatest benefit from sexuality will be available as you relinquish the restraints imposed by the ancient declaration of sexuality as evil. To do that, it is likely that you will require help: psychotherapist, sexual therapist, and/or a spiritual teacher. I suggest that you accept that the unravelling of the imprint of many centuries of repression is going to take sustained attention, commitment, and practice.

To encourage you and set you in a possibly new direction to find the truth of who you are and the means by which you might live in love and abundance (not necessarily riches), I will share with you some of my process with my teacher.

Seeking awareness of myself, I participated for ten years in the activities of the Deertribe, the name given by my teacher to the group studying ancient Native American transformational practices. During three of those years, I was an apprentice to the medicine man, knowing that there was a me that I did not know, a higher consciousness in me that was aware of a larger slice of the universe and my ability to participate in it. I committed myself to these experiences immediately after my marriage ended and I was free to pursue the threads of my own reality without the constant need to explain and justify myself.

Inherent in the program was preparation to become available for the high-level orgasm that would open my senses to awareness of a bigger reality. High-level orgasm occurs when participants come to the experience as their higher selves, the human they are meant to be, unburdened by distortions of trying to fit in and belong, which are manifest when we do not know or trust who we are. To this end, I participated in purification lodges, which occurred about once a month in the Deertribe. The low willow hut of the purification lodge and the steam from water poured on red-hot rocks offered an intimate and powerful contact with the Great Spirit. From my prayers and the responses I sensed in the vapors, I felt opened to my own reality as a physical manifestation of what the Great Spirit offered of Itself in me. Little by little I felt myself grow into what felt like an authentic being, no longer needing to try to be any way but the way I was. I began to know that I was being guided into an authentic practice of human being.

I took at least one vision-quest journey a year (often three or four), making deeper and deeper connections with the Great Spirit and experiencing an unwinding of the realities of life that I had twisted around myself as an encasement, restricting my awareness and my motion as I tried to be an acceptable human being, unaware that my birth and natural growth had naturally made me acceptable. For the vision-quest, I was alone in a remote place (in the Santa Inez Valley, in Joshua Tree, in Tujunga, in the high Sierras, near Santa Margarita, in Arizona and in Mexico). I mentioned in Chapter II that my ancestors responded to the seven shakes of the rattle, coming in turn from all eight directions of the universe to teach me. After once experiencing the presence of the ancestors and the opening of the universe to my awareness, these prayers became fervent, filled with the knowledge that they would be answered by informed energy all around me. I came to know the answers to my questions and the sense of my own life missions. I deposited the messages in my notebook, clearing each from my mind to make room for the next one to enter my awareness. Days and nights of the quests were spent asking for knowledge and recording these incoming messages. The prescribed vision-quests were in graduated intensity and longer duration, requiring deeper questions and allowing wider awakening.

My first vision-quest was over one night alone in the wilderness at Joshua Tree National Park, California. The next was in a chamber

6 feet by 4 feet by 4 feet. I dug my hole near enough to the main altar where the leader would be spending the night so that she could secure the plywood covering of my burial site at sundown. Burial ceremonies made death my ally, spurring me on to accomplish the mandates of this life without wasting valuable moments of my time on Earth. I learned that death became an ally when I accepted the reality that my life will be finite, making every moment valuable in terms of what I am able to discover in it about who I am and how I am meant to interact with life. In creating my own death and accepting it, I waste no more energy resisting the reality of death and make use of every available moment to actualize my own reality—no more sit-coms and other wasted entertainment time.

Then I stayed two nights in the wilderness, and later, two nights in the grave, three nights in the wilderness, and three nights in a cave. I continued the progress to the core of myself, performing all aspects of the ceremonies: casting a circle of rocks each representing a compass direction, sealing the circle with tobacco, cornmeal, cayenne, and garlic salt to welcome the ancestors and keep out negative energy, constructing an altar, smoking my pipe with prayers for a useful ceremony, dancing around the altar with prayers for self-recognition, rattling with seven shakes of my gourd to call the ancestors in from each compass direction to bring their knowledge of who I am. The lack of food and greatly restricted water resulted in an altered state, allowing me to learn what I needed to know about myself, my relationship to life and everything in it, and what I needed to do. The walls of the reality I had accepted since childhood vanished and insight arrived. I began to know myself as multi-layered and felt comfortable in the unseen world that has always been my home.

For my last supervised vision-quest, I was escorted on a long hike into Oak Mountain north of Porter Ranch at the northern edge of the San Fernando Valley. A longtime purification lodge participant who had roamed the mountain all his life took me to a ridge that jutted out over what is now Stevenson Ranch. The sage grew so densely along the ridge of the top that I had to follow close behind his powerful frame while he spread the plants for us to pass. Finally, we came to a 12-foot boulder with a cave that broke through the center so that I had a view of the east and the west, and a passageway from one side to the other. It was a very powerful spot from which to ask for a vision. During that vision quest, which lasted six days and nights, the ancestors instructed me to travel in search of the Goddess tradition foundations on which the cultures of England, Malta, and Greece are built so that I could experience the roots of the Goddess traditions. At the end of the six days and nights my guide came back for me, bringing on his back enough water to quench my thirst and shower. After that, my vision quests became journeys for discovery along the path I had entered: I was called to Agua Azul in Mexico, to Palenque, to Chechen Itza, to Tulum, to Isla Mujeres, to Peru, to Bolivia, to Greece, to Malta, to Avebury (a stone circle in England), and to Bali. In each location, I discovered another level of the buried feminine and my own truth as a woman.

I have shared these experiences as a way of saying that the shift I had to make was extreme and required extreme means. Each reader is in his/her own life situation and will require personalized means. I encourage you to find your way to deepen your experience of the full possibility of your life. You will find your path to yourself when the mandate is clear and the need imperative.

My Native American teacher, Harley SwiftDeer Reagan, instructed in Quodoushka—sexual rites of passage drawn from spiritual practices of the Olmec, Mayan and Toltec cultures, and secret societies within the Cherokee Nation. These were designed to assist the apprentices in their experience of themselves as balanced in all aspects of their beings: giving with their emotions; holding with their physical bodies; receiving with their minds; determining with their spirits; and catalyzing with their sexuality. Each, he warned, must be "standing in his/her own circle of self, not a victim or at the effect of another person, place, or thing." He called the powerful sexuality in love relationships between actualized people that can be created for growing and learning, "fire-medicine."

I will share here some of the principles I learned through SwiftDeer's teachings, which I believe to be universal and open to adaptation by anyone motivated to expand their sexual awareness. You might find them useful until you find your teacher and your own path to full awakening.

Of continual concern in SwiftDeer's teaching was the enactment of the two sacred laws in all interactions, particularly shared sexual intimacy:

1. Everything is born of woman
2. Nothing be done to harm the child or the child within

Apprentices were often reminded to honor the one with whom we were connecting. We were taught that sexual magic could be experienced in all five aspects of our beings (emotions, mind, body, sexuality, and soul):

Emotions are charged with the chemistry and energy of which we are made when excited by people, places, events, and ideas. Our emotions show us what is true. Paying attention to the value of our emotions frees us from false doctrines, myths, and dogmas so that we can be truly present with freedom and in harmony with everything that is.

Our mind reads and interprets the signs of reality offered by everything around us, giving us access to what we must know to make appropriate choices, decisions, and actions. Thus, our mind can tell us where we are in our journey of life so that we can be in balance, acting as the best of what we are. Our minds are not meant as tools to compete and make ourselves appear better than all our brothers and sisters.

Our body, where spirit resides, offers gifts of powerful sensations. Our body responds to incoming sensations as comfort or discomfort, stimulation or repulsion, giving us awareness of the nature of our place in our surroundings. We must become aware of spirit's presence so that our sexual unions can be spiritual, allowing us to see beyond the reality we believe we live in.

Our sexual systems give spirit the mechanisms within our body to raise our energy to its highest potential of pleasure and access to knowledge on a plane closer to the Great Spirit.

Our soul allows us to experience the highest state of pleasure, in which we have total union with everything that is. It is the house of spirit in our being that recognizes that we are part of the creative energy of the Creator (The Great Spirit for Native Americans, and the Goddess for earlier ancestors) who brought us into substance as humans so that It might see Itself. The soul is the interpreter of moments, events, and feelings that are not trapped in the mundane problems of existence, such as relishing the vibrant glow of glistening clean hair as a gift instead of a chore.

The Teacher

Again, you will find your own way to make a transition from the ordinary reality in which you may now live into one that feels like a continuous celebration of life.

I have relied on the instruction of my teacher, Harley SwiftDeer, and I offer some of his gifts here as illustrations of what steps might be taken to heal this ongoing tragedy: the loss of sexual function that has afflicted humankind for 5,000 years. His teaching about orgasm awakened me to a powerful experience of my own sexuality as, during the same time, I gained more recognition of my ancestors, the Goddess worshippers, who had engaged in worship of their Goddess by raising their energy to its highest vibration in sacred sexual ceremonies.

SwiftDeer's grandmother was Cherokee, and his Grandfather was Irish. When he returned from Vietnam, where he had served as a Marine, he worked with a Navaho medicine man who he said was Don Genero in the popular Carlos Castaneda tales. Fundamental to sharing the traditional healing techniques he had learned from that medicine man and other elders, for the purpose of eventually healing the strife in the dominant white culture, Harley believed the secrets he taught us had allowed Native Americans to live as creations of the Great Spirit, in constant contact with that consciousness that had created everything. Sexual practices were prominent in his teaching because he believed that sexual ignorance deprived everyone of the energy needed to achieve successful enactment of the blessing of life. Orgasm, he believed, is a fast track to living as our "higher self," the truth of who we are born to be as awake and walking spiritual beings.

In our weekly classes, SwiftDeer gave us techniques for healing ourselves from impediments to knowing our higher selves, so that beyond coming together for healing sexual experiences, we would come together as our higher selves to explore sexual magic mirroring and reflecting for one another, creating together a pure song of harmony with all that exists. He told us, "The mother made medicine and the medicine was love."

The Fundamentals

There are three main aspects of SwiftDeer's teaching that have allowed me to move forward in healing and reclaim my sexuality as a spiritual function of life, more fully manifesting the reality of who I am.

The first is the ways energy is accumulated and moves through our bodies, and how that energy may be blocked by the ways our past experiences impact our minds, our bodies, our emotions, our sexuality, and our connection to spirit. Purification lodges, vision quests and prayer dances were the continuous processes by which I made discoveries of how I was blocked and how I might step forward. Without understanding how we are personally blocked, we cannot hope to experience the healing and celebration of our sexuality, or the power our sexual energy offers us to live at our highest potential. Cleared of the resistance and interference of old stories we tell ourselves, which diminish our sense of who we are and what we are capable of, we are freed to experience our sexuality, employing all our gifts. You might find that the higher level of sexual experience itself turns the tide to self-discovery. It can work both ways. Our sexual experience has the ability to raise our energy to even higher frequencies where we can participate in the larger reality of our spiritual selves.

The second major teaching that was out of the ordinary is the various means of perceiving energy beyond eyes, ears, taste, smell, and touch that give us information beyond the physical world with which we are familiar. Science has given us a lot of information that confirms what our ancestors knew: that reality extends beyond what we can interpret with our dominant senses.

For instance, SwiftDeer taught about the **Ten Eyes**—these extend our vision into psychic receivers in order to perceive psychic-kinetic energy and allow us to see through our inner vision. We learned to trust what we see that we cannot see with our physical eyes, with an awareness of information coming from all around us. Looking into the distance, I formulate my response to a question, gathering what I do not yet know with my mind, but trust I have access to inside of myself. **The Five Ears**—these extend our hearing and allow us to hear through our inner hearing. In the lodge, I trust what I heard that had not been spoken. Listening with full attention, I began to know what the other could not put into words. The wind and breaking waves began to inform me of a broader reality.

The third category of teachings from SwiftDeer's accumulation of knowledge is some of the techniques he gave us to maximize the possibility of raising sexual energy to its highest potential. These involved attentive, varied, and sensitive stroking and touching, always maximizing the connection without any time restraint. Sexual magic works best when it is an authentic expression of love between people who care about each other (or for you when you are truly caring about and for yourself). Of central concern is the freedom with which our energy moves throughout the body to produce the highest-level orgasm, the manifestation of our energy at its highest level. There is much that a higher level of your own sexuality can teach you.

The subject of this book is the possibility of increasing our vibratory rate through attention to and participation in orgasmic experiences so that we might be more aware of what is hidden in the higher rate of vibration in the world that is hidden from view. In the pursuit of that awareness, I have a few suggestions that follow.

Masturbation as a Tool for Self-Awareness

It is the right of every human to experience the gift of sexual pleasure, which allows us to celebrate life at the highest level. If we are now awakening to the possibility that something might have been missing in our sexual experience, what can we do? To whom do we turn? I suggest that the first step is to break down the barriers to masturbation that have been erected in our culture against our natural tendency to arouse ourselves to heightened awareness and pleasure.

There is much that a higher level of your own sexuality can teach you. Exploring our own sexuality is a way of extending into knowledge of ourselves. How much access into the core of our being can we find? The words "orgasm" and "masturbation" have become bad words for sacred pleasures and means of locating the truth of our own energy. Becoming experts on our own sexual needs and methods for achieving high-level orgasms frees us from wanting what another may be unable to provide, and/or accepting relationships that are otherwise inappropriate to gain sexual satisfaction. Masturbation is one of the gifts of freedom my teacher gave me.

A woman who has healed herself by learning her own sexual nature through masturbation comes to her experience with a partner as a whole person and a full participant in the sexual dynamic. Masturbation is a tool of self-awareness and actualization in the hands of every woman. She must move past the prohibition and the inhibition to claim this magical tool for opening to herself, and bring about her own orgasm, her own highly vibrating energy, and her own healing.

Touch produces sensation. I focus my attention on the sensation and let the sensation guide my attention. Touching and stroking my breasts, my belly, my armpits, my neck, the inside of my leg, feeling the sensation of the touch or the stroke, and holding my attention on the sensation as my touch travels across the surface of my body, not trying to feel anything, not directing the movement of my hand, simply feeling the feeling and following the sensation to its next excitation.

The sensation becomes more and more intense as my hand travels and my attention holds. When that hand finally reaches the most highly erogenous zone — the genital area and, finally, the clitoris — the sensation builds more and more intensity. I am not asking the sensation to go anywhere in particular; I am following with my attention to the place the sensation leads my hand.

SwiftDeer taught that the physical body is one of the ways the Great Spirit/Goddess manifests itself; the physical body is, therefore, a form of energy, of light, of consciousness. This is what high-level orgasm brings to our awareness. He told us that we are the Great Spirit/Goddess energy slowed down until it can be seen and see Itself and as we find ways to raise the vibration of our energy we become more like the energy that created us.

Raising Orgasm to Its Highest Vibration

I am including these actual exercises that I learned in Swift-Deer's Quodoushka workshop in the hope that your exploration of techniques for raising sexual energy will allow you to achieve amazing results and encourage you to pursue active sexual training in order to move beyond what might have become perfunctory sexual performance.

My apprehension about sharing details of my sexual history with the other apprentices diminished over the ten years that I worked with Harley and attended Quodoushka workshops. As I grew in awareness and experienced higher and higher-level orgasms, I anticipated the weekends as very special treats of more and more profound pleasure and insight. The workshops started Friday evenings and ended Sunday night. We practiced individually, with a partner, and as a group.

Individually, we learned that finding access to our own orgasm with breaths and the touch of masturbation puts us in command of our sexual experience, allowing us to reach the highest possible vibration of our own molecules, whether or not we are with a partner, and whatever the partner's knowledge and ability. I grew out of wanting and into giving to myself. Satisfying my own sexual needs takes the burden off relationship to provide and frees intimate moments with another to grow into their unique potential.

All sexual encounters, even those with myself, are ceremonies to connect with the Great Spirit/Goddess for gaining knowledge because sexuality is about raising our energy to its highest level of vibration, *parallel to the higher vibration of the invisible world.* It begins with creating a ceremonial setting to enhance the experience and calling forth its power. The moment must be planned and anticipated. Unlimited time and privacy are essentials. Light candles to guide mysterious forces; burn incense to awaken the senses; set out flowers, beautiful fabrics, and pillows; put on music to enhance the mood. Set the intention that a sacred moment is about to be created, fashioning a mood in the place and the participant(s) *that transcends everyday reality.* My favorite partner and I liked to dance as an introduction to sharing sexual energy. Trust in the pattern of giving and receiving, receiving and giving is required. Slow deep breathing and sometimes synchronized breathing is important. Seek to connect each other's heart chakras, then first chakras (at the root of the spine). Be willing to follow the impulse of the moment, with deep and caring attention to the other and to the self, remaining vigilant of the steadily mounting energy, not proceeding ahead of it.

Being available to the pleasure that is possible in any and all parts of the body, and being willing to give pleasure propelled by awareness that pleasure is being received, allows the process of sharing intimacy to grow into higher and higher vibrations of pleasure, each level leading to the next with no restraint, propelled by full engagement in the process, stimulated by what is being given and what is received, following an unseen path of pleasure to its next level in a spiral into the unknown.

Body Imprints Exercise for Raising Sexual Energy

The physical body is one of the manifestations of the Great Spirit/Goddess. It is, therefore, a form of energy, of light, of consciousness. In Swiftdeer's teachings, we are the Great Spirit/Goddess energy slowed down until it can be seen and see Itself. These physical bodies store our memories from all time, including unpleasant ones that may block our access to pleasure. The Body Imprints exercise allows the body to awaken to its full potential for sexual expression, in part because barriers are identified and illuminated by the focus of the subject and the healer's attention. This exercise is best done with a partner of your sexual preference.

This technique is performed by one partner on the other. Sometimes we have been able to do body imprints on both of us as part of the shared intimacy, but more often the energy would rise in both of us and the second would receive the blessing at a later date.

After making a strong connection by gazing into each other's eyes, my partner lies face down. In the first sequence, I am the gentle, caring, accepting healer. My partner, breathing deeply to become thoroughly relaxed, breathes opening into his mind to become totally available to what the healing session I am about to give him releases to his awareness. In this pattern, I use my hands to stimulate his awareness passing over his body slowly with each technique, from his left foot, up the left side, out and back along the left arm, around the head, out and back along the right arm, down the right side and across to the left foot to begin again. I do the entire circuit three times for each kind of movement. He brings his awareness to each touch.

In the first movement, **I hold my hands about three inches from his body and move them together** up the left side and down the right. Throughout the healing practice I remain vigilant for peculiarities in my partner's body, speaking to the areas that feel particularly hot or cold, open or closed. My attention is entirely on his response as my hands and attention move over him.

Next, **touching gently but firmly with my whole hand, I sweep my hands, hand-over-hand,** along the entire path of the prescribed pattern.

Then, with my **hands next to each other and fingers curved around limbs, I move my hands in opposite directions in a gentle wringing motion** along the path of the prescribed pattern, always keeping my attention on the response of his body along the whole path. I sustain the motion on any area that requires more attention.

Next, I **gently hold a section of skin between my thumbs and index fingers in tender pinches, pulling up slightly, moving along the path, hand over hand, gently squeezing out resistance and allowing something new to enter.**

Lastly, I **stoke him gently with my fingertips.** Occasionally I surprise him with a feather sequence.

The pattern and the techniques are performed on the front as well. Brushing genitals feels wonderful but dwelling there short-circuits the process. Keep going so the energy has a chance to rise to its highest level. We try to repeat the healing on the other, but often that must wait until we find the time for this journey again.

You can see why the development of higher vibration takes time. Sexuality as a sacrament requires an agreement that this is an important part of life and of your commitment to each other so that plenty of time can be allotted.

Body Awakening and Grounding for Raising Sexual Energy

The energy rises very fast with this version of body imprints: First, my partner is on his back, and **I trace my fingertips up from the left foot, this time encircling the genitals and the head, down the right side, across to the left foot** repeating three times.

Second, my partner puts his **feet together, and I begin by blowing gently into the space his arches create, following the same pattern, but this time blowing directly on to the head of the penis. When it is my turn, he blows directly onto my clitoris.** A feather is wonderful here as well. We try to move right along to the other's turn, but, again, often that one must wait—but we never forget who is going first next time.

Practicing these techniques until they felt natural, my partner and I achieved higher and higher-level orgasms, inexplicable pleasure, flowing visions, and a sense of participating in the truth of life.

There is no need to hurry. The main event is the whole process. The strokes and breaths of foreplay raise the wave length and frequency of the vibration. Intent and focus maximize the bond of intimacy. There must be complete openness to and acceptance of the other. Where is the energy in the self, between the two and in the other? The vibrations become more and more intense and frequent. The vibration travels up the chakras from the first, second, and third to the heart, throat, third eye and crown, and out to its return to the Great Spirit.

For humans, sexual pleasure is of much longer duration and much greater intensity than other animals, with the human female capable of repeated orgasm—primarily longer-lasting, pleasurable associations that encourage cooperation between the sexes. Being awake, aware, and alert to this process makes it a spiritual act, a sacred enactment of the original creation.

Orgasm

Orgasm is one of the most pleasurable states we can experience. It alters our perception of reality, opens our hearts, allows love to flow unconditionally, and opens the direct link to our higher self and the Great Spirit—the Everything (which Goddess worshippers called the Divine or the Great Creatrix). For partners, two life forces become one, or one becomes more. SwiftDeer taught that it was "the most spiritual and sacred process available to human beings."

Although orgasm had played an important role in my life before I found the Deertribe, my experience with Quodoushka showed me an orgasm I had not known as a means of blasting into another world with two, three, four, and sometimes five climaxes and often ejaculations (which I had not known were possible for women). Each orgasm had its unique energy and brought its own revelations.

The deeper the participants relinquish their own bodies to the opening between them, and the sensations of the stimulations, the more intense orgasms become, and the more doors open to the unseen mysteries of life. No trying is required. Letting go and relishing the journey accomplishes the end of gaining maximum pleasure and knowledge. Being in the pleasure of each moment allows that moment to develop into all that it can be. Accepting the pleasure of each moment allows the pleasure of the next to be added. Pleasure builds on pleasure in a journey to the highest peak with full knowing of what is being achieved and the full ability to receive the maximum gift and give it back to the giver with the increased energy of the accumulated gifts. This process is not to be rushed but savored in order that all the flavors may be extracted. In the savoring of each level of pleasure comes the recognition of the mysteries that are hidden from those who forget to allow themselves to be thoroughly aroused. Knowing that there is no established end to the journey you are taking, relishing each new discovery, relaxing into the next level allows each event to become an unfolding into the deepest mysteries of life.

Engaging in the possibility of spiritual growth and awakening as the purpose and potential of the sexual encounter goes far beyond the quickie you might want in the morning before work or the tired enactment just before sleep. This book is an entreaty to remember and to practice sexuality as the sacrament it is meant to be. Revealing the discoveries of each to the other increases the bond and the growth of each, giving purpose to the unions life provides us. Laugh, play, and cry together. Find the reasons you have found each other. Let yourself be in the bliss of the other. Let yourselves merge into one being as a representative of all that is sacred. Search every inch of each other's body for all available pleasure of touch, stroke, kiss, and tongue. Employ your whole body as giving and receiving tools: stroke with fingers and toes; suck on fingers and toes; find the erogenous sites under the arms and at the top of the thighs, in the arch of the foot. It is an adventure each time into places you have not been, awakening new understandings.

Touching is a way of stimulating each other to keep frequencies high, shattering the barriers to openness. Touching breasts stimulates the heart chakra, a sometimes-forgotten function of these sustainers of life. All the erogenous zones are there to be explored and employed on the journey to full opening between lovers. Try the ears, the nose, the belly, the buttocks, the fingertips, the elbows, the shoulder blades. It is an infinite and powerful journey to the clitoris and the head of the penis to be actualized and enjoyed along the whole path.

Look deeply into each other's eyes for the truth you will find there. Give yourself totally without restraint or regret. Receive without apology or resistance, giving yourself totally to the awakening that reaches your center. Lovemaking is an adventure into the unknown of pleasure. Each event presents its own wonder of discovery awarded to the practiced explorer surrendering to the process, and the wonder of traveling into the unknown. Continue these practices as you grow together to the perfection you are meant to be.

In the appendix to this chapter I offer further concepts by which SwiftDeer directed his apprentices to experience unseen realities that our ancestors knew were significant contributors to the experience of living.

For additional help with the developing the process of removing restraints to the freedom of energy to move within, I recommend the Deertribe website: www.dtmms.org (Deertribe Metis Medicine Society). There you will find a schedule of their teaching program and events and may wish to make a commitment to gaining recognition of your encumbrances and engaging in transformational healing ceremonies in a journey to becoming aware of your inner self. SwiftDeer is no longer on the planet, but his people are carrying on. The Deertribe headquarters are in Scottsdale, Arizona now: P.O. Box 12397; 48267; (480) 443-3851.

Intimacy Reveals the Truth of Who We Are

Humans free of their anxiety about who they are and the need for someone outside of themselves to identify their value are free to expose themselves to the fully bonded connection of intimacy, the kind of joining in which the soul of each is exposed to the other.

I believe that the purpose of relationship and true intimacy is to share what we are and discover what the union of knowledge from the inner depth of each is meant to birth as higher and higher recognition of life's potential. We must be willing to truly open to ourselves and the other to have access to all that is available in our deepest nature: wisdom. This is why we must allow plenty of time for intimacy to evolve to its most open state. Trusting pleasure allows the opening to knowledge at the highest frequencies of life. Keeping our awareness and focus on the place and the sensation of excitation allows the energy to build there.

I encourage you to practice this high purpose of sexuality so that you gain higher vibratory energy for the way you see and go about living. Sexuality that wants to replicate pornography as a violent exchange between people who care nothing for each other and are indifferent to the possibility of energy rising between them is not what the Great Spirit and/or the Supreme Creatrix had in mind when the gift of sexuality was given. Nor does "hooking up" with whomever you happen to be sitting near qualify as sacred sexuality. There must be agreement that something profound is taking place. There must be honoring and caring between the participants. There must be awareness that life itself is sacred, and that the union is about celebration of the life of each. Time and technique are required to stimulate the highest possible vibratory rate, achieving a rate closer to that of the Creatrix/Great Spirit. There must be a recognition that the explosion of orgasm is meant as a re-creation of the moment of the original creation of all things. These enactments must not be wasted on trivia and indifference.

Allowing sexuality to be an expression of love for yourself and the other transcends the limitations of hooking up as the destination, and pornography as the roadmap, and brings us into the realm of life as a celebration with sexuality the means.

Love and Sexuality

How does love come into the picture?

Love begins the cycle; sexuality becomes all that it can be as an expression of love. We find love when we care deeply for another; love is the feeling that invites intimacy. Intimacy breaks down the walls. The electrical current of attraction moves freely. Trust builds; maps for stimulation are exchanged; energy builds; we learn from each other what the deepest hidden places of excitation have to offer as energy builders; we find the pathway to our own inner light, and we find the inner light of the other as well.

This flood of light illuminates who we are as humans. In this exploration of what was lost when the Goddess was driven away, we are defining the difference between love and sexuality. We must be sure that we know what love is (including love for ourselves) before we can fully experience what sexuality is: the energy of the divine (Goddess/Great Spirit) released by expressions of love, finding our way to ourselves and to each other through opening to intimacy. Love is the divine alive in us giving our sexuality permission to explode into full realization of who we are as divine, and fully recognizing the divine in the other. Sacred sexuality, then, is a marriage of the divine in the partners.

Our sexuality is the generator of action, continually creating the spark of life (the orgasm of being). Healing of our cultural difficulties will be possible when sexuality is given a prominent position in the equation of human behavior, where it will generate humans at their highest creative potential, as dictated by the plan for life. The orgasm of being is the electrical firing of each electron in the atom (the spark of life).

This power cannot be ignored or considered irrelevant. This is who we are. We must ask and seek answers to the main issue of sexuality, currently locked mainly in the background: What is the power of our sexual energy and what are we supposed to do with it? This question should be coming up first, not last, so that we bring the best of what we are to the exploration of each event, experience, and situation.

Those questions we now consider to be the first—those of war and wealth—would be of little importance if we learned to satisfy ourselves with the gifts given to life as blessings. Experiencing our own balance, harmony, beauty, humor, and health in the sparkling of our full orgasm leaves us satisfied, not wanting more. We have the chance to experience all the blessings and gifts that were given with our own life. Sexual energy gives us access to the fullness of who we are, and we can learn again to access that power. High levels of intelligence, intention, and ability to act do not bring perfection in life if sexuality is not integrated and honored. Accepting that letting go to the present moment, appreciating what is there and what we must do, is in the electronic firing of each electron of our own atoms: THIS IS THE ORGASM OF BEING.

As we remember to give more time, attention and importance to our sexual events, we will evolve once again into the humans that were intended when we were given this sacred capacity to be orgasmic, a gift unique to humans.

Making Sure Your Sexual Event Causes an Explosion

An orgasm capable of blasting through our inner barriers to make connection with the divine requires freedom and drive to maximize the sexual experience. This will not necessarily take place after sunset in the total darkness of the bedroom after the children are asleep, providing no one has a headache.

Instead, moving out of denial, forgetfulness, and repression, lovers anticipate experiencing the power of their own orgasm. The male will cherish the female. She will allow herself to feel cherished and return the gift. They will expose sacredness of their beings to the light of life.

First loving the reality of who we actually are—dancing the

dance that is in us—and bringing that true thing to be revealed to the other, provides a portal to the source of our own human vibration, the depth of our own being that has the capacity to connect to that same place in the other who is unafraid, unrestricted, and willingly revealing his/her own inner source. My authentic dance shows my lover how to make love to me: it must come from my love of myself. The female figures you see in these pages, bronze ecstatic female figures I have created, have broken free of the constraints of history and expectation. They vibrate with what is possible. They speak the inner truth exploded by the intense spark of life ignited by orgasm.

I must not distort my own dance with wanting love or sexual advances. I must be giving of myself from my source for the love of giving. And I must receive the gifts back with open acceptance of their blessings. If the receiver cannot receive, the gift cannot be given; if there is no gift given, the receiver cannot receive. The plant world shows us giving until our appetites are satisfied (and beyond), not only until they are ready to stop giving. Sexuality is a shared intimacy that shows each more of who they are as it magnifies and expands the energies of the union.

If, when the music starts you know only to mimic what others are doing in their dance; if you do not trust and allow the mechanism that connects your vibration to the sound of the music, your dance will not be truthful. Show the truth of who you are; make the connection with the other at the source. The purpose of sexuality is to raise both to a higher level and clearer understanding of who they are.

Our life purpose is to find our own dancer — the one who responds to all the musical qualities of life from our own core, the source of our own vibration. Sexuality is the gift provided to allow this full celebration to occur continuously throughout our lives.

GAIA SAYS:

The intimacy is human to human recognition of aliveness.

CHAPTER XIII

PARENTING OUR CHILDREN TOWARD FULLY SEXUAL LIVES

Nowhere in our culture is our dysfunction more pronounced and apparent than when bringing up the subject of children and sexuality. The legacy of shame and denial we have inherited from the 5,000 years of systemic sexual repression, generation after generation, perpetuates a profoundly unhealthy effect on our own legacy. This heritage—religious and cultural taboos, and our own inadequate sexual experiences—has made it nearly impossible to prepare our children for healthy sexual lives. We are so afraid of our own pleasure, so immersed in our own sexual dysfunction, that we muddy the waters for our children, and they do the same for theirs.

It is not a stretch to say that the vast majority of parents in our culture rarely, if ever, speak frankly to their children about sex. My parents' failure to prepare me created a fear of the unknown, and a fixation on solving the mystery. In high school, most of my relationships with boys were carried out in my mind. I had several major crushes that never developed even into conversations, let alone holding hands or kissing (except for the first time in 9th grade when kissing produced wetness in my panties). Major high school political successes and plenty of popularity among the girls did not make up for my fear and discomfort with boys (this may be common for girls from all-girl families) and led to an eruption of repressed sexual energy in college. This happened in October of my freshman year in the back seat of a Pontiac on the way to the Berkeley homecoming football game, with my sister and future brother-in-law in the front-seat. All kissing and petting, it was sufficiently sexual to signify a permanent relationship in the cultural doctrine I had accepted: these were things you did only with someone you would marry. A handy blanket was provided. I never bothered to find out much about him in the two years we dated (that became another explosion after three children and twenty years of marriage). In the sudden experience of sexual pleasures during that long drive, I lost my momentum into seeing a larger picture of who I was becoming. For me the pendulum swung from serious attention to the business of making my way in the culture I was in (which had led to a fabulous honor on graduation from high school) to the isolation of falling in love with sexuality (I called it "being engaged"), which took all my attention.

Instead, my process of becoming ended with marriage, and was not resumed until re-entry into the university many years later. Lost were those early years of my personal growth. If sexuality had not been forbidden and frightening, but a more natural part of my overall development, there could have been balanced development in all aspect of my being (mental, physical, emotional, spiritual, and sexual). As it was, the build-up of energy that had found no expression in high school blasted me off my personal course of development when I was making decisions about my direction in life during college years. I fell into a yawning sexual gulf, putting me in the place where there was only one choice: marriage. It could also be that I was acting out Betty Friedan's myth of the *"feminine mystique"* that encouraged marriage as a way of diverting my course from full adult development and commitment to personal goals.

In addition to the minister who preached the evilness of sexuality and abstinence and told of the tale of the serpent's temptation and the apple that had required God to banish Adam and Eve from the Garden, sex education for me had been left to the physiology teacher, who taught that coupling was necessary to create a child and that men had the penis that, with my equipment, would make this possible, though there were no pictures, and I had never seen a penis. I did know how to plug in the light cord.

It is absurd and crippling that this important aspect of life, essential to our continued existence and for our experience of intimacy and pleasure in life, is mostly left to schools, and only those schools where ignorant, frightened parents have been unable to ban sexual education. Even so, such an education focuses on only the mechanical and biological processes of sex, with an emphasis on fear of sexually transmitted diseases and pregnancy, without ever talking about the beauty and celebration of life through sexuality. Our misgivings translate to negligence, forcing young people's encounters underground and outside the conversations that could help them be safe and satisfying.

When my own children were in junior and senior high school, sex education in the school was a scare tactic the parents conferred on the schools so parents would not have to say anything about syphilis, gonorrhea, or finally, AIDS. Certainly no one could utter the words "penis," "vagina," "orgasm," "masturbation," or "intercourse." By the time I became a university instructor, many restrictions had vanished, but so had intimacy. Students were "hooking-up," something like having a coffee with someone you have just met and may never see again: no caring, no intimacy, no magic, nothing sacred, and of little importance.

In contrast, many Native American communities at the time of European encroachment had Phoenix Fire People: a man for the girl, and a woman for the boy, to teach how to make love powerfully, teaching the techniques and activities that produced not only plea-surable satisfaction, but also high-level, high-frequency orgasms that awaken and celebrate spirit inside of them. Full enactment and enjoyment were not left to chance experience. The elders took responsibility for ensuring the success of the young people as they ventured into this human territory. The children grew into this natural activity with the guidance of their elders who gave importance and understanding to the changes that were occurring in the adolescent, and a pathway into the mysteries that were being glimpsed, calling the children into a special, previously unknown to them, part of what it meant to be alive. What are we going to do to bring sanity to our pubescent children and launch them into adulthood celebrating their sexuality? Our misgivings and denial of responsibility translate to negligence and cause confusion and inappropriate behavior.

Despite all of our current talk about family values and responsible parenting, we have a huge blind spot when it comes to enlightening our children about something so important to their future happiness. Our children will be supplied with hormones. The hormones are given to serve an important function in their lives: the pleasurable stimulation for bonding and sexuality that raises the activity of human molecules in excitation, increasing the likelihood of intercourse and reproduction, and providing a means to celebrate life and the Creator of life with our greatest pleasure. Children have a right to know and honor those functions. Isn't it time we truly become responsible parents and set them on the right path? Preparing them for the physical, emotional, mental, spiritual, and sexual differences that will begin to appear in their lives as they reach puberty is *our job* as parents.

Instead, children are left to gain what knowledge they can from friends, TV, movies, the Internet, and by trial and error. Without positive adult guidance, the information may be distorted and confusing, and in the case of pornography, misleading. Instead, we must find ways to bring our children into this awareness of sexuality as an important and satisfying aspect of what it means to be alive.

The first step to doing so must be to gain a more positive perspective on *our own sexuality*. We cannot teach what we don't ourselves know. We must reawaken to sexuality as a sacred event that magnifies the best in life, sharpens our minds, nourishes our bodies and emotions, and is our connection to the highest energy. We must discover the high level of vibration possible in orgasm, and the techniques for achieving them. Then we can open that path to our children, protecting them from the danger of sexuality as a profane act of dominance, or indifference, with the insufficient intimacy that many of us have too often experienced.

Sexual Problems Attributable to Failed Sexual Education

Masters and Johnson, the team that pioneered research into the nature of human sexual response in the last half of the 20th century, discovered one possible outcome for women of the familial silence about sexuality: faked orgasms. Why do women fake orgasm? Are they afraid to admit that stimulation has been insufficient? Are they afraid to be fully present or fully open to receive pleasure? Are they unfamiliar with their own physical process by which orgasm is achieved? Do they fear that they are unable to have an orgasm? Do early feelings of guilt or fear associated with abuses interfere? For these women, there is little pleasure in sexuality, and no connection to a higher purpose and energy in life. Again and again the moment of greatest pleasure and celebration is missed. A tragedy like this could be avoided by parents who take responsibility for positive sexual education.

Sexual abuse is a terrible disruption in the lives of far too many women. The woman who has been abused may allow the trauma of the attack to cause her to shy away from her sexuality and fail to discover for herself the spark of pleasure of orgasm, which can ignite her ability to choose pleasure in her life and choose how the evolution of her being unfolds through her thoughts and actions.

The American author and feminist, Naomi Wolf, talked about "hooking-up" in her first book, *Beauty Myth*. About 2010, while I was teaching at California Lutheran University, I heard her lecture on the contents of her book in which she expressed sadness at the way "young people have been short changed: they are exhausted and stressed with no time for romance but still have the longing for connection and sex...For many the mystery has been stripped from sexuality [which is commodified] by pornography...in which women are not real women ... men do nothing to bring women to orgasm ... there is no intimacy or tenderness ... desensitizing sexuality so that men have trouble responding to real women."[1]

Young women learn to act like perfectly made-up dolls. Comparing herself to the mannequin beauty of the porn star, the young woman loses confidence in her own appearance and ability to attract a man. Images from porn take the place of what is happening in real-life sexual experience. Porn films rarely show a full body response in orgasm, and young people are unaware of the frequency of the high vibration at the peak of a sexual experience. There is no evidence of the kind of intimacy required to reach maximum pleasure, satisfaction, and opening to knowledge. Without other guidance, young people accept the farce of pornography as a legitimate guide to their sexual practices. Our children need a better guide.

In her book, *Sacred Pleasures*, Riane Eisler discussed some of the ways sexuality has been distorted. Parents may gradually learn to deny to themselves that there was anything wrong with what was done to them as children, and in turn do it to their own children.[2]

Particularly destructive is generationally repeated incest "which works to maintain male sexual control over women."[3] Eisler calls attention to "abusive child-rearing practices that teach submission to authority—selling young children to slavery and girls to prostitution."[4]

Teaching parental skills may be an important requirement to prevent children from learning to associate love with earning a reward and associating coercive touch with the necessity to obey. Eisler reminds her readers that Chinese mothers bound the feet of their own daughters, telling them that the restrictions, pain, and suffering were necessary if they were to find husbands. Alice Walker, in *Possessing the Secret of Joy*, revealed a similar situation in Africa where grandmothers perform clitorectomies on the pubescent girls. Eisler tells us that Homer, in the *Iliad*, portrays the young girl as "'no more than a piece of property, of female sexual slavery.'" And Hera is reported "to be afraid to disobey Zeus lest he beat her."[5]

Sharing the Gifts of Understanding with Our Children

We share our love of books, of surfing, of music, of language, of mechanics. Let's not leave out the fabulous part of our pleasure, our emotions, and our sensations. It is our responsibility as guides to our children to provide safe ways for them to try out what they are feeling and learning. A young woman must begin to know and offer her knowledge: "I like to be touched here, like this." The man also must know what he likes. Intimacy and sexual knowledge must be honored as legitimate goals for young people. If we leave this as a forbidden mystery, how will our children get past their fears and learn practices that will give them the most satisfaction and the highest level of vibration in their orgasms?

Masturbation is the safest form of learning our own part of the sexual experience. We come to know the fullness of our own sexuality beginning with self-pleasuring, a natural activity of small children, one that must be allowed so that sexual nature can mature. We must take care not to interfere with our children's private explorations. We may be more comfortable with this development if we encourage their privacy.

Finding sexual balance in the culture *must* include intentional attitude toward the development of our children's sexual practices. We must allow our child to be sexual with him or herself. Curtailment of masturbation interrupts the natural tendency to self-pleasure, self-knowledge, and self-awareness. Disallowing or condemning self-pleasuring interrupts the child's natural growth, placing a negative burden on sexuality. Suppression of sexual energy and the resultant craving for satisfaction may lead to hormonal explosion in adolescence in which sexual activity becomes wonton with inexperienced partners, resulting in the development of sexual practices that are profane in that they don't reflect the sacredness of the act. Young people who have become experts on their own sexual potentials are not driven by them.

The idea that a woman must be with a man in order to be sexual is a form of bondage and burdens the other with full responsibility for her whole sexual experience. For the women whose pleasure is her own responsibility, sexual encounters are a free flow of energy. She communicates to the giver where her most sensitive spots are. The giver is relieved of fumbling for the special places—and missing them.

The subject of sexuality should be treated as a life-enriching goal for children as they gain the hormones that stimulate attraction. In place of instilling fear, we should introduce sexuality as one of life's blessings that can be made more and more wonderful as skills are gained and intimacy developed. Modern methods of preventing pregnancy could be providing space for this conversation. Sexual exploration and development need have none of the risk it once had of juvenile parents.

Our children's growth and awareness must not be left to chance as it was to a group of eight-year-olds in a school near me. Confused, ill-informed children in 3rd grade damaged each other greatly when one girl was challenged to give a boy a blow-job, then ostracized because she did. What did these children know about what they were doing? Will the distortion of something so wonderful ever leave them? Where were the parents and the teachers as the guides and protectors of this sacred act? I am reminded of a box of matches left unattended found by an infant who had no idea of the terrible danger he was in.

By overcoming the embarrassment in and cultural impediments to talking about how important sexual experiences are to us, we could promote a positive attitude toward the beauty of sexuality and its function to bring us all to our highest level of energy and imagination. We must open the door so that the sexual act may become for our children the source of pleasure it is meant to be, not the tangle of hidden and inept experiments demanded by their hormones and the rigid silence of, or condemnation by, their elders.

Open dialogue with sexually-balanced adults can lead children to an understanding of the sacredness of sexuality and orgasm as elements of a sacrament for celebrating the divine in life. Profane sexuality that does not open the adolescent to a higher knowledge of self and of life can be avoided. The sexually active and aware adult must teach the techniques for achieving high-level orgasms that bring the greatest pleasure and illuminate recognition of inner divinity and the divine source of life: sexuality as sacred is a gift to be used for the full celebration of life. Young people must know—and do not automatically know—of the potential for orgasm to illuminate inner and outer divinity. Sexuality can be offered to the adolescent as a gift to be used for the full celebration of life with a partner who also understands this as the purpose of sexuality. Sexuality must be put on the main menu of what it means to grow into adulthood with the potential to grow into higher and higher levels of celebration and consciousness.

What we have left for the schools we must retrieve as a parental responsibility. Leaving to the schools to discuss with our children the array of possible sexual traumas is a parental method of curbing sexual activity through fear without ever talking about sexuality. Frightening young people and forcing their encounters underground and outside the conversations that could help them be safe and satisfying does not lead to their gaining skills for developing intimacy. If we are as a culture to claim ownership of sexuality as a blessing, we must find the way to make it so for our children by allowing them to experience their own sexual gifts. Finding sexual balance in the culture must include intentional attitude toward the development of our children's sexual practices allowing them to blossom into full sexual awakening, enjoying sexual gifts to fully celebrate life.

Talking to Children About Sexuality as a Celebration

What can we say to children about sexuality that would enhance their life? We might begin with this:

"The entire body is gifted as an instrument for giving and receiving stimulation that enhances the sexual experience by raising the vibratory rate. In love-making, even with self, there is an infinite cycle of giving and receiving in which the giver is able to give when the receiver is open to receiving; the gift is incorporated and returned to the giver by the receiver who has become the giver. An infinite cycle giving and receiving creates the mounting energy of excitation. The spiral of giving and receiving cocoons the lovers in a feather-home, a containing web of total connection infinitely continuous into infinite time and space. Each is lost to the other in shared sensations of pleasure and joy. The process allows each to go within to experience the divine. Our own divine core recognizes the sacred that is all around and has created us.

"There is no script for the developing process. The acts of giving and receiving script themselves. The touch, the breath, the kiss, the gaze become their own dynamic, one act given and creating a response which becomes a gift and is followed by a response continuously without effort or thought in a natural flow of pleasurable sensations.

"The hands can be the givers, or the lips, or the toes, or the elbows, or the nose, and all of these can be the receivers as well. Touching breasts stimulates the heart chakra. Touching is a way of transmitting our emotions and stimulating each other's increased vibratory frequency. Each investigates the other's body to discover the most receptive, most sensitive erogenous zones. Those are the places the gifts must be deposited. The receiver is aware of the gift, the touch, the loving sound, the odor, the gaze, and actively receives it, transmitting the sensation to his/her heart where the response is initiated. Each discovers the response capacity of each part of the other's entire body. Each cell learns to give and to receive the transmissions.

"It is easier to be present when you let yourself feel something. That is how you are present: *YOU FEEL.* You are so close you touch with your awareness. You are 'in' the situation. Your intention, attention, and consciousness are there: the creative moment builds to climax. *THE VIBRATION IS FELT.*

"As the celebration continues the appropriate time for coupling is known. The pleasure of intense sensations when genitals engage will grow and expand. The highest peak of excitation (and vibration) is approaching. Do not hurry. Allow the moment of climax to overwhelm and explode between you. Witness the spark of orgasm. Be aware of the revelations lit by the fire of climax.

"Lovers enter the chamber of their loving and expand to fill the entire area with touching, with movement, with sound, with pleasure and joy."

This is the story that should be told by the elder to the younger. Someone in each child's life needs to tell this story, to give form to the mystery of sexuality. If it is not the parent, then who? Someone must prepare the child for what lies ahead. It is our job in life, our right to know and experience all our bodies are able to experience. Children must be made aware of their right and their potential to celebrate in pleasure and joy.

The Swedish and the Norwegians know. The ancient Chinese knew (Han Dynasty taught sexuality as a blessing and had special words: "precious pearl" and "golden gateway" for female anatomy). Some Tantric practitioners know. And the Goddess worshippers knew. Along with our preparation to earn a livelihood and otherwise expand into our full mental, physical, emotional, and spiritual potentials, there must be education toward full sexual experiences that will provide the realm of joy and celebration that is meant to be a full part of the substance of living.

❧ ❧ ❧

Sexuality is one of life's blessings that can be made more and more wonderful as skills are gained and intimacy developed.

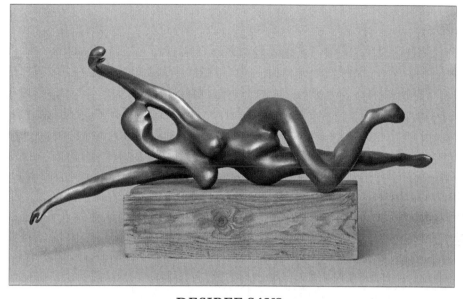

DESIREE SAYS:

The Nexus of spiritual life and life fully acknowledged and lived is where sexuality and love come together.

CONCLUSION

REMEMBERING THE TRUTH OF OUR OWN BEING

In this writing I have dared to proclaim sexuality as the vitalizing force and our gift from the Creator that is a means to celebrate life continuously in a form that reflects the perfection of all the gifts given with life itself. We must reconnect with our sexuality as a powerful tool, a personal energy source, a spark that lights our purpose and holds the possibility of returning life to a constant source of pleasure and celebration, a magnification and a directional aim of our own energy gifted so that life on earth might be enacted in an abundance of joy. The energy that is life is heightened by sacred sexual practices that expand awareness.

We have all come into life with special gifts and a special role representing the original perfection of being and the sacredness of life. Our full participation in our own lives as celebrants leads to our recognition of who we are. The source of energy and mental illumination for full enactment of our lives is high-level orgasms.

With Awareness and Conscious Effort, We Can Re-Awaken Our Connection to Creation

The blessing of our highest self belongs to each of us and is not a product of competition. Competition to identify the best among us makes no sense since we are all created to be perfect as we are. The false mask many of us present cannot be better than the perfection of who we naturally are, and it distorts and distracts from our essential being. It takes a tremendous effort to maintain this false appearance, which actually serves to hide the beauty that we have been made to be. Others in our life may be presenting a false mask as well, adrift in the uncertainty that ignorance of his/her own perfection allows. Both are engaged in a drama of proving themselves to each other, an unnecessary drama since the beauty of the truth of each could be shinning instead. All we need do is allow ourselves to be present, illuminated in our own natural truth.

The spark that initiated life fires continuously as our cells divide and unite. Allowing that spark reveals us to ourselves continuously expanding ourselves and our awareness into a wider and wider range of existence. That spark can be the shaft of light showing us the way to life as a continuous gift.

It is time to recall *the sweetness of the fully developed fruit of life*, like discarding the cardboard taste of fruit in the supermarket, picked before the sun has finished its job because commerce demands it. For thousands of years it has not mattered that the plant knows its way to full development of its fruit. In its fullest expression the fruit is fragile, subject to wind, rain, and heat, and strong as life itself, sweet and rich in its own purpose. The original creators of orchards have been denounced in the name of quick wealth. Their true nature and purpose is still diminished by men and women who do not know or remember what had been and what happened to disrupt a harmonious and balanced way of life that recognized the blessing of sun-sweetened fruit.

The power generated by sexuality will bring forth the voice saying who we are and what we must do. Within the re-creation of creation of each orgasm exists a flash of memory and insight into who we are and what we know. This voice will have the courage to shout, "We will not allow you to destroy this earth out of greed, lust, indifference, and narcissism. Stop what you are doing … it is not working."

Given full voice, women will offer questions and solutions beyond what men have already initiated or have the ability to perceive. We will:

- Stop our mad pursuit of progress and wealth
- Include all people as legitimate recipients of emotional, financial, and physical well-being
- Look for the ways we can live together celebrating each other and our diversity
- Look for the ways each can participate in the culture, enacting our true gifts
- Evaluate what exists as cultural imperatives and whether these imperatives reflect the most prudent use of the life-force energy in harmony and balance with *what naturally is* on this planet
- Address the problems of adapting our lives to the reality of climate change
- Help us construct new ways of being and doing that have nothing to do with money
- Search for conflict solutions that do not involve war. Life is too valuable to be given or taken in war. Another way must be found that honors life— our own and our enemy's
- Establish a renewed awareness that life is sacred, a gift to be treasured, for everyone

A whole new way of life will emerge, one that is more balanced, more joyful, and more sustainable.

Each woman holds within her own being an authentic, truthful, relevant, purposeful, specific energy that is required for her to do her life in the way it is meant to be. This is an energy that sparks a voice that speaks its own truth, a truth that is required to balance the truth of the masculine, spoken from the perspective of the woman and required to establish the harmony we are seeking.

Estrogen has something to say that testosterone has not noticed.

Woman Must Come Forward with What She Knows from Her Gut: War Is Not the Answer

The dialogue concerning what is important in life is subsumed by the life-and-death struggles of war. The blood spilling from fear of each other and greed-based engagements of human energy and attention rob the creative spirit of its place in us, its value, respect, and room to operate. Reading Steve Coll's *Ghost Wars: The Secret History of the CIA*, an account of the nation's convoluted struggle to control what happens in Afghanistan and the minions of that nation's Saudi guest, Osama bin Laden, I see how lopsided our government's policies are. There is no time, space, or interest in celebrating life. Within our government there is the belief that terrible things might happen, and it is government's responsibility to prevent them, but they are unable to do so. Instead, the government perpetuates the cycles of violence and war.

STOP MAKING WAR. The enemy is not the one who blocks our way to the oil or the gold, but the one inside who still believes oil and gold obtained by any means are essential for life. The enemy is the one inside who doesn't see the value of life itself. The enemy keeps pushing for more and better, not seeing the abundance and beauty all around us! The luscious capacity to celebrate life is squeezed out and diminished in importance as we maintain stances of offense and defense.

Women who bring forth all lives must reclaim their position of nourishing and protecting life out of respect for themselves and life itself. Negotiation is required to establish the needs of all parties and the means of satisfaction. This kind of negotiation comes from the heart with understanding at its core. It cannot proceed when one speaker has a gun at the heart of the other. I weep with shame at the methods of my country's "leaders" acting brutally in the name of peace. We cannot afford to wait any longer. Our tools for destroying each other have been fine-tuned and made available to everyone.

It is time to bring ourselves into alignment with the celebration of life that is possible and necessary in order to change the destructive direction humankind is now taking.

Remembering How to Love Our Lives: Our Emotions Tell Us What Is in Our Heart

Instead of war, let's practice life as love. Love is the way of life that honors and cares for everything, and aims to expose us to wonder, thankfulness, and joy witnessing and confirming beauty. We are each made perfect to reflect Great Spirit back to itself by manifesting spirit on Earth. Spirit, the creative energy, is manifest in beauty and in love.

As our ancient foremothers stopped cringing in fear and began to investigate their environment, they discovered the abundant supply of materials on this earth that benefited them. They discovered the regularity of the pattern of natural events and how to prepare and engage. They learned to keep warm when it was needed and save rain for dry spells. They learned which plants and animals they could eat, which needed to be cooked and how, which could solve medical issues, and which to avoid. They learned how to engage with what was around them and how to sustain, honor, protect, and celebrate themselves, their creator, and the fact of life. They did not forget to love life, to love themselves and each other.

Love is the sense of self encased in well-being—warm and comfortable, knowing that all is as it should be, that we have been given all that is needed to glow in our lives, and that we have the capacity to meet challenges. Love is the certainty that what we encounter is a portion of the gift of life, and that its properties will blend with our own to enhance our vibratory rate. Love is feeling our vibratory rate increase and our sense of ourselves expand in response to what is in our environment. As our vibrations increase, we become more of the sacred that we are, the highest vibration: The Creator. Love is drinking in and experiencing this expanded feeling of the perfection of our own being and life itself.

Trying to *get* love blinds us to the love *that is*. The love we are seeking is always there. Remembering this forgotten truth allows love to be present. It is in everything, always available. It is our forgetting that must be overcome.

Love does not look like what it became after the Indo-European invasions: Lot offered his daughter to be raped by the unruly crowd; Jesus died to redeem mankind's sins; Christian soldiers were sent off to battle, often against women; knights, cowboys, cops, space cadets are celebrated for their heroic killings. In the name of love, evil has been unleashed as suspicion, blame, fault-finding, confrontation, and general pain and anxiety, drowning out the best of what it is to be human: the "enormous capacity for consciousness, choice, empathy, and love," as Rianne Eisler describes it.

The sense of love we must remember is the ingredient required for life itself to emerge. It was the love of the Great Spirit/Goddess that suggested the possibility of life as visible form, which It caused to emerge from the amorphous energy that was Its own consciousness (known to me as a Native American Creation story). This was a loving act expressing the Creator's love for Itself, a love that wanted to see Its own perfection. We are that love and that perfection. We have largely forgotten that this is who we are: love and perfection celebrating the Creative force so that It will know Itself and be in celebration.

The reason for this book is to remind us of the tool the Great Spirit/Goddess gave us to celebrate love and perfection as the gifts of life: orgasm. Sacred sexuality—honoring the orgasm as a sacrament—allows us to experience our lives as the Creator (Great Spirit/ Goddess) intended: as a celebration. When we come to ourselves and to each other glowing in the love expressed by the Creator in our creation, our orgasm is a re-creation of our own creation. We are in the love of life, the love of the Creator, the love of ourselves, and the love of each other.

This is the love that we recognize in the eyes of the other as the connection becomes more intimate. This is the love that arouses us and fuels our desire. This is the love that unites us as one and transmits through our orgasm, the re-creation of the moment of creation.

It is obvious that greed and taking are not good formulas for sustaining life and happiness. Behind a gun or a bomb is hate; in front are death and chaos. Our approach has not rewarded us with lasting peace and a sense of well-being and security. We have not tried love and celebration for a very long time. The situation is so severe, and our ability to cope and find solutions so limited, that it seems the moment has come when feminine strategies could again be applied: love and celebration as the way of living instead of hate and war.

Love is a larger perspective, bright and clear. Life looked at through the window of love is wise, abundant, beautiful, joyful, pleasurable, exciting, enthusiastic, open, honest, enacted with integrity, compassionate, filled with laughter—all expanders which allow the Great Spirit/Goddess to express itself through us.

Beauty is Infused with the Love of the Creator

In beauty, we recognize the perfection of what has been created. It teaches us how to be in love of life. Being in our own beauty sparks freedom to participate in the magic of life unfolding in and around us, and we continually gain energy for further investigation and creative action.

I do not believe that the same God created warring with cannons, bombs, land mines, and drones also created rushing waters, breaking waves, mountainsides covered with poppies or lupines, a bright blue sky with floating clouds, and gentle breezes. When I hear the birds and the deep constant movement of the breeze through the tall ponderosas, and the distant tumbling of water over rocks, my heart opens to life. All is good. There is nothing to fear. This feeling is the love of life. I look out on what the Great Spirit/Goddess gave us: the deep blue waters, the radiant sky, the lush and plentiful growth from the rich earth. Why do we ever want? Everything is here, more than we know how to appreciate or use. In love of life, we feel the richness of every moment and every gift.

The Difference Between Love and Sexuality

Love is a state of being, a recognition of the blessings of life and an immersion into its beauty and perfection. I open the flow of love by recognizing love all around me in the blessings of creation. Sexuality is energy—engaging in the energy of Spirit—an increase in the frequency of life's vibration. Sexuality, beginning with a deep intimacy (an exchange of inner realities), becomes an expression of love, the love first expressed when the Great Spirit/Goddess created all things out of Its love for Itself and its desire to see Itself. We must be sure of what love is before we can fully experience what sexuality is. Love is viewing life and everything in it as a blessing to be celebrated, a sense of joy at being part of everything that is, a delight in every discovery, a thrill at the prospect of participating, a knowing that the Great Spirit/Goddess is there, and that we are being protected and guided. This is love. Its expression is sexuality, the increase of vibratory rate. We begin loving by loving ourselves as creations of the Great Spirit/Goddess. We celebrate that reality by raising our energy, laughing, singing, dancing, and making love!

Love Between Two People

The purpose of relationship and true intimacy is to share what we know and find out what the union of that knowledge from the inner depth of each is meant to birth. Sharing the truth of who we are, there is no need to try to be or prove ourselves. Desire is the signal of the unconscious motivator, the spark. Pleasure is the fulfillment.

We begin loving by loving ourselves: then we are prepared to love another. Love of another is an enactment of the love of the Great Spirit/Goddess who created out of love, the love of ourselves, and the love that is the basis of all life. Your love opens me to a deeper love of myself. This deepens my love for you and my love for everything that is. When you see my true beauty, it helps me see it. Love serves as the sun that provides the energy by which we each grow. I ask for what I desire and serve your desires. In the energy field of the beauty of our love, I feel the natural grace of who I am. Masculine and feminine are blended in us as in the Great Spirit. As the masculine knows itself as the giver, it becomes exposed and vulnerable; as the woman opens herself fully, she ejaculates. As each gender becomes aware of itself as a blend of genders, it knows a deeper level of itself.

It is not about trying to get love; being present and open, allows love access and emits love. Trying to get love, I miss the love that is there. Giving back the gift received keeps the cycle moving. Perpetually dealing with each other's stuff and pulling each other down causes both to drown in the relationship. This is what, too often, we now call love. Manipulation and need make a natural response impossible, and likely to be judged inadequate and inferior. When we are truly taking care of ourselves, our own stuff, there will be no desire to try for love that is not there (a hopeless pursuit). Separation (sufficient to know ourselves and take care of our own stuff) allows for true union. From the perception of the known qualities of their own soul, each can see the other more clearly than from the self-ignorant outpost of wanting. A heart willing to be vulnerable to the possible pains of love and life is capable of feeling the blessings of both.

When we return to reverence for the Great Spirit/Goddess and memory of celebrating our Creator and ourselves with sacred sexuality, we will return to love of life itself.

In the purification lodge I felt the love, the mutual support, the appreciation of each other—what we each bring, what we each encounter—all the stories and all the courage. I am sure it is this love that has kept me going to find the way of saying these things that I pray will awaken us once again to loving our lives.

Healing Will Proceed When Life Is Recognized as Continuous Creativity

Each person must know that their life is always part of the creative process of life. The creative artist, the mother, developing fetus, and each person must be reinforced in their roles of allowing creation to manifest Itself through them. We must allow ourselves to remember that we are creation itself being manifest. Creation is the invisible making Itself visible. Each moment is birthed into being as creation evolves. When we live in the creation of each moment, we are allowing the mystery of *what is* to reveal itself. We do not know what the next moment holds, but the potential for "wonderful" is always present. We can all begin to be open to the whole realm of possibility. When we remember that creation is continually occurring through us, through our thoughts, our perceptions, and our actions, we connect to the blessing of our life. Then the possibilities for celebration are infinite.

We will find healing for ourselves and our planet when we return to the practice of sexuality as a re-enactment of the creation of all things, a sacrament that keeps us connected to the sacredness of our lives and all life. Orgasm is our means of tapping the source of energy contained in our being and truly being in our own divinity, recognizing this creative principle underlying existence.

APPENDIX FOR CHAPTER VI:
BIBLICAL REFERENCES TO EVIL
SEXUALITY AND THE LAST TRACES OF THE
GODDESS RELIGION

Injunctions Against Women's Sexuality

Here are a few examples of the Levite injections into the Holy Bible that were part of their program to remove women of their position in society by robbing them of the sexual freedom they had experienced for thousands of years:

Hosea: I will put an end to all her rejoicing, her feasts, her new moons, her Sabbaths, and her solemn festivals. I mean to make her pay for all the days she offered burnt offerings to the Baal and decked herself with rings and necklaces to court her lovers, forgetting me. It is Yahweh speaking."[1]

Ezekiel tells of people in temples of Jerusalem facing east with twigs to their nostrils (probably branches from Asherah, whom the Book of Kings suggests was worshipped alongside Yahweh in his temple in Israel) and weeping for the death of Tammez.[2]

The appellation "son of man"—priests no longer considered themselves sons of women.

Jezebel was condemned for celebrating the religion of

her parents — the Queen of Heaven and her Baal — and was murdered gruesomely as warning to all wayward women.[3]

II Kings …that Jehu and his men murdered every member of the congregation, then finally made a "latrine" of the building itself.[4]

Hebrews who dared worship in the ancient religion of the Queen of Heaven and Her Baal were victims of a violent religious persecution, words that were translated into murder and destruction explained as having been ordered by Yahweh.[5]

Hebrew male's daily prayer: "Blessed art Thou O Lord our God, King of the Universe, who has not made me a woman."[6]

Mohammed stated, "When Eve was created, Satan rejoiced."[7]

Jeremiah warned, "…the women who openly announced their intention to continue the worship of the Queen of Heaven…would meet with famine, violence, and total destruction as a result of their religious beliefs."[8]

St. John Chrysostom: "The women taught once and ruined everything [referring to the teaching from the apple of the Tree of Life]. On this account, let them not teach."[9]

"Because of what she had done at the very beginning of time she was expected to submit obediently."[10]

"A warning to any women who wished to defy Yahweh's declaration that it had been just such a woman as she who had caused the downfall of mankind."[11]

"Into the myth of how the world began, the story the Levites offered as explanation for the creation of all existence, they placed the advisory serpent and the woman who accepted its counsel, eating of the tree that gave her the understanding of what "only the gods knew"—the secret of sex—how to create life."[12]

"In male religion, sexual drive was not to be regarded as natural biological desires of women or men that encouraged the species to reproduce itself but was to be viewed as women's fault."[13]

"Proof of the admission of her guilt was supposedly made evident in the pain of childbirth women were assured was their eternal chastisement for teaching men bad habits."[14]

The writers and religious leaders who followed Christ assumed the same prose of contempt for the female, continuing to use religion to lock women further into the role of passive and inferior beings, and more easily controlled property.

Women were to be regarded as mindless, carnal creatures, both attitudes justified and "proved" by the Paradise myth.[15]

Eph.5:22-24 — Paul's letter to Ephesians: Wives, submit yourselves to your own husbands as you do to the Lord. For the husband is the head of the wife as Christ is the head of the church, his body, of which he is the Savior. Now as the church submits to Christ, so also wives should submit to their husbands in everything.[16]

1Tim.2:11-14 — "Let the women learn in silence with all subjection. But I suffer not women to learn, nor to usurp authority over men, but to be in silence. For Adam was first formed and then Eve and Adam was not deceived, but the women being deceived was in the transgression."[17]

1Cor.11:3,7,9 — "The head of every man is Christ; and the head of every woman is man; and the head of Christ is God. For a man indeed ought not to cover his head for as much as he is the image and the glory of God, but the woman is the glory of man. Neither was man created for woman, but woman for the man."[18]

Statements were carefully designed to suppress the earlier social structure continually presented the myth of Adam and Eve as divine proof that man was to hold the ultimate authority.

So intent was Paul in declaring maleness to be first that he blinded himself to the biological truth of birth: "For the man is not of the woman but the woman is of the man."[19]

Last Breath of the Goddess

Finally, there was little known of the Goddess outside of hidden pockets in out of the way places. The remaining temples were finally closed.

300 A.D. Emperor Constantine put an end to the sanctuary of Ashtoreth at Aphaca

380 A.D. Emperor Theodosius closed down the temple of Goddess at Eleusis, Rome; Diane (Artemis) in Ephesus in Western Anatolia

The Parthenon on the Acropolis (a Goddess site from 1300 B.C. to 450 A.D.) was turned into Catholic Church in 450 A.D.[20]

5th century Emperor Justina converted the remaining temple of Isis to a Christian church

Arabia — 7th century. Mohammad brought an end to the national worship of the sun goddess, Al Lat [21]

APPENDIX TO CHAPTER XII:
ACHIEVING HIGH-LEVEL ORGASMS

Vision-Questing

During my training with Harley Swiftdeer, I took at least one vision-quest journey a year, making deeper and deeper connections with the Great Spirit, and experiencing an unwinding of the realities of life that I had twisted around myself as an encasement, restricting my awareness and my motion as I tried to be an acceptable human being, unaware that my birth and natural growth had naturally made me acceptable. For the vision-quest, I was alone in a remote place (in the Santa Inez Valley, in Joshua Tree, in Tujunga, in the high Sierras, near Santa Margarita). I was instructed to call on my ancestors to come and teach me with seven shakes of my gourd rattle in each of the compass directions and call for the universe to join them. After once experiencing the presence of the ancestors and the opening of the universe to my awareness, these prayers became fervent, filled with the knowledge that they would be answered by informed energy all around me. The answers to my questions and the sense of my own life missions become known to me. I deposited the messages in my notebook, clearing each from my mind to make room for the next one. Days and nights of the quests are spent asking for knowledge and recording these incoming messages. The prescribed vision-quests were in graduated intensity and longer duration, requiring deeper questions and allowing wider awakening.

My first vision-quest was over one night alone in the wilderness. The next was in a 6 by 4 by 4 foot chamber. I dug my hole near enough to the main altar where the leader would be spending the night so that she could secure the plywood covering of my burial site at sundown. Burial ceremonies made death my ally, spurring me on to accomplish the mandates of this life without wasting valuable moments of my time on Earth. I learned that death became an ally when I accepted the reality that my life will be finite, making every moment valuable in terms of what I am able to discover in it about who I am and how I am meant to interact with life. In creating my own death and accepting it, I waste no more energy resisting the reality of death and make use of every available moment to actualize my own reality—no more sit-coms and other wasted entertainment time.

Then I stayed two nights in the wilderness, and later, two nights in the grave, three nights in the wilderness, and three nights in a cave. I continued progress to the core of myself, performing all aspects of the ceremonies: casting a circle of rocks each representing a compass direction, sealing the circle with tobacco, cornmeal, cayenne, and garlic salt to welcome the ancestors and keep out negative energy, constructing an altar, smoking my pipe with prayers for a useful ceremony, dancing around the altar with prayers for self-recognition, rattling with seven shakes of my gourd to call the ancestors in from all directions to bring their knowledge of who I am. The lack of food and greatly restricted water resulted in an altered state, allowing me to learn what I needed to know about myself, my relationship to life and everything in it, and what I needed to do. The walls of the reality I had accepted since childhood vanished and insight arrived. I began to know myself as multi-layered and felt comfortable in the unseen world that has always been my home.

For my last supervised vision-quest, I was escorted on a long hike into Oak Mountain north of Porter Ranch in the San Fernando Valley. A longtime purification lodge participant who had roamed the mountain all his life took me to a ridge that jutted out over what is now Stevenson Ranch. The sage grew so dense along the ridge of the top that I had to follow close behind his powerful frame while he spread the plants for us to pass. Finally, we came to a 12-foot boulder with a cave that broke through the center so that I had a view of the east and the west, and a passageway from one side to the other. It was a very powerful spot from which to ask for a vision. During that vision quest, which lasted six days and nights, the ancestors instructed me to travel in search the Goddess tradition foundations on which the cultures of England, Malta, and Greece are built so that I could experience the roots of the Goddess traditions. At the end of the six days and nights my guide came back for me, bringing on his back enough water to quench my thirst and a shower. After that, my vision quests became journeys for discovery along the path I had entered: I was called to Agua Azul in Mexico, to Palenque, to Chechen Itza, to Tulum, to Isla Mujeres, to Peru, to Bolivia, to Greece, to Malta, to Avebury (a stone circle in England), and to Bali. In each location, I discovered another level of the buried feminine and my own truth as a woman.

Finding my way to my higher-self within the teaching of the Deertribe Metis Medicine Society included the following concepts of restricting and moving energy, and the maps of those energy movements entering and moving throughout the body.

Dark, Light, and Rainbow Arrows:

Dark:

As I proceeded through the transformational ceremonies Swiftdeer prescribed, I gradually understood how I held the "dark arrows," how I was "at the effect of people, places, and things," gauging my own worth by how others saw me. The door was opened to my **attachment** to the acceptance of my family and friends, in whose esteem I found my self-esteem. Little by little, ceremony by ceremony, I saw the ways my path was blocked by the need for verification outside of myself (**dependency**). I saw how I protected myself by **judging** others against my own strongly held beliefs. I found others to associate with who would support my claims (**comparison**). I became aware that I was not operating in the present because I **expected** things to be as I had come to believe they should be from past experiences. It was appalling to realize as the ceremonies revealed to me that, though I had grown and participated in life as an adult, a **needy child's voice** inside of me needed to be assured by others who would take care of me and make me feel okay. In all this suffering of need, I demonstrated the belief that I was the most important element in life (**ego self-importance**).

Light:

Sitting time after time on the mountain through the night while vision-questing, calling the ancestors from each direction to be my teachers, the dim glow of "light arrows" began to appear. Little by little I could hear the voice of my own being calling to my awareness, showing me how to be in balance and harmony by focusing on **awareness** of me within myself. The ancestors brought knowledge of my gifts, strengths, and weaknesses, and I let go of my need for constant recognition and support from others. I could love and honor my specialness (**self-appreciation**) in relation to others, deriving pleasure from being myself (**self-pleasure**), and I began to know that I am perfect as I am even if I make mistakes, and that I can learn from them (**self-acceptance**). I began to find joy and pleasure in my own way. Loving myself, I no longer need to be loved and accept the love that comes my way with the openness of the love within me (**self-love**). The ancestors helped me understand that I am in my own Sacred Dream that is developing as I access my higher-self in response to the influence of the universe (**self-actualization**). I need never be "at the effect of anyone or anything, at any time in any way." I am at the center of my own circle of power of self "following the maximum efficiency/minimum effort law of never taking self or life too seriously; seeking knowledge and pleasure [has become my] meaning for life [giving me] power" (**Impeccability: Warrior's Freedom***)*.

Rainbow:

The "rainbow arrows" remain a work in progress. I believe that as I open myself to the teachings of each moment I come closer to the being that I was meant to be when I came into this life. **Gaining illumination** is the goal of finding pleasure and knowledge in everything around me, and I sometimes can feel this. **Gaining introspection,** aligning myself with all the worlds—plant, animal, human, and mineral—with the four directions, and the cycles of life is sometimes possible. **Gaining trust, innocence, and perfection,** knowing that all things are connected, often allows me to give freely of my essence without expecting anything in return. This writing is an example of freely giving. **Gaining wisdom, alignment, and harmonic resonance** with all forms of all things adds to my comfort in life and the prevalent sense of how beautiful life is. **Gaining full open heart-to-heart communication** allows me to walk through my life saying what I have come to know and seeking others who also speak from their hearts. I am able to connect with **a balance of my own male and female energy** as I learn to bring the joy of sexual awakening into each moment. This is when I sustain high-energy and enthusiasm. **Gaining abundance and prosperity** feels closer as I hold more of the Rainbow arrows longer. I include the ideas of the Rainbow arrows to set the direction of the reader toward a higher possibility of living life in joy which I am pursuing.

Adapted from Swiftdeer's Quodoushka Manual,
pp. 13-19

Star-Maiden Circle:

This has been a main tool for retuning to my center since Swiftdeer introduced me to it nearly forty years ago. On a full moon or a new moon, on the solstice or the equinox, on my birthday, or whenever I feel off balance, this ceremony has been a bridge to my higher self out of a stuck place into a state of divine understanding. Many of Swiftdeer's teachings were accomplished in the sacred circle of a medicine wheel. For the Star-maiden Circle ceremony, each direction on the compass is assigned characteristics that help us choreograph our energies for a "Dance of Life" that most accurately reflects our gifts and potentials. Each position has both a light and a dark mirror. By identifying a dark mirror of our lower self that keeps us stuck, we can focus our attention on opening that symbol to the light mirror of our higher-self, releasing the energy and the truth of who we are.

I include these teachings as a tool for climbing out of a stuck place in the lower self that holds dark arrows, which interfere with achieving a high-level orgasm. The Star-Maiden Circle ceremony can lead us to experience our full power in our higher-self. It is performed sitting in the center of a circle of stones each representing one of the eight directions of the compass. It is a powerful tool for gaining insight into our psyche—our actions, reactions, desires, beliefs, goals, etc.

Standing in the center of this circle, beginning by facing the South and proceeding clockwise to the

Southeast, the ancestors may be called from each direction with groups of six shakes of the rattle, alternated with six stamps of the left, then the right foot, repeated until the presence of the ancestor is felt. Ancestors bring information of which Dark Arrows we hold and how we can open ourselves to the Light Arrows and, eventually, the Rainbow Arrows.

South: Mythology and Entertainment: Mythologies, created by internalization of teachings from childhood experiences, parents, family and friends, tell the stories of "who we are, what life is about, what relationships are like." Entertainment is the way we enact our mythologies by the way we live, either in pleasure and joy, or indulging in continually painful re-enactments. On the dark side we might be telling ourselves that we are worthless; on the light side we might know of ourselves as brilliant." Through understanding our emotional myths [we] open to the past and see the blocks that have kept [us] from total emotional sexual enjoyment. [We] learn to trust our emotions."

Southwest: Symbols of Life Experience: Symbols are the picture in our minds created by each word or phrase we hear. They carry the energy of feelings based on the experiences we have had with a specific symbol. The word "sex" will bring up horrible images for one person and beautiful images for another. We fear and do not want to look at dark or closed symbols, so they become limitations on our lives. Opening those symbols "gives us a sense of power and freedom...at cause in our lives." We are no longer at the effect of them. Through a constant and continuous action of fully opening our sexual symbols, [we] begin to understand the full range of the [possible sexual experience].

West: The Daydream: Our dreams are first conceived in this place of introspection and intuition. "This is the place where the seed meets the egg, and gestation begins on ideas, desires, hopes, and fears, and all the things we wish to create for ourselves." We dream what could be that we might nurture into existence. "It is the dark void from which all possibilities may flow." On the dark side, we are so stuck in what might be that nothing is actualized. On the light side, these daydreams are raw material for what is manifest in our lives such as imagining our eminent meeting with our lover, including the beauty of the environment, the sound of the music, and the twinkle in his eye. "Through full use of [our] introspection [we] bring [our] everyday daydreams new images of [our] body and [our] physical sexuality."

Northwest: Rules and Laws: These are the ways we know how things should be. "They are the limitations and boundaries we place on ourselves and others to govern conduct." The limitation and imprisonment by rules and laws that are not in accordance with Sacred, Natural, Magical, or Universal laws are on the dark side. Sacred laws are on the light side, and they are in "proper alignment with proper energy movement." I have mentioned two sacred laws: everything is born of woman and nothing be done to harm the child or the child within. "Through the power of [our] own dream symbols, [we] begin to open and examine the rules and laws, which we use to establish our own sexual morals. As [we] rid ourselves of the dogmas [we] begin to see the new images of [ourselves] as the God/Goddess of love...."

North: Philosophies and Belief Systems: The generalized "framework we create about ourselves, life, and others...as our minds attempt to validate our myths, and to set up a system that supports them." Philosophies and belief systems that restrict and limit us are on the dark side. On the light side, they empower us and promote our free learning and growth...Through developing the power of clarity [we] open [our] mind to the full potential of the actualized thought-form...[we] use wisdom and knowledge to develop [our] mental-sexual philosophy free of limiting belief systems."

Northeast: Choreography of Energy Movement: This is the place from which "we design the flow of energy in our life process." As part of the animal kingdom, we trust that all the required resources are given, including the energy of Spirit. On the dark side, we choreograph our energy in such a way that we are out of balance with ourselves, others, and our world. On the light side, we are aware of the universal flow of energy and harmonize with it. "Through the full use and contact with [our] [higher self] [we]begin to see [our] own needs, and design [our] energy movements to express the fullness of [our] power to choose—to become the God/Goddess of Love."

East: Fantasy: This "is the fire within spirit; it is imagination flowing freely; it the elaboration and blossoming of what was birthed in the Daydream." Fantasies on the dark side keep us in illusion or are harmful to others. This is the place from which we live the fantasy of our life's experience, gain approval, recognition, etc., from others instead of doing what we are here to do." On the light side, fantasy allows us to honor ourselves and know that anything is possible. The artist totally absorbed in a new project, a dancer letting go of restraint in responding to the music, the business person engaging in a new project, the mother engaged in the play of her two-year-old are letting go to fantasy. "Through the full use of [our] imagination [we] create fantasies, which bring [us] to full realization, [our] actual expression of our spiritual/sexual reality."

Southeast: Concepts of Self: From this life and all our past lives we have developed concepts of who we are in all aspects of our being. On the dark side we hold the Dark Arrows of attachment, dependency, judgments, comparison, expectation, and the self-importance of the needy child, which pull us off balance as we seek validation for ourselves from others. "We give our power away to others." On the light side we gain validation for ourselves from inside our being, which is empowered by the Light Arrows of self-awareness, self-appreciation, self-acceptance, self-pleasure, self-love, self-actualization, and impeccability. This is the person finding joy in the pursuit of her own goals knowing fully that she is capable and will succeed. "Through use of all five senses, [we] bring the pleasure of touch into the spiritual realm of self-stimulation;

learning self-control and full self-release [we] reach total self-awareness and the concept of [our] God/Goddess self."

From Swiftdeer's Quodoushka Manual

Flowering Tree Ceremony:

On occasion, the ceremony may be enacted. It is performed in a remote space where there will be no interruptions. There should be a tree in each of the cardinal positions of the compass. The procedure is: Sitting with your back against the South tree ask: WHO AM I? Write the answers in a journal; move around the tree and with your back to the tree in the West ask: WHERE DO I COME FROM? Write the answers in the journal; move to the North of the tree and with your back against the tree ask: WHAT ARE MY GIFTS? Write the answers; move to the East of the tree, and with your back against the tree ask: WHAT IS MY PATH WITH HEART? (WHAT AM I SUP-POSED TO DO?). Write the answers as they come in. Continue to the North tree, the West tree, and the East tree asking the same questions in the procedure described for the South tree. Conclude the ceremony by asking from the Center which direction requires your attention. Throw tobacco in that direction. Thank each tree with a tobacco offering. For this ceremony, a bundle is held in the left hand at the navel throughout the process. The bundle is created from essences of the plant, animal, mineral, and human (hair or spit) worlds found on the way to the spot. The bundle is buried in the center when ceremony is complete.

From the Teachings of Harley Swiftdeer

For a comprehensive teaching of the Native American healing tradition of principles, techniques, and ceremonies contact the Deertribe Metis Medicine Society in Scottsdale, Arizona: dtmms@dtmms.org; http://ddtmms.org; P.O Box 12397, Scottsdale, AZ 85245; 480-443-3851.

ABOUT THE AUTHOR

Dina Pilaet, Photographer

LYNN CREIGHTON'S development as an author and an artist has paralleled her personal growth as an active participant in Native American philosophies and ceremonies. She apprenticed with a medicine man and, under his direction, pursued a deeper and deeper connection to a divine creative source and came to a deeper knowledge and understanding of herself and her place in the universe. It is her continued transformational practices (leading purification lodges, vision-quests, and other ceremonies) that inform her work, both sculptural and literary.

Ms. Creighton has prepared this statement of her findings from ceremonial and sculptural work in her book, *Reclaiming the Sacred Source: The Ancient Power and Wisdom of Women's Sexuality*. It is her intention to establish a way forward in which the gift of sexuality will be enacted as the magical treasure given when life is given in order that humanity will always celebrate itself and each other.

A sculptor for forty years, Ms. Creighton has taught for over thirty at the college and university level and shown her sculpture throughout the United States, in Japan, in France, in Luxemburg, in Italy and in South Africa. Her sculptures have won many awards and been the subject of many media reviews, and she has frequently been invited for television interviews. The Ventura County Museum mounted a retrospective of Ms. Creighton's sculpture in 2019. Ms. Creighton has traveled with her work to gatherings celebrating feminine spirituality; she created ceremonial experiences for women and men of the re-emerging feminine; and she recalled the sacredness of sexuality in workshops for women in numerous locations across the United States (including Hawaii) and South Africa. Ms. Creighton makes her home in Southern California.

NOTES

Chapter 3 Endnotes: Sexuality as a Celebration of the Divine

1. Rianne Eisler. *Sacred Pleasure: Sex, Myth, and the Politics of the Body.* Harper Collins, 1995, p. 227.
2. Ibid., 180.
3. Ibid., 198.
4. Ibid., 198.
5. Ibid., 93.
6. Ibid., 94 (from Reich).
7. Ibid., 376.
8. Ibid.,
9. Jacquetta Hawkins. *Dawn of the Gods: Minoan and Mycenaean Origins of Greece.* The Arcadia Press, 1968, p. 131.
10. Ibid., 53.
11. Ibid., 77.
12. Ibid., 170.
13. Ibid., 78.
14. Ibid., 66.
15. Ibid., 70.
16. Ibid., 25.
17. Ibid., 30.
18. Ibid., 30.
19. Ibid., 222.
20. Simone de Beauvoir. *The Second Sex*, Vintage Books, 1952, p. 75. 27. Ibid., 75.
21. Ibid., 88.
22. Ibid., 88.
23. Ibid., 181.
24. Ibid., 4.
25. Ibid., 5.
26. Ibid., 222.
27. Ibid., 88.
28. Ibid., 88.
29. Ibid., 181.
30. Ibid., 4.
31. Ibid., 5.
32. Ibid., 6. 3
33. Ibid., 18.
34. Ibid., 175.

Chapter 4 Endnotes: When the Goddess Reigned

1. Marija Gimbutas. *The Language of the Goddess*, San Francisco. Harper and Row, 1989, p. xiii.

2. Ibid., xix.

3. Ibid. xix.

4. Ibid. xv.

5. Marija Gimbutas. *The Goddesses and Gods of Old Europe*, Berkeley and Los Angeles, University of California Press, 1974 and 1982, p. 236.

6. Marija Gimbutas. *The Language of the Goddess*, San Francisco. Harper and Row, 1989, p. xiv.

7. Ibid. 111.

8. Ibid., 3.

9. Ibid., 236. 14. Ibid., xix.

10. Marija Gimbutas. *The Goddesses and Gods of Old Europe*, Berkeley and Los Angeles, University of California Press, 1974 and 1982,, 95.

11. Ibid., 236.

12. Ibid., 236.

13. Ibid., 80.

14. Marija Gimbutas. *The Language of the Goddess*, xix.

15. Marija Gimbutas. *The Goddesses and Gods of Old Europe,* 58

16. Ibid., 93.

17. Marija Gimbutas; *The Language of the Goddess; p.316*

Chapter 5 Endnotes: The Unravelling of Goddess Worship by God-Fearing Groups

1. Merlin Stone. *When God Was a Woman*, New York and London, Harvest/HBJ. 1976, p. 22 (from Robert Graves, *The Golden Ass*).

2. Ibid., xxv.

3. Ibid., 23-24.

4. Ibid., 37-38.

5. Ibid., 47 (from /George Glotz. *The Aegean Civilization*, London: Routledge and Paul, 1925.).

6. Ibid., 47 (Alexiou Stylianos. *Minoan Civilization*. Iraklion Crete, The Archeological Museum, 1969).

7. Ibid., 47 (from Jacquetta Hawkes. *The First Great Civilization*, London: Hutchison, 1973.).

8. Ibid., 64.

9. Ibid., 43.

10. Ibid., 28.

11. Ibid., 42-43.

12. Ibid., 44.

13. Ibid., 44.

14. Ibid., 45.

15. Ibid., 46 (from Charles Seltman. *Women of Antiquity,* London: Pan Books, 1952)

16. Ibid., xx.

17. Ibid., 67.

18. Ibid., 67.

19. Ibid., 72.

20. Ibid., 72.

21. Ibid., 71.

22. Ibid., 74.

23. Ibid., 81.

24. Ibid., 90.

25. Ibid., 93.

26. Ibid., 95.

27. Ibid., 95.

28. Ibid., 51 (from Robert Graves, *The Greek Myths*, Harmonsworth: Penguin, 1969).

29. Ibid., 52 (from E. A. Butterworth. *Some Traces of the Pre-Olympian World,*1966).

30. Ibid., 51 (from E.A. Butterworth, *Some Traces of the Pre-Olympian World*).

31. Ibid., 101.

32. Ibid., 101.

33. Ibid., 107.

34. Ibid., 108.

35. Ibid., 110.

36. Ibid., 114.

37. Ibid., 114.

38. Ibid., 115.

39. Ibid., 115.

40. Ibid., 123.

Chapter 6 Endnotes: The Holy Bible as a Tool for Repression

1.Merlin Stone. *When God Was a Woman*, New York and London, Harvest/HBJ, 1976, p. 26.

2. Ibid., xxv.

3. Ibid., xxv.

4. Ibid., 117.

5. Ibid., 168.

6. Ibid., 169.

7. Ibid., 169.

8. Ibid., 172.

9. Ibid., 168.

10. Ibid., 179.

11. Ibid., xxvi.

12.Riane Eisler. *Sacred Pleasure,* San Francisco, Harper and Row, 1995, p. 32.

13.Merlin Stone. *When God Was a Woman*, New York and London, Harvest/HBJ, 1976, p. 195. 14. Ibid., xxvi.

Chapter 7 Endnotes: Women Asleep to Themselves Are Unavailable for Solving Cultural Problems

1. Simone De Beauvoir. *The Second Sex*, New York, New York, Vintage Books of Random House, 1952.

2. Betty Friedan. *The Feminine Mystique,* New York, New York, W. W. Norton & Company, Inc., 1963, p. 106., 72. 5. Ibid., 77.

Chapter 8 Endnotes: How the Women's Movements Failed

1.Betty Friedan. *The Feminine Mystique,* New York, New York, W. W. Norton & Company, Inc., 1963, p. 81.

2. Ibid., 82.
3. Ibid., 83.
4. Ibid., 82.
5. Ibid., 85-86.
6. Ibid., 86.
7. Ibid.,86.
8. Ibid., 87.
9. Ibid., 87 (from Yuri Suhl. *Ernestine Rose and the Battle for Human Rights,* New York, 1959, p.158).
10. Ibid., 87.
11. Ibid., 97.
12. Ibid., 98.
13. Ibid., 98.
14. Ibid., 125.
15. Ibid., 104.
16. Ibid., 113.
17. Ibid., 117.

18. Ibid., 119.
19. Ibid., 104.
20. Ibid., 71.
21. Ibid., 68.
22. Ibid., 54.
23. Ibid., 65.
24. Ibid., 52.
25. Ibid., 16.
26. Ibid., 32.
27. Ruth Rosen. *The World Split Open,* New York, New York, The Penguin Group, 2000, p. 221.

Chapter 9 Endnotes: The Sham of Gender Equity

1.Merlin Stone. *When God Was a Woman,* New York and London, Harvest/HBJ. 1976, p. 154.

Chapter 10 Endnotes: Freud and Reich

1.Wilhelm Reich. *The Function of Orgasm: Sex-Economic Problems of Biological Energy,* New York: Farrar Straus and Giroux, 1940, p. 89.
2. Ibid., 96.
3. Ibid., 136.

4. Ibid., 210 (from Sigmund Freud. *Civilization and Its Discontents;* New York: Norton and Co. 1962).

5. Ibid., 211.

6. Ibid., 220.

7. Ibid., 220.

8. Ibid., 222.

9. Ibid., 155.

10. Ibid., 221.

11. Ibid., 71.

12. Ibid., 5.

13. Ibid., 6.

14. Ibid., 7.

15. Ibid., 8.

16. Ibid., 12.

17. Ibid., 17.

18. Ibid., 18.

19. Ibid., 18.

20. Ibid., 59.

21. Ibid., 148.

22. Ibid., 155.

23. Ibid., 158.

24. Ibid., 200-7.

25. Ibid., 161-2.

26. Ibid., 179.

27. Ibid., 185.

28. Ibid., 179.

29. Ibid., 103-7.

30. Ibid., 108.

31. Ibid., 200-1.

32. Ibid., 202.

33. Ibid., 230.

34. Ibid., 232.

35. Ibid., 9.

36. Ibid., 233.

37. Ibid., 240.

38. Ibid., 237.

39. Ibid., 237.

40. Ibid., 240.

41. Ibid., 242.

42. Ibid., 244.

43. Ibid., 244.

44. Ibid., 116.

45. Ibid., 186.

46. Ibid., 188.

47. Ibid., 221.

48. Ibid., 232.

49. Ibid., 222.

50. Ibid., 233.

51. Ibid., 224.

52. Ibid., 228.

53. Ibid., 362.

54. Ibid., 274.

55. Ibid., 282.

56. Ibid., 379.

Chapter 11 Endnotes: Electromagnetic Energy Cannot Be Denied

1. Peter Redgrove. *The Black Goddess and the Unseen Real,* New York: Grove Press, 1987, 105.

2. Ibid., 172.

3. Ibid., 110.

4. Ibid., 47.

5. Ibid., 47.

6. Ibid., 126.

7. Ibid., 48 (from B. Nicholson. *"Does Kissing Aid Human Bonding by Semiochemical Addiction?" British Journal of Dermatology*, vol. III, 1984, pp.623-7).

8. Ibid., 97.

9. Ibid., 135 (from Barbara Walker, *The Women's Encyclopedia of Myths and Secrets*, San Francisco, Harper and Row 1983, p. 613).

10. Ibid., 134 (from William Anderson. *Dante the Maker*, London, Routledge and Kagan, 1980, p. 92).

11. Ibid., 131-2.

12. Ibid., 134-5 (from William Anderson. *Dante the Maker*, London, Routledge and Kagan, 1980 p. 110)

13. Ibid., 135.

14. Ibid., 135.

15. Ibid., 169.

16. Ibid., 169.

17. Ibid., 172.

18. Ibid., 172.

19. Ibid., 172.

20. Ibid., 172.

21. Ibid., 117.

22. Ibid., 167 (from Barbara Black Koltuv, *The Book of Lilith*. Maine, Nicholas-Hays, 1986).

23. Ibid., 168.

24. Ibid., 117.

25. Ibid., 164.

26. Ibid., 164.

27. Ibid., 161.

28. Ibid., 162 (from Whitney Chadwick, *Women Artists and the Surrealist Movement*, London: Thames and Hudson,1985, p.143)

Chapter 12 Endnotes: Parenting our Children Toward Fully Sexual Lives

1. Naomi Wolf: from lecture at California Lutheran University about 2009.

2. Riane Eisler. *Sacred Pleasure*, San Francisco: Harper and Row, 1995, p, 187.

3. Ibid., 281.

4. Ibid., 185.

5. Ibid., 103-4.

Appendix Chapter 6 Endnotes: Biblical Injunctions against Women's Sexuality

1.Merlin Stone. *When God Was a Woman;* New York and London; Harvest/HBJ; 1976; 185.

2. Ibid., 186.

3. Ibid., 188.

4. Ibid., 189.

5. Ibid., 187.

6. Ibid., 224.

7. Ibid., 224.

8. Ibid., 185.

9. Ibid., 226.

10. Ibid., 221.

11. Ibid., 223.

12. Ibid., 217.

13. Ibid., 221.

14. Ibid., 221.

15. Ibid., 221.

16. Ibid., 224-5.

17. Ibid., 225.

18. Ibid., 225.

19. Ibid., 225-5.

20. Ibid., 194.

21. Ibid., 195.

BIBLIOGRAPHY

Anand, Margot. *The Art of Everyday Ecstasy.* New York, New York. Broadway Books, a division of Random House, Inc. 1998

Anand, Margot. *The Art of Sexual Magic.* New York, New York. G.P. Putnam's Sons. 1995.

Blair, Nancy. *Amulets of the Goddess – Oracle of Ancient Wisdom.* Oakland, CA. Bookpeople. 1993.

Blum, Jeanne Elizabeth. *Woman Heal Thyself.* Boston, Massachusetts. Charles E. Tuttle Co., Inc. 1995.

Bolen-Shinoda, Jean M.D. *Gods in Everyman.* New York, New York. Harper & Row. 1989.

Brokaw, Tom. *Boom: Voices of the Sixties: Personal Reflections on the '60's and Today.* New York, New York. Random House, Inc. 2007.

Carson, Rachel. *Silent Spring.* New York, New York. Houghton Mifflin Company. 1962.

Dodson, Betty. *Sex for One.* New York, New York. Crown Publishers, Inc. 1987.

De Beauvoir, Simone. *The Second Sex.* New York, New York. Alfred A. Knopf. 1952.

Eisler, Riane. *Sacred Pleasure.* San Francisco: Harper and Row. 1995.

Ephron, Nora. *Crazy Salad.* New York, New York. Bantam Books, Inc. 1972.

Ephron, Nora. *When Harry Met Sally...* New York, New York. Alfred A. Knopf. 1990.

Feuerstein, Georg, Ph.D. *Sacred Sexuality: The Erotic Spirit in the World's Great Religions.* Rochester, Vermont. 2003.

Fleming, Anne Taylor. *Motherhood Deferred, A Woman's Journey.* Ballantine Books, a division of Random House, Inc. 1994.

Friday, Nancy. *My Mother Myself.* New York, New York. Dell Publishing. 1977.

Friedan, Betty. *The Feminine Mystique.* New York, New York. W. W. Norton & Company, Inc. 1963.

Gimbutas, Marija. *The Goddesses and Gods of Old Europe.* Berkeley and Los Angeles. University of California Press. 1974 and 1982.

Gimbutas, Marija. *The Language of the Goddess.* San Francisco. Harper and Row. 1989.

Griffin, Susan. *Woman and Nature.* New York, New York. Harper & Row Publishers, Inc. 1978.

Harris, Helaine Z. *Are You In Love with a Vampire?* Encino, CA. An Awakening Publishing Company. 1997.

Howard, Michael. *Earth Mysteries*. Great Britain. St. Edmundsbury Press Ltd. 1990.

Jong, Erica. *Sappho's Leap.* New York, New York. W. W. Norton & Company. Inc. 2003.

King, Karen L. *The Gospel of Mary of Magdalena: Jesus and the First Woman Apostle*. Santa Rosa, California. Polebridge Press. 2003

Leonard, Linda Schierse. *The Wounded Woman.* Boston, Massachusetts. Shambhala Publications, Inc. 1982

Lubell, Winifred Milius. *The Metamorphosis of Baubo*. Nashville and London. Vanderbilt University Press. 1994.

Mataare (Channeled by). for Anamika & Carolyn Hawkins. *The Soul's Guide.* Santa Barbara, CA. Mountain Cat Productions. 2004.

McGaa, Ed (Eagle Man). *Mother Earth Spirituality*. New York, New York. HarperCollins Publishers, Inc. 1990.

Metzger, Deena. *The Other Hand.* Los Angeles, CA. 3Red Hen Press. 1999.

Moore, Thomas. *The Soul of Sex*. United States of America. HarperCollins Publishers, Inc. 1958.

Nelson, James B. *Sexuality and the Sacred.* Louisville, Kentucky. Westminster/John Knox Press. 1994.

Neumann, Erich. *The Great Mother*. Princeton, N.J. Princeton University Press. 1966.

Norwood, Robin. *Women Who Love Too Much*. Los Angeles, CA. Jeremy P. Tarcher, Inc. 1985.

Orbach, Susie. *Fat is a Feminist Issue*. New York, New York. Paddington Press. Ltd. 1978.

Orenstein, Gloria. *The Reflowering of the Goddess.* New York, New York. Pergamon Press, Inc. 1990.

Perera, Sylvia Brinton. *Descent to the Goddess*. Toronto, Canada. Inner City Books. 1981.

Piercy, Marge. *Small Changes*. United States of America. Doubleday and Company, Inc. 1972.

Piercy, Marge. *Woman on the Edge of Time*. New York, New York. Ballantine Books. 1976.

Preiss, Byron. *Herstory – Women Who Changed the World.* New York, New York. Penguin Books, USA, Inc. 1995.

Purce, Jill. *The Mystic Spiral.* New York, New York. Thames and Hudson, Inc. 1974.

Qualls-Corbett, Nancy. *The Sacred Prostitute – Eternal Aspect of the Feminine.* Toronto, Canada. Inner City Books. 1988.

Ransom, Victoria. and Bernstein, Henrietta. *The Crone Oracles.* Samuel Weiser, Inc. 1994.

Reagan, Harley. *The Sweet Medicine Sundance Teaching of the Chuluaqui-Quodoushka.* Quodoushka 1/11 training manual. USA. Deer Tribe Metis-Medicine Society. **1986**.

Redgrove, Peter. *The Black Goddess and the Unseen Real: Our Unconscious Senses and Their Uncommon Sense.* New York: Grove Press. 1987.

Rice, Anne. *Merrick.* New York, New York. Alfred A. Knopf. 2003.

Rosen, Ruth. *The World Split Open*. New York, New York. The Penguin Group. 2000.

Samples, Bob. *Mind of Our Mother.* Philippines. Addison Wesley Publishing Company, Inc. 1981.

Stassingopoulos, Agapi. *Gods and Goddesses in Love*. New York, New York. Paraview Pocket Books. 2004.

Steinem, Gloria. *Outrageous Acts and Everyday Rebellions*. New York, New York. Holt, Rinehart and Winston. 1983.

Stone, Merlin. *Ancient Mirrors of Womanhood.* Boston, Massachusetts. Beacon Press. 1979.

Stone, Merlin. *When God Was a Woman.* New York and London. Harvest/HBJ. 1976.

Walker, Alice. *In Search of Our Mothers' Gardens*. Orlando, Florida. Harcourt Brace Jovanovich, Publishers. 1983.

Walker, Barbara G. *The Crone*. New York, New York. Harper & Row Publishers, Inc. 1985.

Warter, Carlos, M.D., Ph.D. *Recovery of the Sacred*. Deerfield Beach, Florida. Health Communications, Inc. 1994.

Whitmont, Edward C. *Return of the Goddess*. New York, New York. The Crossroad Publishing Company. 1982.

Wolf, Naomi. *The Beauty Myth.* New York, New York. HarperCollins Publishers, Inc. 1991.

Woolf, Virginia. *A Room of One's Own*. New York and London. Harcourt, Brace & World, Inc. 1957.

Zweig, Connie. *To Be a Woman – The Birth of the Conscious Feminine.* New York, New York. St. Martin's Press. 1990.

Made in the USA
Las Vegas, NV
22 November 2022

60047371R00166